# KIDS' KNITS

# KIDS' KNITS

## Lesley Anne Price

**BALLANTINE BOOKS · NEW YORK**

# CONTENTS

**Editor** Jemima Dunne
**Art Editor** Anne-Marie Bulat
**Designers** Gill Della Casa, Nick Maddren
**Managing editor** Amy Carroll

First published in Great Britain in 1983 by
Dorling Kindersley Limited
9 Henrietta Street
Covent Garden, London WC2E 8PS

Copyright for patterns © 1983 Lesley Price
Copyright © 1983 Dorling Kindersley

All rights reserved under International and
Pan-American Copyright Conventions.
Published in the United States by Ballantine
Books, a division of Random House, Inc.
New York, and simultaneously in Canada by
Random House of Canada Limited, Toronto.

This edition published simultaneously in hardcover
and trade paperback.

Library of Congress Catalog Card Number
83-91275

ISBN 0-345-31968-0 (hdcvr)
ISBN 0-345-31500-6 (trd pbk)

Manufactured in the United States of America

First Edition: August 1984

10 9 8 7 6 5 4 3 2 1

Lesley Price has always been interested in textiles but began knitting and designing children's clothes after the birth of her twin sons, Casper and Alexis, now seven years old, and her daughter Amber, now two and a half years old. The clothes she made were extremely individual and universally admired – in fact, so many people asked for her patterns that she felt compelled to offer them in some form. She began by writing the patterns down and ordering the yarns from her own suppliers in the Shetlands. This was the start of *Knitkits,* eventually launched in January 1982, a business in which she markets her designs for clothes for babies and young children in a readily accessible kit form. In these kits she supplies her patterns together with *everything* required to make the garments except the needles.

A great many of Lesley's ideas, especially her use of color and garment shaping derive from the different tribal "uniforms" that exist all over the world. She and her husband spent nearly five years travelling extensively throughout Europe, the Middle East, India, Africa, Australia and South America, during which time she saw a wealth of different styles of weaving, embroidery, printing on textiles, knitting and pattern motifs. She has successfully grafted these influences onto traditional garments most particularly from the British Isles and has recently broadened her range to include well-loved clothes from all over the world. For example, she uses a Fair-Isle pattern on a Peruvian bonnet, and has a Chinese cap in Shetland wool.

In this volume she has included a complete range of interesting and very unusual children's clothes – everything that a child will need for the first five years short of diapers, rainhats and rubber boots. There is a complete range of summer and winter sweaters along with party outfits and sportswear. Moreover, she has included a range of toys and other useful baby items. Every knitter will find something delightful to make – from simple garments worked with bulky yarn and large needles, such as the *Chunky Fair-Isle,* to the more complicated patterns worked with fine yarn on fine needles such as the *Christening Set* with its *Cobweb Shawl.*

Because all the patterns in this book are based on traditional designs, they will not date and, if they are made carefully, they will outlast the child and can be put away for the next generation. Where possible all the patterns are given in six sizes so that brothers and sisters can all be dressed similarly. The garments are sized according to the chart on page 136, but it is important to measure any child carefully before you start because young children grow at different rates and as a result vary a great deal in size and shape so you may need to adjust the pattern slightly.

Almost all of Lesley's patterns are made with natural fibers: Shetland wool, cottons and silks. Playsuits, which are likely to get particularly dirty, may be more practical made in a machine-washable acrylic. You shouldn't have any difficulty finding the recommended yarn types – as they are widely available. Check the suppliers' addresses on page 143 for more specific information.

**Chunky knits**
Two traditional "uniforms" the shorts based on German Lederhosen, left, and the Fair-Isle pattern jacket, below, are ideal for inexperienced knitters. There are easy-to-follow patterns, with clear colorful graphs for both garments and, worked in bulky Shetland yarn, they are both really quick to knit.

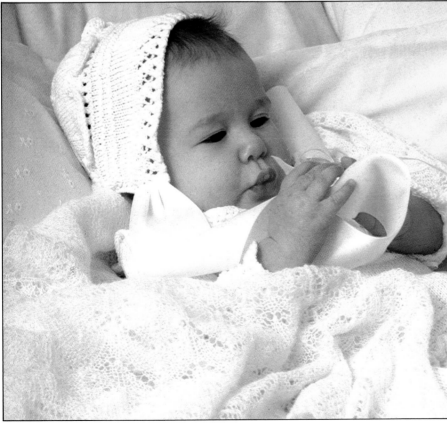

**Clothes and accessories for all ages**
Almost all the patterns in this book are suitable for both boys and girls. There are some clothes especially for babies such as the Christening set, left, but most can be worked in all six sizes.

# Cute Clown

Warm and cosy baby's playsuit which is smart enough for a
special occasion. Make it in acrylic yarn so that it is easy to wash
and care for.

## PLAYSUIT

### Yarn
Yarn A $5\frac{1}{4}$ ($5\frac{1}{4}$, $5\frac{1}{4}$)oz acrylic knitting worsted
(white)
Yarn B $3\frac{1}{2}$ ($3\frac{1}{2}$, $5\frac{1}{4}$)oz acrylic knitting worsted
(blue)

### Needles
1 pair no 5 (6, 7)

### Notions
$10\frac{3}{4}$in zipper (white)

### Stitch gauge
26 sts and 44 rows to 4in over garter st on no 5
needles; 22 sts and 40 rows to 4in over garter
st on no 6 needles; 18 sts and 34 rows to 4in
over garter st on no 7 needles (or size needed
to obtain given tension).

## Measurements

To fit sizes 1, 2, 3 only

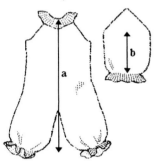

**a** Length $17\frac{1}{2}$ (20, $24\frac{1}{2}$)in
**b** Sleeve seam $6\frac{1}{4}$ ($7\frac{1}{2}$, $8\frac{3}{4}$)in

## Body

Cast on 40 sts using yarn A. Work in garter st
throughout knitting 2 rows yarn A, then 2 rows
yarn B – the right side will have clean unbroken
stripes.
*Shape crotch:* Work 13 rows without shaping.
With wrong side of work facing cast on one st
at beginning next and following 2 alternate
rows (crotch end). Work 1 row without shaping.
Cast on 2 sts beginning next row (crotch end) –
45 sts. Work 1 row without shaping.
*Shape body:* Wrong side facing, cast on 55 sts
before first st on needle and knit across all 100
sts. Work 9 rows without shaping, ending at
neck edge. Cast on 2 sts beginning next row –
102 sts. Knit 1 row.
*Shape armhole:* K2tog beginning next and
every alternate row until 85 sts remain. Work 7
rows without shaping.
*Reverse shaping:* Increase 1 st beginning of
next and every alternate row (armhole edge)
until there are 102 sts on needle. Knit 1 row.
Bind off 2 sts at beginning of next row. Work 9
rows without shaping. Beginning at neck edge,
bind off 55 sts. Knit 1 row. Bind off 2 sts
beginning next row. Knit 1 row. Then, k2tog at
beginning next row and following 2 alternate
rows – 40 sts. Work 12 rows without shaping
and bind off.
Work other half similarly.

## Sleeves

Starting with yarn B cast on 30 sts. Work 3 rows
without shaping. Then increase 1 st beginning
next and every alternate row until there are 47
sts on needle. Work 7 rows without shaping.
K2tog beginning of next and every alternate
row until 30 sts remain, work 4 rows without
shaping and bind off.
Work other sleeve similarly.

## Ankle ruffs

Right side facing and using yarn A, pick up and
knit 1 st from base of each white stripe – 35 sts.
Work 7 rows without shaping. Double sts: k
into front and back of each st – 70 sts. Knit 3
rows. Double sts again and knit 3 rows – 140
sts. With right side facing, bind off with yarn B.

## Wrist ruffs

As for ankles but pick up 20 sts doubling to 40
then 80 sts.

## Neck ruff

Right side facing and using yarn A, pick up 24
sts around neck. Knit 1 row. Double sts: k
into front and back of each st on needle – 48
sts. Knit 3 rows. Double sts again – 96 – and
knit 8 rows. Right side facing bind off with
yarn A.

## Finishing

Assemble all pieces of garment and fit zipper
in place in the back of suit.

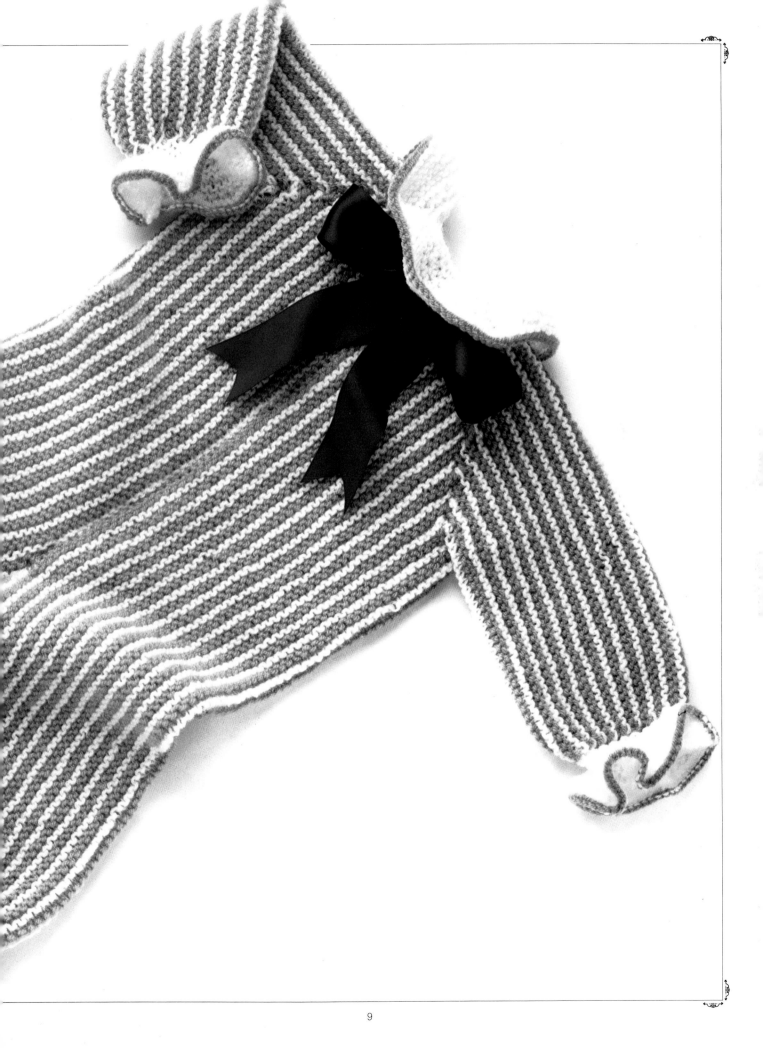

# Spring Fair-Isle

This multi colour bordered cardigan made from 2-ply Shetland yarn looks great worn with matching legwarmers and Peruvian-style hat.

# CARDIGAN

## Yarn

Main yarn M 2 (2, 2, 3, 3, 3)oz 2-ply Shetland (white)
Yarn A 1 (1, 1, 2, 2, 2)oz 2-ply Shetland (blue)
Yarn B 1 (1, 1, 1, 1, 1)oz 2-ply Shetland (green)

## Needles

1 pair size 3¼ (3¾, 4, 3½, 3¾, 4)mm
Similar size circular (or set of 4 double-pointed)

## Notions

Cardigan – 7 small buttons
Jumper – 2 small buttons

## Tension

28 sts and 36 rows to 10cm over st st on 3¼mm needles; 26 sts and 34 rows to 10cm over st st on 3¾mm needles; 24 sts and 32 rows to 10cm over st st on 4mm needles (or size needed to obtain given tension).

## Measurements

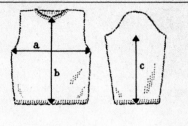

 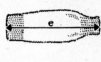

### Cardigan
*To fit sizes 1, 2, 3, 4, 5, 6*
**a** Chest 47 (51, 55, 59, 64, 69)cm
**b** Neck to hem 21 (25, 29, 33, 37, 41)cm
**c** Sleeve seam 17 (19, 22, 24, 26, 28)cm

### Hat
*To fit sizes 1–2, 3–4, 5–6*
**d** Around face 42 (45, 48)cm

### Legwarmers
*To fit sizes 1, 2, 3, 4, 5, 6*
**e** Length (top to base of ankle) 16 (18, 23, 25, 29, 31)cm

## Body

With yarn A cast on 132 (132, 132, 166, 166, 166) sts. Work 7 rows in garter st. Change to st st and, working appropriate edge sts as indicated, work 30 rows following pattern on graph A. Change to yarn M and continue in st st until work measures 12 (16, 19, 23, 26, 30)cm from beginning (or more or less as required), ending on a p row.

*Shape armholes:* Knit 31 (31, 31, 38, 38, 38) sts, cast off 4 (4, 4, 8, 8, 8), k62 (62, 62, 74, 74, 74), cast off 4 (4, 4, 8, 8, 8), k31 (31, 31, 38, 38, 38). Continue working on these last 31 (31, 31, 38, 38, 38) sts only. Decrease 1st at the beginning of next 3 knit rows (arm edge). Then, work next 16 rows following pattern on Graph B or 16 rows plain.

*(Three largest sizes only: work a further 6 rows st st.)*

*Shape shoulder:* Cast off 10 (10, 10, 12, 12, 12) sts at neck edge, purl to end. Decrease one st at beginning of every alternate row (neck edge) until 14 (14, 14, 19, 19, 19) sts remain. Continue without shaping until work measures 21 (25, 29, 33, 37, 41)cm from beginning (or more or less as required). Cast off.

*Shape back:* Wrong side facing, rejoin yarn to 62 (62, 62, 74, 74, 74) sts on needles. Work 6 rows st st, decrease 1st at the beginning of each row. Work 16 (16, 16, 22, 22, 22) rows without shaping, incorporating pattern from graph B if desired.

*Shape neck:* Purl 18 (18, 18, 22, 22, 22) sts, cast off 20 (20, 20, 24, 24, 24), p18 (18, 18, 23, 23, 23). Turn and complete as before. Finish other shoulder similarly. Wrong side facing, rejoin yarn to remaining 31 (31, 31, 38, 38, 38) sts and continue as before, reversing shaping where appropriate.

## Sleeves

With yarn A cast on 40 (40, 40, 50, 50, 50) sts.

Work 5 rows garter st, increasing 8 (8, 8, 10, 10, 10) sts evenly across last row – 48 (48, 48, 60, 60, 60) sts. Continue in st st. Work 6 rows in pattern following Graph C. Change to yarn M and work without shaping until work measures 6¾ (7½, 8¾, 9½, 10¼, 11)in from wrist (or more or less as required).
*Shape sleeve head:* Bind off 3 (3, 3, 5, 5, 5) sts, at beginning of the next 2 rows. Decrease one st at the beginning of every row until 24 sts remain, then decrease at both ends of every row until 8 sts remain. Bind off working k2tog. Work another sleeve similarly.

## Finishing

Sew sleeve and shoulder seams. Press work well with warm iron and damp cloth. Set sleeves into armholes.
### Cardigan only
With right side facing, using circular needle or set of 4 and yarn A, pick sts evenly from hem to neck on right front, around neck and from neck to hem on left front. Work 5 rows garter st, increasing one st at neck edge corners in each row and making 7 evenly-spaced buttonholes on 3rd row; yfwd, k2tog. Bind off loosely. Sew on buttons to correspond with buttonholes.
### Pullover only
Measure 3in down on left back, and, with right side work facing, using circular needle or first needle of set of 4 and yarn A, pick up sts from this point, up left back, around neck, ending at same depth on right back. Work 5 rows garter st, increasing 1 st at neck edge corners in each row, making 2 buttonholes on 3rd row of right back; yfwd, k2tog. Bind off loosely. Sew up back seam, tucking left side edging inside work but leaving right side out. Sew the base of edgings to work. Sew on buttons to correspond with buttonholes.

## HAT

### Yarn
Main yarn M ½oz 2-ply Shetland (white)
Yarn A ½oz 2-ply Shetland (blue)
Yarn B ½oz 2-ply Shetland (green)
### Needles
Set of 4 double-pointed no 2 (3, 4)
### Notions
Size C crochet hook
### Stitch gauge
30 sts and 38 rows to 4in over st st on no 2 needles; 28 sts and 36 rows to 4in over st st on no 3 needles; 26 sts and 34 rows to 4in over st st on no 4 needles (or size needed to obtain given tension).

## Method

With yarn A, cast on 126 sts evenly over 3 needles and work 3 rounds. Work 23 rounds following pattern on Graph D. Change to yarn B and work as follows:
**Round 28** *Knit 5, k2tog, rep from * to end.
**Rounds 29 and 30** *Knit 3 yarn A, k3 yarn B, rep from * to end.
**Rounds 31 and 32** Change to yarn A: knit.
**Rounds 33 and 34** *Knit 3 yarn B, k3 yarn A, rep from * to end.
**Round 35** *Knit 4 yarn B, k2tog, rep from * to end.
**Round 36** With yarn B, knit.
**Round 37** *Knit 1 yarn A, k1 yarn B, rep from * to end.
**Round 38** *Knit 1 yarn B, k1 yarn A, rep from *

to end.
**Round 39** *Knit 3 yarn B, k2tog yarn M, rep from * to end.
**Round 40** *Knit 1 yarn M, k1 yarn B, rep from * to end.
**Round 41** *Knit 1 yarn B, k1 yarn M, rep from * to end.
**Round 42** *Knit 2 yarn A, k2tog, rep from * to end.
**Round 43** With yarn B, knit.
**Rounds 44 to 46** With yarn M, knit.
**Rounds 47 and 48** With yarn A, knit.
**Round 49** As round 37.
**Round 50** As round 38.
**Rounds 51 to 54** With yarn A, knit.
Continue in yarn M only.
**Rounds 55 and 56** Knit.
**Round 57** K2tog, *k2, k2tog, rep from * to end.
**Round 58** *Knit 1, k2tog, rep from * to end.
**Round 59** *K2tog to end.
Thread yarn through remaining sts and fasten off securely.

## Finishing

### Earflaps
Pick up 15 sts either side of work and using yarn A, work 14 rows garter st. Bind off 1st at the beginning of each row until 7 sts remain. Bind off.
### Edging
Working from the earflaps around the face, and using yarn M, crochet little points around base of work: chain, single crochet, double, treble, double, single crochet, chain. Outline points and earflaps with a round of slip-stitch in yarn B, working picots into treble sts and around the earflaps at evenly-spaced intervals.
### Chains and tassels
Make tassel using remnants of yarns M, A and B. Crochet 4in chain of yarn A. Attach tassel to one end of chain, then sew other end of chain to top of bonnet.

Work two 6in cords of yarns M, A and B, and attach to ends of earflaps.
Press bonnet well with damp cloth and hot iron.

## LEGWARMERS

**NB** *This pattern can be adapted to make socks or slippers (see pp. 100–103).*
### Yarn
Main yarn M ½oz 2-ply Shetland (white)
Yarn A 1 (1, 1, 2, 2, 2)oz 2-ply Shetland (blue)
Yarn B ½oz 2-ply Shetland (green)
### Needles
1 pair no 2 (3, 4, 2, 3, 4)
### Stitch gauge
30 sts and 38 rows to 4in over st st on no 2 needles; 28 sts and 36 rows to 4in over st st on no 3 needles; 26 sts and 34 rows to 4in over st st on no 4 needles (or size needed to obtain given tension).

## Method

Working from the top using yarn A, cast on 51 (51, 51, 67, 67, 67) sts. Work in k1, p1 rib for 20 rows.
**Next row** Knit 5; *k into the front and back of next st, k1, rep from * to last 4 sts; k4 – 72 (72, 72, 96, 96, 96) sts.
Purl 1 row. With st st, follow pattern on Graph E until work measures 5 (6, 7, 7¾, 9, 9¾)in from beginning (or more or less as required).
**Next row** Right side facing, change to yarn A, k2tog across all sts.
Work in k1, p1 rib for 10 (10, 15, 15, 20, 20) rows for ankle. Bind off in k1, p1 rib. Work another legwarmer similarly.

## Finishing

Press well and sew up leg seams.

**Graph A**

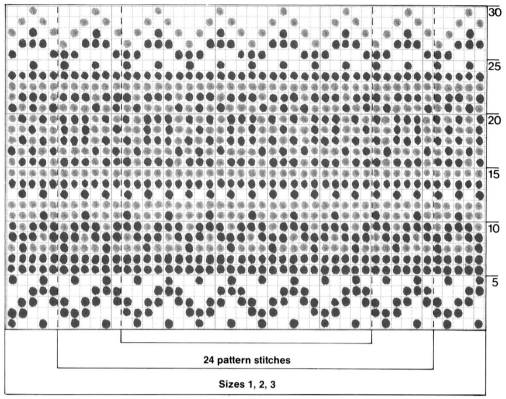

24 pattern stitches

Sizes 1, 2, 3

Sizes 4, 5, 6

**Graph B**

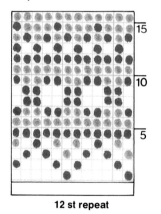

12 st repeat

**Graph C**

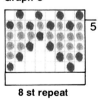

8 st repeat

**Graph D**
(3 color hat)

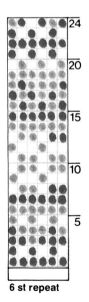

6 st repeat

**Graph D**
(5 color hat,
see photograph, left)

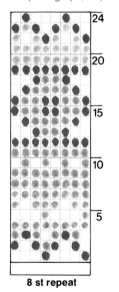

8 st repeat

**Graph E**

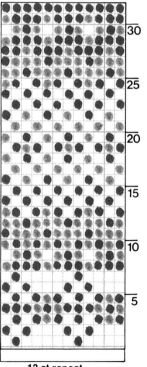

12 st repeat

# CORNISH KID

Cute and warm, this pullover is designed for hard wear and is bound to outlast your child, so make it large. Knit it in one of the traditional colors: navy blue, white or scarlet.

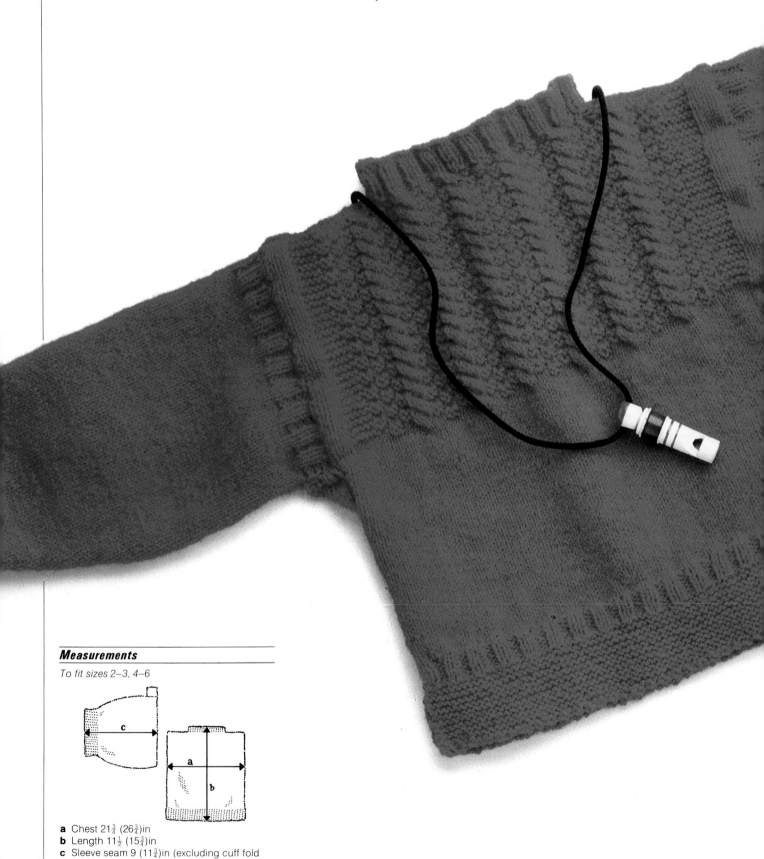

## Measurements

*To fit sizes 2–3, 4–6*

**a** Chest 21¾ (26¾)in
**b** Length 11½ (15¾)in
**c** Sleeve seam 9 (11¾)in (excluding cuff fold back)

## SWEATER

### Yarn

$8\frac{3}{4}$ ($12\frac{1}{4}$)oz 5-ply Guernsey yarn or knitting worsted

### Needles

Three no 0 for sleeves and chest
no 0 circular (or set of 5 double-pointed) for body and neck.

### Notions

Stitch holder or 2 large safety pins

### Stitch gauge

31 sts and 47 rows to 4in over st st on no 0 needles (or size needed to obtain given tension).

## Body

**NB** *Body can also be worked on two needles in two pieces, if preferred. In which case ignore instructions for false seam.*
*Shape welt:* Cast on 80 (100) sts using knotted-edge method and straight needles. Work 20 rows garter st. Make another welt similarly, then change to circular needle (or set of 5) and work across both welts.
*Begin main section:* Work 6 rounds k2, p2 rib, purling the st above both side slits in hem to make false seam.
Continue in st st still working purl st for false seams and work as follows:
**Next row** *Knit 15 (19), increase by knitting into front and back of next st, rep from * to end – 170 (210) sts.
Continue in st st until work measures 6 ($9\frac{3}{4}$)in from beginning (or more or less as required).
*Shape back:* Change to straight needles and work on 85 (105) sts for back. Smaller size only, work further $1\frac{1}{4}$in st st then *all* sizes work in pattern as follows:
**Row 1** Right side facing, k10; *k2, p2, k2, c4f, rep from * 5 (7) times; k2; p2; k2; k9.
**Row 2** Purl 4; k5; *p2, k2, p2, p4, rep from * 5 (7) times; p2; k2; p2; k5; p5.
**Row 3** Knit 10; *p2, k2, p2, c4f, rep from * 5 (7) times; p2; k2; p2; k9.
**Row 4** Purl 4; k5; *k2, p2, k2, p4, rep from * 5 (7) times; k2; p2; k2; k5; p5.
Repeat these 4 rows until work measures $10\frac{3}{4}$ ($15\frac{3}{4}$)in from beginning.
Work other half body similarly.
*Shape shoulder:* With back and front on separate needles, wrong sides of work together, points of needles at the same end,

k2tog through first 2 loops (1 st from each needle). Repeat with next loops (1 st from each needle) and bind off first st. Continue in this way until 17 (27) sts have been bound off from each needle.
*Neck gusset:* Knit 1 st from front needle, turn. Sl 1, p next st and p1 from back needle, turn. Continue taking up one st from front and back needles alternately until 7 sts on needle. Break yarn and leave 7 sts on stitch holder or large safety pin.
Slip remaining sts of front onto empty needle (point of needle will be at armhole edge). Repeat with sts of back. Rejoin yarn to work and shape shoulder and work neck gusset as before. With remaining 100 sts (including sts on stitch holder) and circular needle (or double-pointed needles), work 6 (8) rounds k2, p2 rib and bind off loosely in rib.

## Sleeves

Cast on 48 (60) sts using knotted-edge method and straight needles. Knit 1 row. Work 2 ($2\frac{3}{4}$)in k2, p2 rib for cuff. Change to st st and increase sts as follows: *Knit 7 (9), k into front and back next st, rep from * to end – 54 (66) sts. Continue in st st increasing 1 st both ends every 4th row until there are 70 (90) sts. Continue until 9 ($11\frac{3}{4}$)in have been worked from beginning, ending with a wrong-side row.
*Commence gusset shaping:* Cast on 10 sts beginning next row. Work 6 rows st st over all sts. Then k 6 rows k2, p2 rib, work gusset sts st st. Bind off.
Work another sleeve similarly.

## Finishing

Sew sleeve seams and set into armholes. Press work gently.

### Knotted edge cast on

Cut 2 yards of yarn and fold in half. Wind double yarn towards you and twice around thumb. Using single strand of yarn, knit through all four strands together pulling double strands through carefully and knot will be formed. Bring yarn forward and repeat.

# JACOB'S COAT

A collection of four glorious tops can be made from this simple shape – a cardigan, vest, pullover or pullover vest – using lots of beautiful colors. You can use the pattern to make them in plain shades if you prefer.

## MATERIALS

### Yarn
Main yarn M *2oz* 2-ply Shetland (navy or camel)
*1oz* each 11 different shades 2-ply Shetland

### Needles
1 pair no 2 (3, 4, 2, 3, 4)

### Notions
Length bias binding for neatening seams
3 (3, 4, 5, 6, 7) $\frac{1}{2}$in buttons

### Stitch gauge
30 sts and 38 rows to 4in over striped st st on no 2 needles; 28 sts and 36 rows to 4in over striped st st on no 3 needles; 26 sts and 34 rows to 4in over striped st st on no 4 needles (or size needed to obtain given tension).

## Measurements

To fit sizes *1, 2, 3, 4, 5, 6*

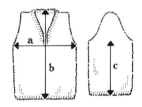

**a** Chest 19$\frac{3}{4}$ (21$\frac{1}{4}$, 23, 23$\frac{1}{4}$, 24, 24$\frac{3}{4}$)in
**b** 8$\frac{1}{4}$ (9$\frac{3}{4}$, 11$\frac{1}{2}$, 13, 14$\frac{1}{2}$, 16$\frac{1}{4}$)in
**c** 6$\frac{1}{4}$ (7, 8$\frac{1}{4}$, 9$\frac{1}{2}$, 10$\frac{1}{4}$, 10$\frac{3}{4}$)in

## Back

**NB** *Because up to 5 shades are used in any one row, it may help you to make several small card bobbins to hold short lengths of different shade yarns. Wrap a 10 or 20 yard length of yarn around the base of the bobbin; this will help to keep the yarns untangled.*

With yarn M cast on 66 (66, 66, 80, 80, 80) sts using 2-needle method. Work 10 rows in st st. Refer to graph A for pattern, select yarn for first stripe. Using this yarn, k through st picking up corresponding cast-on loop to make row. Continue in this way to end of row. Work in stripes as graph until work measures 4$\frac{3}{4}$ (5$\frac{1}{2}$, 6$\frac{3}{4}$, 8$\frac{1}{4}$, 9$\frac{1}{2}$, 10$\frac{3}{4}$)in from hem fold (or more or less as required), ending with a purl row.

*Shape armhole:* Bind off 3 (3, 3, 5, 5, 5) sts at the beginning of the next 2 rows. Bind off one st at the beginning of the next 6 (6, 6, 8, 8, 8) rows – 54 (54, 54, 62, 62, 62) sts. Continue working in st st stripes until work measures 7$\frac{3}{4}$ (9, 10$\frac{3}{4}$, 12$\frac{1}{4}$, 13$\frac{3}{4}$, 15$\frac{1}{4}$)in from hem fold ending with a purl row.

*Shape neck:* Knit 17 (17, 17, 18, 18, 18) sts, bind off 20 (20, 20, 26, 26, 26), k17 (17, 17, 18, 18, 18). Continue on last set of sts and work as follows:

**Row 1** Purl.
**Row 2** K2tog, k to end.
**Row 3** Bind off 6, purl to end.
**Row 4** As row 2.
**Row 5** As row 3.

**Row 6** Knit.
Bind off.
Work other shoulder similarly, reversing shaping.

## Front – Cardigan and Vest

With yarn M cast on 36 (36, 36, 45, 45, 45) sts using 2-needle method. Work 10 rows in st st. Catch up hem into cast-on loops on row 11. Purl one row. Refer to graph and work in pattern without shaping until work measures same as back to armhole shaping, ending on a purl row.

*Shape armholes and neck edge:* Bind off 3 (3, 3, 5, 5, 5) sts at the beginning of the next knit row. Bind off one st at the beginning of next 3 (3, 3, 4, 4, 4) alternate rows – 30 (30, 30, 36, 36, 36) sts – simultaneously decreasing one st at neck edge on every row until 16 (16, 16, 17, 17, 17) sts remain. Work without shaping until work measures same as back to shoulder, ending at armhole edge. Bind off 6 sts at arm edge on alternate rows, work one row and bind off remaining sts.

Work another piece similarly but reverse shaping and pattern.

## Front – Pullover and Pullover Vest

With yarn M cast on 72 (72, 72, 90, 90, 90) sts using 2-needle method. Work 10 rows in st st and using next color yarn (as back), catch up hem, p1 row. Refer to graph and work in pattern without shaping until work measures 4 (4$\frac{3}{4}$, 6, 7$\frac{1}{2}$, 8$\frac{1}{4}$, 9$\frac{3}{4}$)in from hem fold ending on a purl row.

*Shape V-neck:* Knit 36 (36, 36, 45, 45, 45), turn. P2tog, p to end. Work 6 more rows, decreasing one st at the beginning of every purl row.

*Shape armhole:* Bind off 3 (3, 3, 5, 5, 5) sts, k to end – 29 (29, 29, 36, 36, 36) sts. Decrease 1st at the beginning of the next 8 rows then, keeping arm edge straight, decrease one st at neck edge on every row until 16 sts remain. Work without shaping until work measures same as

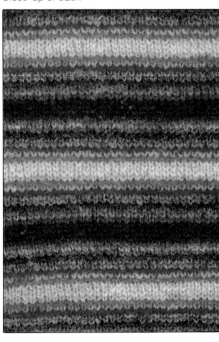

Close-up of back

back to shoulder, ending at armhole edge. Bind off 6 sts at arm edge on next 2 k rows, work one row. Bind off. Work other side similarly but reversing shaping.

## Sleeves

With yarn M cast on 66 (66, 66, 80, 80, 80) sts and work in pattern as front, including hem, without shaping, until work measures 6¼ (7, 8¼, 9½, 10¼, 10¾)in (or more or less as required) from hem fold.

*Shape sleeve head:* Bind off 3 (3, 3, 5, 5, 5) sts at the beginning of the next 2 rows. Bind off one st at the beginning of the next 6 (6, 6, 8, 8, 8) rows, then work without shaping for ¾ (1¼, 1½, 2, 2¼, 2¾)in. Bind off one st at the beginning of the next 10 rows, then decrease one st at each end of the next 7 rows. Bind off by knitting 2 tog.

## Edging bands

*These are needed around armholes of vest and pullover vest, around the neck of pullover and pullover vest and up front and around neck of vest and cardigan.*

### Armhole bands

With yarn M, cast on 15 sts and working in st st, knit a band long enough to fit around armhole. Incorporate a subtle stripe every 7th and 8th row if desired. Work another band similarly.

### V-neck band

Cast on one st. Yo, k1, turn. Purl 2, turn. Yo, k2, turn. Purl 3, turn. Continue in this way until purling 8 sts. Break yarn. Cast on one st. Knit into the front and back of the st, turn. Purl 2, turn. Knit 1, k into the front and back of next st, turn. Purl 3, turn. Continue in this way until purling 7, then knit across the 7 and 8 sts on needle. Work without shaping until band is long enough to go around neck opening and fit over child's head.

*Shape end:* With right side of work facing, k6, k2tog, turn. Purl 7, turn. Knit 5, k2tog, turn. Purl 6. Continue in this way until one st remains. Bind off. Break yarn. Starting at inside edge, k2tog, k to end, turn. Purl one row. Continue in this way until one st remains. Bind off.

### Front edging

Cast on 15 sts and work in st st without shaping. Make a buttonhole on 3rd/4th row then every 12 rows as follows: k3, bind off 3, k3, bind off 3, k3.

**Next row** Purl 3, make 3 sts, p3, make 3 sts, p3. Repeat this as often as necessary until band is long enough to reach beginning of neck shaping. Continue working straight until band is long enough to go around the neck and down the other side. Bind off.

## Finishing

Press all parts of garment well, place right sides together and assemble. Neaten all seams with bias binding if desired. Place open binding against seam and sew through all thicknesses using thread and running st, or a domestic sewing machine. Press seams well and trim all loose ends of yarn to within about ½in of work. Turn binding and catch other edge to work, being careful not to bunch seam on right side. Fold and press edgings and attach to relevant parts of garment. Place buttonhole edging on left front for a boy and right front for a girl. Catch buttonholes together – front to back – and affix buttons.

**Graph A (front)**

This pullover vest was worked using camel as main yarn.

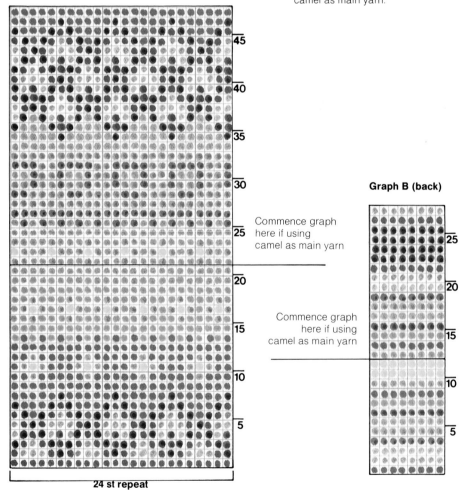

Commence graph here if using camel as main yarn

**Graph B (back)**

Commence graph here if using camel as main yarn

**24 st repeat**

# Lucy's Pocket

This little shoulder purse together with its matching dolls will delight every child and is an ideal way of using up left-over yarn. It is extra smart if it is made to match a particular outfit.

## PURSE

### Yarn

Main yarn M *1oz* 2-ply Shetland (light blue)
Yarn A *½oz* 2-ply Shetland (pink)
Yarn B *½oz* 2-ply Shetland (white)

### Needles

1 pair no 3
1 crochet hook

### Measurements

Approx 6in deep

### Method

With yarn M cast on 60 sts. Change to yarn A and work 6 rows garter st. Change to yarn M and work a row of eyelets as follows: k1; *yfwd, k2tog, rep from * to last st; k1. Work 25 rows st st ending with a purl row.
*Shape base:* *K2tog, k8, rep from * to end.
*Next and every alternate row:* Purl.
**Next row** *K2tog, k7, rep from * to end.
Continue decreasing in this way until 6 sts remain. Break yarn and thread through sts. Sew up seam.

## Chains

Crochet 2 × 11¾in chains and one short chain using 2 strands yarn M. Thread long chains through eyelet holes in opposite directions starting from opposite sides. From yarns M, A and B make 3 tassels and affix to ends of chains. Fix short chain to base of purse. Crochet a long chain yarn M to make a shoulder strap and affix to top edge of purse.

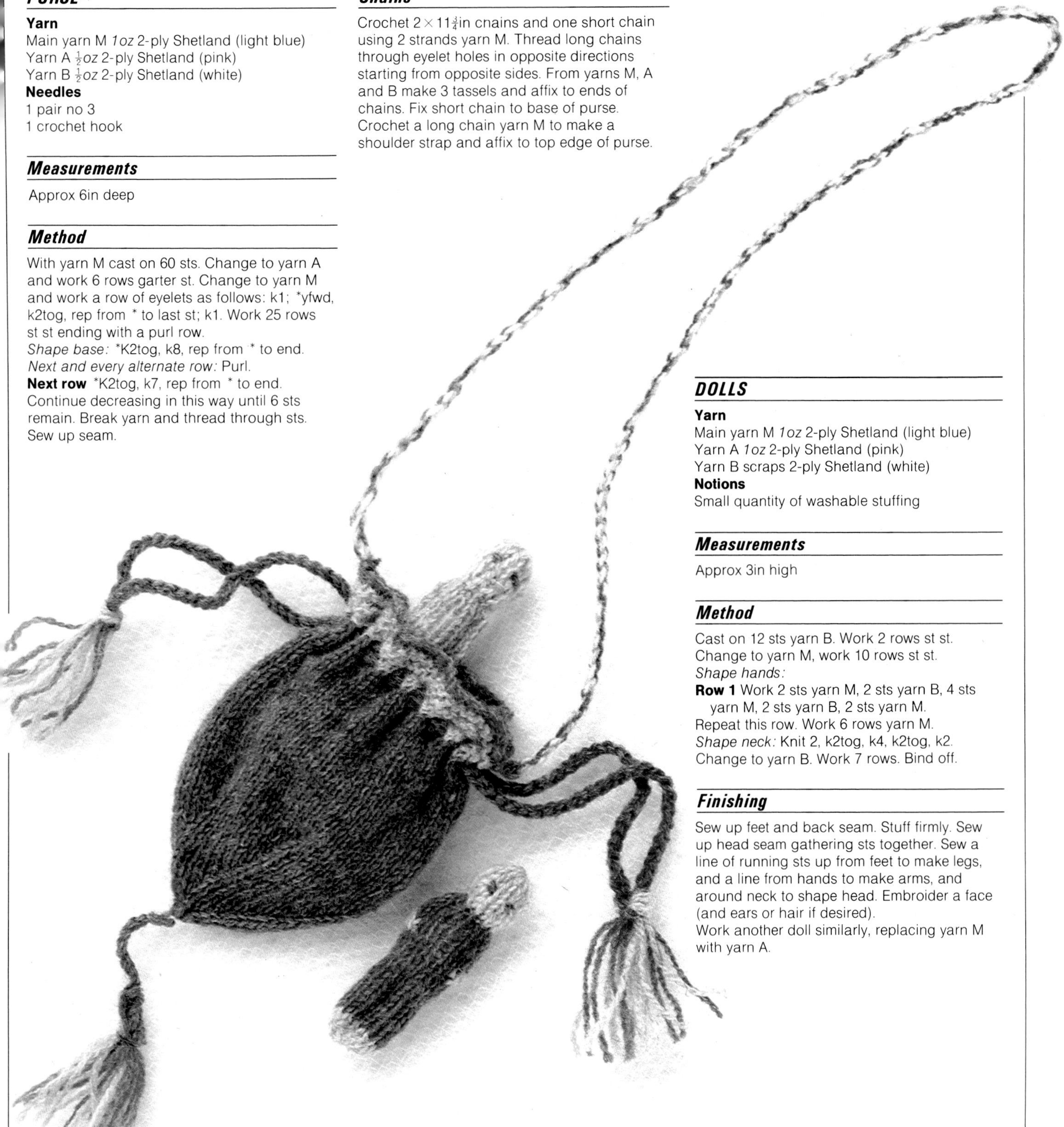

## DOLLS

### Yarn

Main yarn M *1oz* 2-ply Shetland (light blue)
Yarn A *1oz* 2-ply Shetland (pink)
Yarn B scraps 2-ply Shetland (white)

### Notions

Small quantity of washable stuffing

### Measurements

Approx 3in high

### Method

Cast on 12 sts yarn B. Work 2 rows st st.
Change to yarn M, work 10 rows st st.
*Shape hands:*
**Row 1** Work 2 sts yarn M, 2 sts yarn B, 4 sts yarn M, 2 sts yarn B, 2 sts yarn M.
Repeat this row. Work 6 rows yarn M.
*Shape neck:* Knit 2, k2tog, k4, k2tog, k2.
Change to yarn B. Work 7 rows. Bind off.

### Finishing

Sew up feet and back seam. Stuff firmly. Sew up head seam gathering sts together. Sew a line of running sts up from feet to make legs, and a line from hands to make arms, and around neck to shape head. Embroider a face (and ears or hair if desired).
Work another doll similarly, replacing yarn M with yarn A.

# COUNTRY COUSIN

This traditional English smock can be made in wool or cotton.
It is worked in one size only but will fit a child of 18 months until
he or she is about four years old.

## SMOCK

### Yarn
Main yarn M *7oz* 2-ply Shetland or *12¼oz* cotton
(blue)
Yarn A *1oz* 2-ply Shetland or *1¾oz* cotton in
contrast color (white)

### Needles
1 no 3 circular
1 pair no 3

### Notions
3 buttons (you can make your own, see p. 130).

### Stitch gauge
28 sts and 36 rows to 4in over st st (or size
needed to obtain given tension).

## Pockets

Using yarn M and 2 needles, cast on 50 sts,
then follow pattern on Graph A.
**Row 1** Knit 30 (pocket lining), p9 (flap lining),
k11 as graph.
**Row 2** Purl 11 sts from graph, k9, p30.
Repeat these 2 rows until Graph A is finished,
p 1 row and bind off.
Work another pocket similarly.

## Skirt

Using yarn M and circular needle cast on 200
sts using 2-needle method. Knit 3 rounds then
purl round 4 to make a fold line for hem.
Continue in st st but pick up cast-on row to
make hem on round 9. Continue without
shaping until work measures 7¾in from hem
fold. Mark beginning of next round by threading
small length of contrast yarn behind first st.
Knit 30 sts, bind off 40, k30, mark next st with
contrast yarn, k30, bind off 40, k30.
*Attach pockets:* Knit 30 sts, then with right side
facing, pick up and k 40 sts evenly along row
ends at patterned edge, k60, work second
pocket as before, k30. Continue in rounds until
work measures 14¼in (or more or less as
required) from hem fold.
*Shape armhole gussets:*
**Round 1** Knit 50, *pick up the strand which lies
between sts on needles and k into front and
back of it (making 2 sts for start of gusset)*,
k100, rep from * to *, k50.
**Round 2** (Knit to gusset, k into front and back
next 2 sts) twice, k to end.
**Round 3** (Knit to gusset, k into front and back
next st, k2, k into front and back next st)
twice, k to end.
Continue in this way increasing 2 sts at gusset
on every round until each gusset contains
10 sts.
*Shape bodice:* Referring to Graph B for pattern,
work as follows:
**Next row** Increase 2 sts in first st; (k1, p1)
twice; *p2tog, k2tog, rep from * 7 times; p1;
k9 in pattern; k2, bind off 20, k1, k9 in
pattern, p2tog, **k2tog, p2tog, rep from **
16 times; k9 in pattern; k1; bind off 20; k2;
k9 in pattern; p1; ***k2tog, p2tog, rep from
*** 7 times, turn.
Commence working back and forth on needle.
**Next row** Cast on 3 sts in next st, work 3 sts

moss st, work 17 sts k1, p1 rib as set, p9 in
pattern, p2, turn.
Continue working on these 31 sts, making
eyelet hole for buttons in rows 3, 13, 23 by
working yo, k2tog on last 2 sts.
When graph finishes, p 1 row and bind off.
*Work other side:* Wrong side facing, rejoin yarn
to other 31 sts and work similarly, but reversing
sts and omitting buttonholes. With first 3 sts
moss st, p1, work 16 sts k1, p1 rib, p9 in
pattern, k2.
*Shape front:* Wrong side work facing, rejoin
yarn to remaining 55 sts and k1, k9 in pattern,
35 sts in k1, p1 rib (smocking lines), p9 in
pattern, p1. Continue working on these sts
until graph finishes, then k 1 row and bind off.

## Sleeves

With yarn M cast on 80 sts using 2-needle
method. Work 12 rows st st knitting row 4
instead of purling to make fold line for hem and
picking up hem on row 9.
*Make wrist smocking lines:*
**Row 1** Knit 30; *k2tog, p2tog, rep from * 4
times; k30 – 70 sts.
**Row 2** Purl 30; *k1, p1, rep from * 4 times; p30.
**Row 3** Knit 30; *k1, p1, rep from * 4 times; k30.
Repeat rows 2 and 3 twice.
**Row 8** Purl 30; *k1, p1, rep from * 4 times; p30.
**Row 9** Knit 30, k into front and back next 10
sts, k30 – 80 sts.
Continue without shaping until sleeve measures
9in from fold line, ending with a wrong-side
row. Make shoulder smocking lines as wrist to
Row 8, then work as follows:
**Row 9** Bind off 30, k to end.
**Row 10** Bind off 29, p to end – 11 sts.
Work top of sleeve following pattern on Graph
C when graph finishes, p 1 row and bind off.
Work another sleeve similarly.

## Collars

Cast on 22 sts. Work in st st following pattern
on Graph B working first 12 and last st in yarn
M. Bind off.
Work another collar similarly.

## Smocking

Press st st sections well and smock lines at
front and back bodice, shoulders and wrist
(see p. 132).

## Finishing

Set sleeve into armhole, working from bodice
and back corners. Sew underarm seam.
Carefully catch pocket linings to inside of skirt.
Sew up ends of pocket flaps. Fold collars and
sew ends, and position collars so that they
meet center front, leaving button-bands free.
Sew neatly to neck section. If desired, make
buttons (see p. 130) and attach to correspond
with buttonholes.

**Graph A**

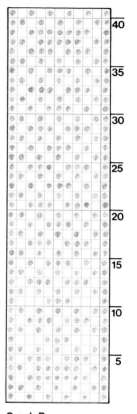

**Graph B**

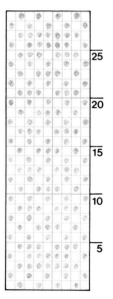

## PURSE

Instructions for purse are given on previous page (p. 19).

### Measurements

**a** Chest 22in (loose fitting)
**b** Neck to hem 19¾in
**c** Sleeve seam 7¾in

**Graph C**

# TOMBOY

Gay cotton overalls which any child would love to have. They are easy to knit and are very practical because they are so easy to launder.

## OVERALLS

### Yarn

Main yarn M 6¼ (6¼, 8, 8, 10½, 11½)oz medium-weight cotton (blue)
Yarn A 1¾oz medium-weight cotton (red)

### Needles

1 no 2 (3, 4, 2, 3, 4) circular
1 pair similar size
Size C crochet hook

### Notions

2 buttons

### Stitch gauge

30 sts and 40 rows to 4in over st st using no 2 needles; 28 sts and 38 rows to 4in over st st using no 3 needles; 26 sts and 36 rows to 4in over st st on no 4 needles (or size needed to obtain given tension).

## Measurements

To fit sizes 1, 2, 3, 4, 5, 6

**a** Chest 18½ (19¾, 21¼, 23¾, 25¼, 27¼)in
**b** Inside leg 9 (11, 13¾, 16¼, 17, 19)in

## Legs

With yarn A cast on 40 (40, 40, 50, 50, 50) sts using 2-needle method. Working back and forth in rows work 32 rows k1, p1 rib. Change to yarn M and k up sts on cast-on row alternating one st from needle with 1 loop from cast-on edge – 80 (80, 80, 100, 100, 100) sts. Work in st st without shaping until work measures 9 (11, 13¾, 16¼, 17, 19)in from hem fold (or more or less as required).
*Shape crotch:* Knit 1 row.
**Row 2** *and every alternate row:* Purl without shaping.
**Row 3** Knit 5, turn.
**Row 5** Knit 10, turn.
Continue in this way until knitting 30 sts, then turn.
**Row 15** Knit to end row.
**Row 16** Purl 5, turn.
**Row 17** *and every alternate row:* Knit without shaping.
**Row 18** Purl 10, turn.
**Row 20** Purl 15, turn.
Continue in this way until purling 30 sts. Break yarn and push sts onto flexible part of needle. Work another leg similarly but do not break yarn.
*Shape body:* Right side facing, work 55 rounds st st over all 160 (160, 160, 200, 200, 200) sts.
Continue working in rounds until work measures 9¾ (11, 11¾, 11¾, 12½, 13¾)in from

crotch (or more or less as required), ending at center side of garment.
*Work pocket:* Using another pair of needles and yarn A cast on 24 sts. Work 20 rows st st. Leave these sts and shape bodice of main garment:
*Work bodice:* With yarn M, bind off 3 (3, 3, 5, 5, 5) sts, k15 (15, 15, 23, 23, 23), k2tog 5 times. Change to yarn A, bind off 24 sts, break yarn. Change to main color, k across 24 sts of pocket lining and k2tog 5 times from sts on needle. Knit 15 (15, 15, 23, 23, 23) sts, bind off 6 (6, 6, 10, 10, 10), k27 (27, 27, 35, 35, 35), k2tog 10 times, k27 (27, 27, 35, 35, 35), bind off 3 (3, 3, 5, 5, 5)
*Work back* as follows:
**Next row** Purl 64 (64, 64, 80, 80, 80).
**K2tog beginning next 10 rows.
*Shape neck:* Knit 15 sts, bind off 24 (24, 24, 30, 30, 30), k15.

*Shape back left strap:* Work on these last 15 sts. Keeping outside (left) edge straight, k2tog beginning next 5 k rows.**
Work 16 (16, 16, 26, 26, 26) rows without shaping on these 10 sts, then k2tog beginning next 6 rows and bind off.
*Shape right strap:* Right side facing, rejoin yarn to back. Keeping outside (right) edge straight, p2tog beginning next 5 purl rows. Finish as back left strap.
*Work front:* Right side facing, rejoin yarn to front. Purl 1 row, then work as back from ** to **
Work 12 (12, 12, 20, 20, 20) rows without shaping.
*Make buttonhole:* Knit 2, k2tog, yfwd, sl 1, k2tog, psso, k3. Purl 1 row. K2tog beginning next 5 rows and bind off.
*Shape right front strap:* Rejoin yarn to inside and keeping outside (right) edge straight, p2tog beginning next 5 purl rows. Finish as front left strap.

Using contrast yarn A and size C crochet hook, make double chains all around top edges (arm, neck and strap).

## Finishing

Sew pocket in place and fix buttons to correspond with holes. Sew crotch seam, or, if preferred for younger child, fit small open-ended zipper for easier diaper changes.

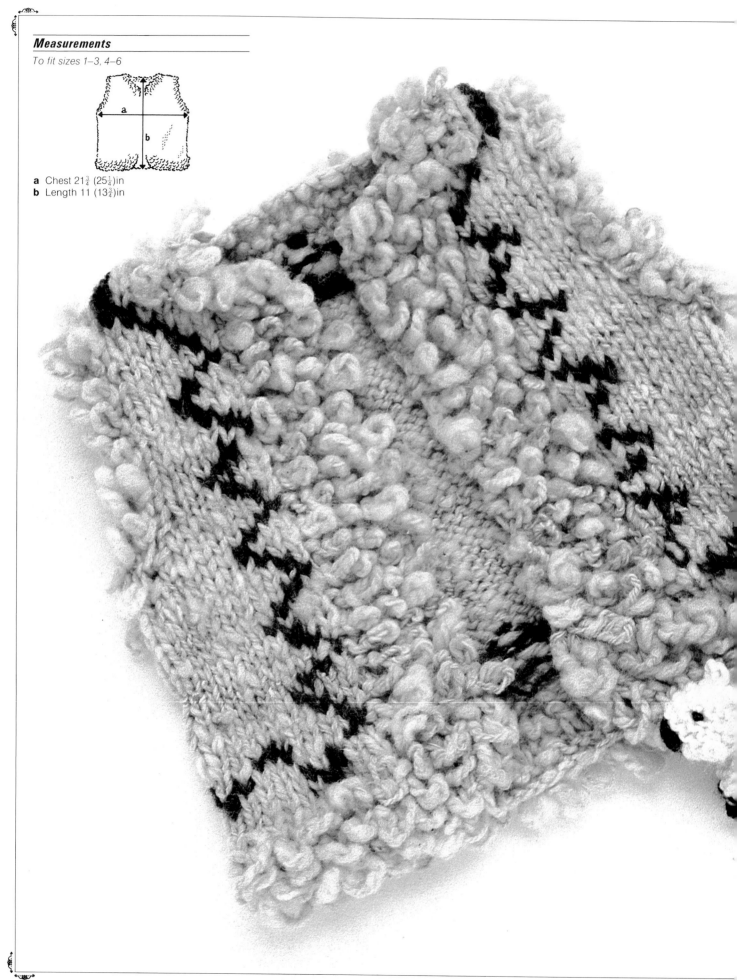

## Measurements

*To fit sizes 1–3, 4–6*

**a** Chest 21¾ (25¼)in
**b** Length 11 (13¾)in

# WOOLLY LAMB

This delightful "ethnic" vest is designed especially for working with homespun yarn, although it can also be made using a similar bobbly material.

## VEST

### Yarn
Main yarn M 5¼oz/3 full spools (7oz/4 spools) 2-ply coarse, uncarded handspun wool, or similar thick knobbly yarn (natural)
Yarn A *1oz* (½ spool) 2-ply fleece yarn (black)

### Needles
1 pair no 9

### Stitch gauge
14 sts and 20 rows to 4in over st st on no 9 needles (or size needed to obtain given tension).

## Body

Using yarn M, cast on 73 (85) sts. Knit 1 row making loop in every second stitch as follows: k1, loop yarn over 2 fingers of left hand, k1, lift loop and k into next st, k1. Knit 1 row. Repeat these 2 rows twice.

With loops hanging on right side of work, continue working first and last 6 sts garter st and central 61 (73) sts st st. Work 2 rows then refer to Graph A for zigzag pattern. Continue in this way without shaping until work measures 5½ (7)in from beginning (or more or less as required).

*Shape armholes:* Knit 16 (18) sts, bind off 4 (6), k33 (37), bind off 4 (6), k16 (18).

*Left front:* Knit 6 sts with loops, p10 (12). K2tog beginning next 3 k rows at armhole edge.
**Continue without shaping until work measures 9¾ (12½)in (and 12/16 lines of zigzag have been worked).

**Row 1** Work 1 yarn M to last 2 sts, work 1 yarn A, work 1 yarn M.

**Row 2** Work 1 yarn M, 1 yarn A, work to end yarn M.

Continue in pattern working straight line yarn A up shoulder.

*Shape neck* as follows: With wrong side facing, k10 (12) sts making loops as above, p3.

**Row 1** Knit.

**Row 2** Bind off 6 (8), k4 making loops, p3.

**Row 3** Knit.

**Row 4** Knit 4 making loops, p3.
Bind off.
Return to sts for back.

*Work back:* P2tog, p to end. Decrease one st beginning next 5 rows, then continue without shaping or pattern until work measures 9 (11¾in)in from beginning. Then work in pattern following Graph B.

*Shape neck:*

**Row 1** Knit.

**Row 2** Purl 6, k15 (19) with loops, p6.
Repeat these 2 rows.
Bind off.

*Right front:* Rejoin yarn to arm edge right front. P2tog beginning next 3 purl rows (armhole edge) working last (and first on k rows) 6 sts garter st with loops and keeping pattern in sequence. Continue as left front from **, reversing shaping.

## Arm edging

Right side facing, k up 40 (55) sts across armhole. Work 3 rows garter st, making loops on right side work. Bind off.

## Finishing

Join shoulder seams. Press work carefully.

**Graph A:** Left front

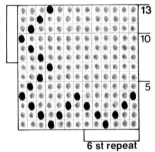

Repeat 5 (7) times

6 st repeat

**Graph A:** Right front

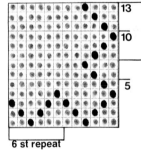

Repeat 5 (7) times

6 st repeat

**Graph B** (Small size)

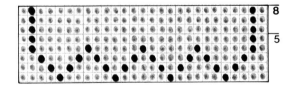

**Graph B** (Large size)

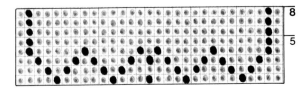

Together this pull-on cotton sweatshirt and matching pants
make a sporty tracksuit suitable for any child.

10

5

4 stitch repeat

## SWEATSHIRT

**Yarn**
Main yarn M 7 *(7, $8\frac{3}{4}$, $8\frac{3}{4}$, $10\frac{1}{2}$, $10\frac{1}{2}$)oz* medium-weight cotton (red)
Yarn A *$1\frac{3}{4}$ ($3\frac{1}{2}$, $3\frac{1}{2}$, $5\frac{1}{4}$, $5\frac{1}{4}$, 7)oz* medium-weight cotton (white)
**Needles**
1 no 2 (3, 4, 2, 3, 4) short circular or pair long double-pointed
**Notions**
20in soft elastic for neck
Stitch holder
**Stitch gauge**
30 sts and 40 rows to 4in over st st on no 2 needles; 28 sts and 38 rows to 4in over st st on no 3 needles; 26 sts and 36 rows to 4in over st st on no 4 needles (or size needed to obtain given tension).

## Measurements

*To fit sizes 1, 2, 3, 4, 5, 6*

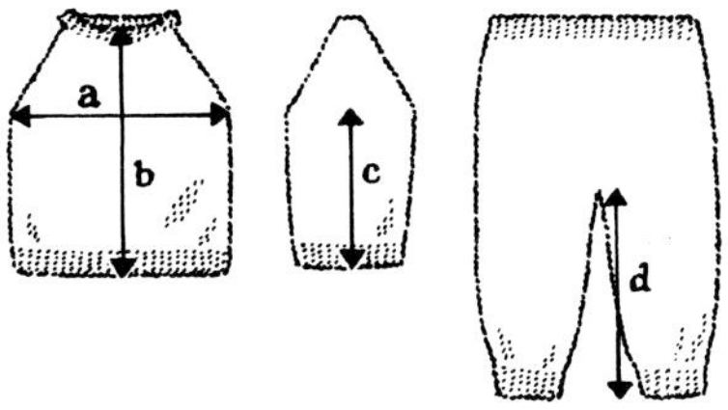


**Sweatshirt**
**a** Chest 22 ($23\frac{3}{4}$, $23\frac{3}{4}$, $24\frac{3}{4}$, $26\frac{1}{2}$, $28\frac{1}{2}$)in
**b** Length: neck to hem $8\frac{3}{4}$ ($10\frac{1}{4}$, $11\frac{3}{4}$, $13\frac{1}{2}$, 15, $16\frac{1}{2}$)in
**c** Sleeve seam $6\frac{3}{4}$ ($7\frac{1}{2}$, $8\frac{3}{4}$, $9\frac{1}{2}$, $10\frac{1}{4}$, 11)in
**Trousers**
**d** Inside leg 9 (11, $13\frac{3}{4}$, $16\frac{1}{4}$, 17, 19)in

## Body

This is worked in one piece with a side seam. With yarn M cast on 126 (126, 126, 141, 141, 141) sts using 2-needle method. Knit 1 row, then work 19 rows k1, p1 rib. Make hem by knitting up one loop from cast-on edge with each st and increase: k1; *yfwd, k3, rep from * to last 2 sts; yfwd, k2 – 168 (168, 168, 168, 188, 188) sts.
Work in st st following pattern from graph. Continue until work measures $6\frac{3}{4}$ ($7\frac{1}{2}$, $8\frac{3}{4}$, $9\frac{1}{2}$, $10\frac{3}{4}$, 11)in from hem fold (or more or less as required) ending on a wrong-side row.
**NB** *Do not break yarn when knit or purl sequence is upset by graph, as on rows 6 and 13, but start same end of row with new yarn.*
*Shape armholes:* Bind off 3 (3, 3, 5, 5, 5) sts, k76 (76, 76, 82, 82, 82), bind off 6 (6, 6, 10, 10, 10), k80 (80, 80, 86, 86, 86), bind off 3 (3, 3, 5, 5, 5).
*Shape back:* Working on last 80 (80, 80, 86, 86, 86) sts on needle and keeping first and last 2 sts of every row in yarn M, work raglan shaping. Purl 1 row.
**Next row** K1, sl 1, psso at beginning and k2tog, k1 at end.
Repeat these 2 rows working in pattern until 46 sts remain. Slip these sts onto holder.
*Shape front:* Work as back until 54 sts remain.
*Shape neck:* Wrong side facing, p20 sts, turn.
**Row 2** Sl 2, k15, k2tog, k1.
**Row 3** Purl 15, turn.
**Row 4** Sl 2, k10, k2tog, k1.
**Row 5** Purl 10, turn.
**Row 6** Sl 2, k5, k2tog, k1.
**Row 7** Purl 7, turn.
**Row 8** Sl 1, k3, k2tog, k1.
**Row 9** Purl 5, turn.
**Row 10** Sl 1, k1, k2tog, k1.
**Row 11** Purl 3, turn.
**Row 12** K2tog, k1.
Wrong side facing, slip all sts onto second needle.
**Row 13** (Right side facing) Knit 1, sl 1, k1, psso, k17, turn.
**Row 14** Sl 2, p17.
**Row 15** Knit 1, sl 1, k1, psso, k12, turn.
**Row 16** Sl 2, p12.
**Row 17** Knit 1, sl 1, k1, psso, k7, turn.
**Row 18** Sl 2, p7.
**Row 19** Knit 1, sl 1, k1, psso, k5, turn.
**Row 20** Sl 1, p6, turn.
**Row 21** Knit 1, sl 1, k1, psso, k2, turn.
**Row 22** Sl 1, p3, turn.
**Row 23** Knit 1, sl 1, k1, psso, k1, turn.
**Row 24** Sl 1, p2 – 42 sts on needle.
Slip these sts onto stitch holder.

## Sleeves

With yarn M cast on 32 (32, 32, 40, 40, 40) sts using 2-needle method. Knit 1 row, then work 19 rows k1, p1 rib.
Make hem by knitting up one loop from cast-on edge with each st and increase by yfwd, k1 to end – 64 (64, 64, 80, 80, 80) sts. Continue in st st following pattern from graph until work measures $6\frac{3}{4}$ $7\frac{1}{2}$, $8\frac{3}{4}$, $9\frac{1}{2}$, $10\frac{3}{4}$, 11)in (or more or less as required) from hem fold.
*Shape armholes:* Bind off 3 (3, 3, 5, 5, 5) sts, work to end. Repeat this row – 58 (58, 58, 70, 70, 70) sts.
Keeping first and last 2 sts of each row in yarn M, *work raglan shaping:* K1, sl 1, k1, psso at beginning and k2tog, k1 at end of every right-side row. Work until 26 sts remain. Slip sts onto holder.
Work another sleeve similarly.

## Neck band

Change to yarn M, knit across all 140 sts 11 rows, k1, p1 rib, k1, row and bind off.

## Finishing

Fold neck back and catch it to inside of main body of work. Thread elastic through this casing. Sew up side seam and sew sleeves to body.

## PANTS

**Yarn**
Main yarn M $5\frac{1}{4}$ *($5\frac{1}{4}$, 7, 7, $8\frac{3}{4}$, $8\frac{3}{4}$)oz* medium-weight cotton (red)
Yarn A *$1\frac{3}{4}$oz* medium-weight cotton (white)
**Needles**
1 no 2 (3, 4, 2, 3, 4)
**Notions**
1yd soft elastic
**Stitch gauge**
30 sts and 40 rows to 4in over st st using no 2 needles; 28 sts and 38 rows to 4in over st st on no 3 needles; 26 sts and 36 rows to 4in over st st on no 4 needles (or size needed to obtain given tension).

## Legs

With yarn A cast on 40 (40, 40, 50, 50, 50) sts using 2-needle method. Working back and forth in rows, work 32 rows k1, p1 rib. Change to yarn M and knit up sts on cast-on row alternating 1 st from needle with 1 loop from cast-on edge – 80 (80, 80, 100, 100, 100) sts. Work in st st without shaping until work is 9 (11, $13\frac{3}{4}$, $16\frac{1}{4}$, 17, 19)in from hem fold (or more or less as required), ending with a purl row.
*Shape crotch:* Knit 1 row.
**Row 2** *and every alternate row:* Purl without shaping.
**Row 3** Knit 5, turn.
**Row 5** Knit 10, turn.
Continue in this way until knitting 30 sts, then turn.
**Row 15** Knit to end of row.
**Row 16** Purl 5, turn.
**Row 17** *and every alternate row:* Knit without shaping.
**Row 18** Purl 10, turn.
**Row 20** Purl 15, turn.
Continue in this way until purling 30 sts. Break yarn and push sts onto flexible part of needle. Work another leg similarly but do not break the yarn.
*Shape body:* Right-side facing, work 55 rounds st st over all 160 (160, 160, 200, 200, 200) sts.
*Shape waist:* With contrast yarn, work 20 rounds k1, p1, rib and bind off.

## Finishing

Sew crotch seam, or, if preferred for younger child, fit small open-end zipper for easier diaper changes.

# Dusky Rose

Beautiful Fair-Isle-pattern dress can be worn with buttons at the front or back, by itself or over other clothes. Make it a complete outfit by knitting matching tights or socks and a hat (see overleaf).

## DRESS

### Yarn
Main yarn M 2 (2, 2, 3, 4, 5)oz 2-ply Shetland (natural)
Yarn A 1 (1, 1, 2, 2, 2)oz 2-ply Shetland (red)
Yarn B 1oz 2-ply Shetland (brown)
Yarn C 2 (2, 3, 3, 4, 4)oz 2-ply Shetland (pink)

### Needles
1 pair no 2 (3, 4, 2, 3, 4)
1 size no 2 circular or similar size 4 double-pointed needles

### Notions
9 (9, 10, 12, 14, 16) tiny buttons

### Tension
30 sts and 36 rows to 4in on no 2 needles;
28 sts and 34 rows to 4in on no 3 needles;
26 sts and 32 rows to 4in on no 4 needles (or size needed to obtain given tension).

## Measurements

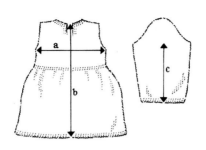

**a** Chest 18½ (19¾, 21¼, 23, 24½, 26)in
**b** Neck to hem 11 (13¾, 15¾, 18½, 21¼, 23)in
**c** Sleeve seam 6¼ (7, 8¼, 9½, 10¼, 10¾)in

## Method

Using 2-needle method and yarn A, cast on 201 (201, 201, 249, 249, 249) sts. Work 3 rows st st then knit row 4 to make fold line for hem. Continue in st st and pick up hem into row 9. Then work 26 rows following pattern from Graph A. Change to yarn M and continue in st st until work measures 7 (8¼, 9, 10¼, 11½, 12¼)in (or more or less as required) ending with a knit row. Then work as follows:

**Row 1** Purl 1 yarn M; *p1 yarn A, p5 yarn M, rep from * to last 2 sts; p1 yarn A; p1 yarn M.

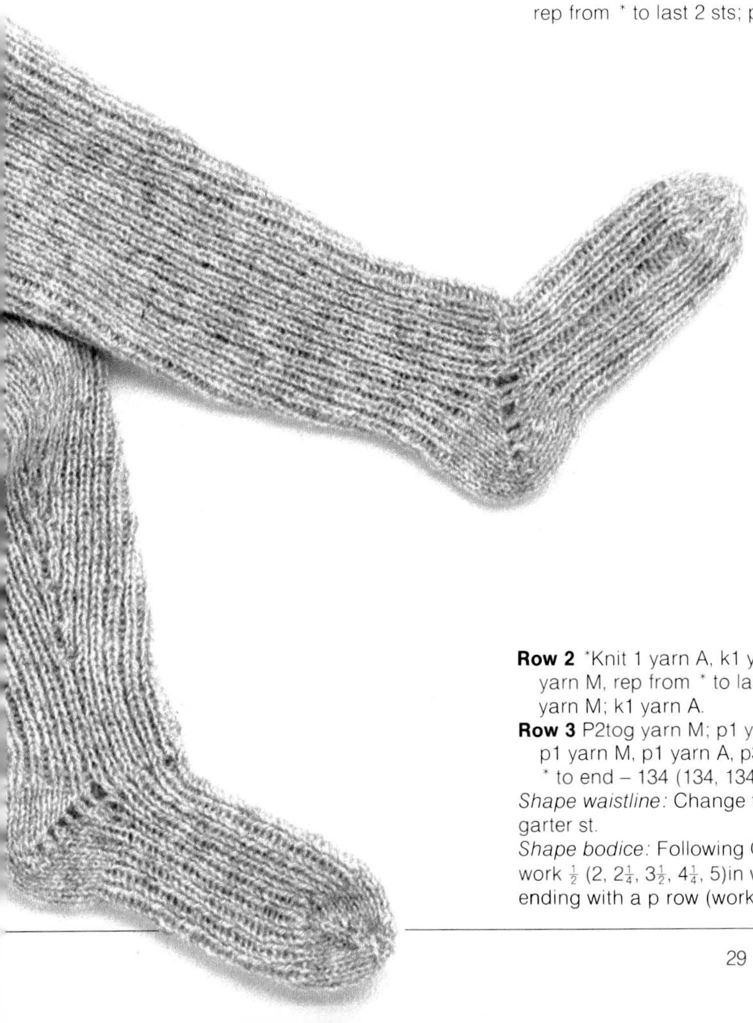

**Row 2** *Knit 1 yarn A, k1 yarn M, k1 yarn A, k3 yarn M, rep from * to last 3 sts; k1 yarn A; k1 yarn M; k1 yarn A.

**Row 3** P2tog yarn M; p1 yarn M; *p1 yarn A, p1 yarn M, p1 yarn A, p3tog yarn M, rep from * to end – 134 (134, 134, 166, 166, 166) sts.

*Shape waistline:* Change to yarn A, Knit 6 rows garter st.

*Shape bodice:* Following Graph B for pattern work ½ (2, 2¼, 3½, 4¼, 5)in without shaping ending with a p row (work in yarn C once

graph is completed). Then, bind off sts for armhole as follows:

**Row 1** Taking care to keep pattern correct, k31 (31, 31, 38, 38, 38); bind off 4 (4, 4, 6, 6, 6), k64 (64, 64, 78, 78, 78), bind off 4 (4, 4, 6, 6, 6), k31 (31, 31, 38, 38, 38).

*Left front:* Continue working on the last 31 (31, 31, 38, 38, 38) sts binding off 1 st at beginning of next 3 alternate rows. Continue without shaping until work measures 10¼ (13, 15, 17½, 20, 21¾)in from hem fold, ending at front edge.

*Shape neck:* Bind off 10 (10, 10, 12, 12, 12) sts beginning of next row. Then decrease 1 st at neck edge at the beginning of every alternate row until 14 (14, 14, 18, 18, 18) sts remain. Bind off and break yarn.

*Work back.* Wrong side work facing, rejoin yarn to left back of work and continue in pattern as graph. Bind off 1 st beginning of next 6 rows. Continue without shaping until work measures 10¼ (13, 15, 17½, 20, 21¾)in from hem fold ending with a k row.

*Shape neck:* Purl 18 (18, 18, 23, 23, 23) sts, bind off 22 (22, 22, 26, 26, 26), p18 (18, 18, 23, 23, 23). Complete as left front (above). Finish other shoulder similarly.

*Right front:* Rejoin yarn to wrong side of work on right front and continue as left front, reversing shaping where necessary.

## Sleeves

Using yarn A, cast on 40 (40, 40, 50, 50, 50) sts. Work 5 rows garter st, increasing 8 (8, 8, 10, 10, 10) sts evenly across last row – 48 (48, 48, 60, 60, 60) sts. Continue in st st and work 7 rows following pattern on Graph C. Change to yarn C and work st st until sleeve measures 6¼ (7, 8¼, 9½, 10¼, 10¾)in (or more or less as required).

*Shape sleeves:* Bind off 3 (3, 3, 4, 4, 4) sts beginning next 2 rows – 42 (42, 42, 52, 52, 52) sts. K2tog beginning every row until 24 sts remain, then k2tog both ends every row until 8 sts remain. Bind off knitting 2 sts tog. Work another sleeve similarly.

## Making up

Press all pieces well. Sew sleeve and shoulder seams, set sleeves into armholes.

## Button-bands

With right side of work facing, using no 2 circular needle and yarn A, pick up sts evenly from hem to neck on right front, pick up 60 (64, 68, 72, 76, 80) sts around neck and continue to pick up sts from neck down to hem on left front. Work 2 rows garter st, increasing 1 st at neck edge corners in each row.

*Buttonholes:* Make 9 (9, 10, 12, 14, 16) evenly-spaced buttonholes on 3rd row by: yfwd, k2tog. Knit 2 rows increasing at neck edges as before. Bind off.

## Finishing

Press well. Sew on buttons to correspond with buttonholes.

**Graph A**

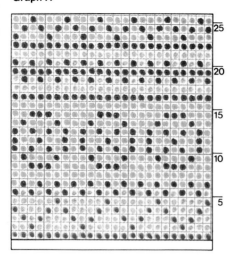

25
20
15
10
5

**24 st repeat**

**Graph B**

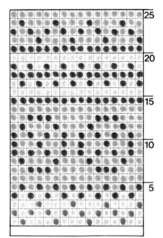

25
20
15
10
5

**16 st repeat**

**Graph C**

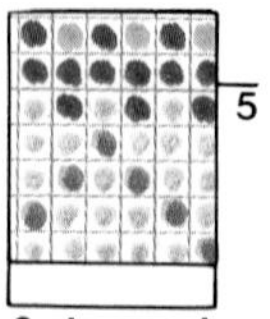

5

**6 st repeat**

Make a hat and socks to match the coat-dress using the pattern for the bonnet on p. 12 and pattern for the pink socks on p. 102.

## TIGHTS

**NB** *These can be knitted in wool, a soft acrylic yarn or cotton yarn.*

**Yarn**
Main yarn M 2 (2, 2, 3, 4, 5)oz 2-ply Shetland (natural)

**Needles**
1 pair no 2 (3, 4, 2, 3, 4)
Set of 4 similar size double-pointed

**Notions**
1yd elastic for waist

**Stitch gauge**
40 sts and 36 rows to 4in over k1, p1 rib on no 2 needles; 36 sts and 32 rows to 4in over k1, p1 rib on no 3 needles; 32 sts and 28 rows to 4in over k1, p1 rib on no 4 needles (or size needed to obtain given tension).

## Measurements

*To fit sizes 1, 2, 3, 4, 5, 6*

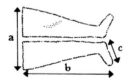

**a** Waist up to 20 (21. 22, 23, 24, 25¼(in
**b** Length 16¼ (18, 21¼, 22½, 23¾, 25¾)in
**c** 3½ (4¼, 4¾, 5½, 6, 6¼)in

## Left leg

*Starting at waist:* Cast on 50 (50, 50, 66, 66, 66) sts using 2-needle method. Work 8 rows st st, then k up cast-on row, to make carrier for elastic. Change to k1, p1 rib and work 5½ (6¼, 7, 7¾, 8¾, 9½)in without shaping.
*Increase sts for crotch:* Increase 1 st beginning next 6 rows. Cast on 3 (3, 3, 5, 5, 5) sts beginning of the next 2 rows – 62 (62, 62, 82, 82, 82) sts.

Change to double-pointed needles and commence working in rounds stitches divided as follows: 20, 20, 22 sts on needles for sizes 1, 2, 3; and 27, 27, 28 sts for sizes 4, 5, 6. Work 6 rounds without shaping, then k2tog both ends every 4th round until 30 (30, 30, 42, 42, 42) sts remain. Continue without shaping until work measures 15¾ (17¾, 21, 21¾, 23, 24¾)in from waist (or more or less as required).
*Shape heel:* Work in k1, p1 rib to last st, turn. Continue in st st working as follows:
**Row 1** Purl 15 (15, 15, 19, 19, 19), turn.
**Row 2** Knit 14 (14, 14, 18, 18, 18), turn.
Continue knitting or purling one less st per row until purling 7 sts. Turn and k 8. Turn and p 9. Continue knitting or purling one more st per row until purling 15 (15, 15, 19, 19, 19) sts.
*Working in rounds again:* Knit 16 (16, 16, 20, 20, 20); *k2tog, k1, rep from * 3 (3, 3, 6, 6, 6) times; k2 (2, 2, 1, 1, 1). Working in rounds k1, p1 rib, continue without shaping until foot measures 3¼ (4, 4¼, 5, 5½, 6)in (or more or less as required) from heel.
*Shape toe:*
**Round 1** K2tog, k9 (9, 9, 14, 14, 14), k2tog twice, k9 (9, 9, 13, 13, 13), k2tog.
**Round 2** *and every alternate row:* Knit without shaping.
**Round 3** K2tog, k7 (7, 7, 12, 12, 12), k2tog twice, k7 (7, 7, 11, 11, 11), k2tog.
**Round 5** K2tog, k5 (5, 5, 10, 10, 10), k2tog twice, k5 (5, 5, 9, 9, 9), k2tog.
*Larger 3 sizes:*
**Round 6** K2tog, k8, k2tog twice, k7, k2tog.
**Round 7** K2tog, k6, k2tog twice, k5, k2tog.
*All sizes:* Knit 1 round and bind off.

## Right leg

Work right leg as left leg but, when working the heel, omit the round in k1, p1 rib when commencing heel shaping and read k for p, p for k.

## Finishing

Sew both sections together at crotch seam. Sew toe seams and thread suitable length of elastic through waist.

# Hop Scotch

Neat Fair-Isle-pattern pullover vest and matching beret with a touch of class. It looks great worn with jeans.

## PULLOVER VEST

### Yarn

Main yarn M *1 (1, 1, 2, 2, 2)oz* 2-ply Shetland (oatmeal)
*½oz* 2-ply Shetland of each of other 5 colors (green, blue, yellow, vermillion and plum)

### Needles

1 pair no 2 (3, 4, 2, 3, 4)

### Stitch gauge

32 sts and 36 rows to 4in over st st on no 2 needles; 30 sts and 34 rows to 4in over st st on no 3 needles; 28 sts and 32 rows to 4in over st st on no 4 needles (or size needed to obtain given tension).

### Measurements

#### Pullover vest

*To fit sizes 1, 2, 3, 4, 5, 6*
**a** Chest 19 (20, 21¼, 23, 24½, 26)in
**b** Length 8¾ (9½, 11, 12¼, 13¾, 15¼)in
**Beret**
*To fit sizes 1–2, 3–4, 5–6*
**c** Around head 15 (16¼, 17½)in

### Back

Using yarn M, cast on 66 (66, 66, 80, 80, 80) sts and work 12 rows k1, p1 rib.
**Next row** Increase 10 (10, 10, 14, 14, 14) sts as follows: *smaller 3 sizes* – *k6, k into front and back next st, rep from * to last 3 sts, k3; *for larger 3 sizes* – *k into front and back next st, k5, rep from * to last 2 sts, k into front and back next st, k1 – 76 (76, 76, 94, 94, 94) sts.
Refer to Graph A and work in st st without shaping until work measures 5 (6, 6¾, 7½, 8¼, 9)in from beginning (or more or less as required) ending with a p row.
*Shape armholes:* Bind off 3 (3, 3, 5, 5, 5) sts beginning next 2 rows, then decrease 1 st beginning next 6 (6, 6, 8, 8, 8) rows. Continue working in pattern until work measures 8¼ (9, 10¾, 11¼, 13½, 15)in from beginning, ending with a p row.
*Shape neck:* Knit 22 (22, 22, 24, 24, 24) sts, bind off 20 (20, 20, 27, 27, 27), k22 (22, 22, 24, 24, 24). Then work on last set of sts as follows:
**Row 1** Purl.
**Row 2** K2tog, k to end.
**Row 3** Bind off 6, p to end.
**Row 4** As row 2.
**Row 5** As row 3.
**Row 6** Knit.
Bind off.
Work other shoulder similarly, reversing shaping.

### Front

Work as back until 8 fewer rows have been worked than back to armholes.
*Shape V-neck:* Knit 38 (38, 38, 47, 47, 47) sts, turn. Continue on these sts, p2tog, p to end. Work 6 more rows, decreasing first st beginning of every p row.
*Shape armhole:* Bind off 3 (3, 3, 5, 5, 5) sts, k to end. K2tog beginning of next 6 (6, 6, 8, 8, 8) rows, then keep arm edge straight and decrease 1 st beginning every row at neck edge until 20 (20 ,20, 22, 22, 2) sts remain. Continue without shaping until work measures the same as back. Then, bind off 6 sts at arm edge next 2 alternate rows, p 1 row and bind off.
Work other side to match, reversing shaping where necessary.

### Neck edging

Using yarn M, join right shoulder. Starting from left front, pick up and knit 36 (38, 40, 44, 48, 52) sts down left front to 1 st from middle (mark with colored thread), pick up same number of sts up right front and 30 (30, 32, 34, 36, 38) sts across back of neck. Work in k1, p1 rib, to last 2 sts before middle front st, k2tog, p1, k2tog, k1, p1 rib to end. Work 5 more rows similarly, decreasing each side of middle st. Bind off in rib, decreasing as before.

### Armhole edging

Join left shoulder seam. Right side facing, pick up and k 56 (60, 62, 72, 76, 80) sts around armhole edge. Work 6 rows k1, p1 rib and bind off in rib.
Work another armhole similarly.

### Finishing

Sew side seams and press work carefully.

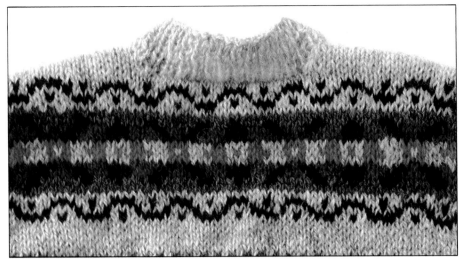

Detail showing back of neck.

## BERET

### Yarn

Main yarn M *1oz* 2-ply Shetland (oatmeal)
*¼oz* 2-ply Shetland each of other 5 colors
(green, blue, yellow, vermillion and plum)

### Needles

1 pair no 3 (4, 5)

### Stitch gauge

30 sts and 34 rows to 4in over st st on no 3
needles; 28 sts and 32 rows to 4in over st st
on no 4 needles; 26 sts and 30 rows to 4in over
st st on no 5 needles (or size needed to obtain
given tension).

## Method

With yarn M cast on 72 sts. Knit 2, *p1, k1, rep
from * to end. Repeat this row 5 times.
**Row 7** *Knit 7, k into front and back next st,
rep from * to end.
**Row 8** *and every even-numbered row:* Purl.
**Row 9** *Knit 8, k into front and back next st,
rep from * to end.
Continue in this way increasing 9 sts every
alternate row until 20 rows have been worked
and increasing 1 st at end of last row – 136 sts.
Refer to Graph B and commence working in
pattern. Work 4 rows without shaping, decrease
1 st at end of last row – 135 sts.
**Row 1** *Knit 13, k2tog, rep from * to end.
**Row 3** *Knit 12, k2tog, rep from * to end.
Continue decreasing in this way on every odd-
numbered row until 9 sts remain. Break yarn,
thread end through remaining sts, draw up and
sew seam.

## Finishing

Dampen work and pull it over small plate or
circle of cardboard to stretch it into shape, and
leave it to dry. Press carefully from outside.

**Graph A**

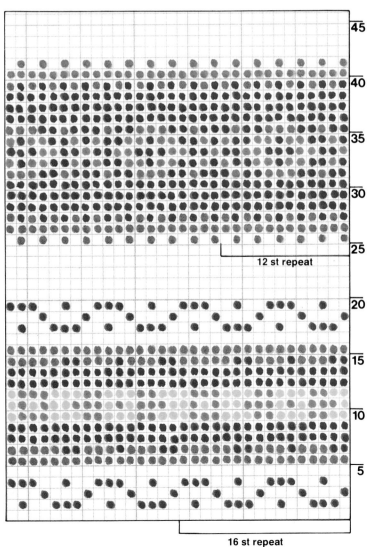

45
40
35
30
25

**12 st repeat**

20
15
10
5

**16 st repeat**

**Graph B**

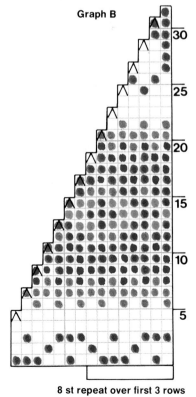

30
25
20
15
10
5

**8 st repeat over first 3 rows**

## Measurements

*To fit sizes 4, 5, 6 only*

**a** Chest 23 (24¾, 27½)in
**b** Sleeve seam 9½ (10¼, 11)in
**c** Inside leg 16¼ (17, 19)in

# RAINBOW TRIM

Big, bright all-in-one playsuit is very simple to make and fine for both girls and boys. It is warm and cosy and, worked in acrylic yarn, it is machine washable.

## PLAYSUIT

### Yarn
Main yarn M $10\frac{1}{2}$ (12$\frac{1}{4}$, 14)oz acrylic knitting worsted (blue)
Scraps 3 colors acrylic knitting worsted (green, yellow, red)

### Needles
1 pair no 4 (5, 6)

### Notions
12in zipper to match yarn M or one color in stripes

### Stitch gauge
24 sts and 32 rows to 4in over st st on no 4 needles; 22 sts and 30 rows to 4in over st st on no 5 needles; 20 sts and 28 rows to 4in over st st on no 6 needles (or size needed to obtain given tension).

## Pockets

With yarn M cast on 30 sts and work 20 rows st st. Then work as follows: Knit 28, turn. Purl 26, turn. Continue this way working 2 less sts per row until purling 6, then turn. Knit to end row. Knitting across all sts, continue in garter st working 1 row yarn M, 2 rows green, 2 rows yellow, 1 row red, and bind off in red.
Make another pocket similarly.

## Body

Using yarn M cast on 60 sts. Work 6 rows garter st, then change to st st. Increase 1 st both ends every 3rd row until 90 sts on needle. Continue until work measures $16\frac{1}{4}$ (17, 19)in (or more or less as required), ending with a wrong side-row. Then k40 sts, bind off 10 for crotch, k40. Working on these last 40 sts and keeping left (outside) edge straight; k2tog beginning next and following 5 alternate rows – 35 sts. Continue without shaping until work measures $28\frac{1}{2}$ (30, 33)in from beginning (or more or less as required). Bind off. Finish other half of work similarly, reversing shaping. Work another body section similarly.

## Sleeves

Using yarn M cost on 60 sts. Work 6 rows garter st, then continue in st st without shaping until work measures $9\frac{1}{2}$ (10$\frac{1}{4}$, 11)in from beginning (or more or less as required). Bind off.
Work another sleeve similarly.

## Arm and shoulder bands

Cast on 84 sts yarn M. Work in garter st as follows: 1 row yarn M, 2 rows green, 2 rows yellow, 2 rows red, 2 rows yellow, 2 rows green, 1 row yarn M. Bind off in yarn M.
Work another band similarly.

## Finishing

Press all 8 pieces carefully. Sew arm and shoulder bands into position along front and back shoulder edge. Sew sleeves to bands and fit into side seams. Sew side seams. Sew back seam and crotch, then fit zipper in place at center front. Center pockets over side seams at hip level and sew in place.
*Finish neck:* Using yarn M, pick up 45 sts evenly around neck and bind off.

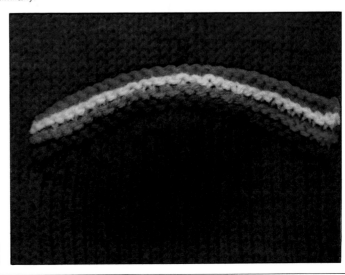

Close up of rainbow-shaped pocket

# CHINESE CAP

Based on a traditional Mongolian design, this hat looks great on little girls and boys alike. Knit it in bright colors for the best effect.

## HAT

### Yarn

Main yarn M *1oz* 2-ply Shetland (red)
Yarn A Scraps 2-ply Shetland (green)
Yarn B Scraps 2-ply Shetland (dark blue)
Yarn C Scraps 2-ply Shetland (yellow)
Yarn D Scraps 2-ply Shetland (turquoise)

**Needles**
Set 4 double-pointed no 2 (3, 4)
1 pair no 2 (3, 4)

## Measurements

*To fit sizes 1–2, 3–4, 5–6*
Around head 17 (18, 19)in

## Method

Cast on 120 sts over 3 needles (40 each) using yarn A. Work 4 rounds garter st. Refer to graph and, working in st st, continue until work measures 4 (4¾, 6)in

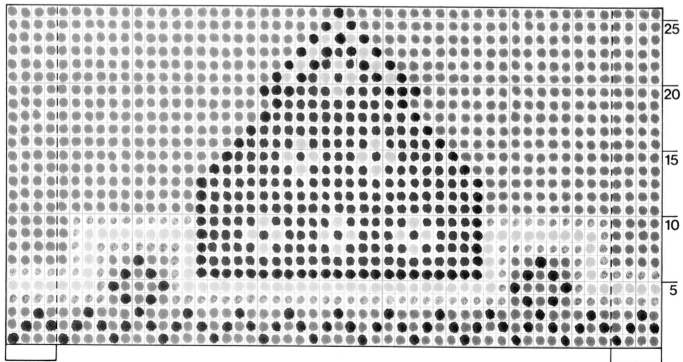

Repeat these sts to end (10 times)

Repeat these sts 9 times

# COSY TOES

Easy and really quick to knit, this pattern can be used to make a pair of cosy bootees that will not fall off a baby, or slippers for an older child. It is an ideal way to use up any extra wool you have around.

*Commence crown shaping:* \*K2tog, k8, k2tog, rep from \* to end.
Work 3 rounds without shaping.
**Next round** \*K2tog, k6, k2tog, rep from \* to end. Work 3 rounds without shaping. Repeat, decreasing 20 sts every 4th row until 20 sts remain. Work 3 rounds without shaping, then k2tog across all sts, k 1 round and break yarn. Thread through remaining sts and secure.

## Neck and earflaps

Cast on 180 sts yarn A. Work 2 rows garter st, then bind off 60 sts at beginning next 2 rows. Work on the remaining 60 sts:
**Row 1** Knit 3 yarn A, k17 yarn D, turn.
**Row 2** Sl 1, p6 yarn D, p1 yarn C, p5 yarn D, p1 yarn C, p3 yarn D, p3 yarn A.
**Row 3** Knit 2 yarn A, sl 1, k1, psso, k1 yarn D, k1 yarn C, k1 yarn D, k1 yarn C, k3 yarn D, k1 yarn C, k1 yarn D, k1 yarn C, k4 yarn D, turn.
**Row 4** Sl 1, p4 yarn D, p1 yarn C, p5 yard D, p1 yarn C, p2 yarn D, p3 yarn A.
**Row 5** Knit 2 yarn A, sl 1, k1, psso, k11 yarn D, turn.
**Row 6** Sl 1 yarn D, p to last 3 sts, k3 yarn A.
**Row 7** Knit 2 yarn A, sl 1, k1, psso, k3 yarn D, k3, k1 yarn C, k4 yarn D, turn.
**Row 8** Sl 1, p3, k1 yarn C, k1 yarn D, k1 yarn C, k2 yarn D, k3 yarn A.
**Row 9** Knit 2, sl 1, k1, psso, k2 yarn D, k1 yarn C, k yarn D to last 7 sts, turn.
**Row 10** Sl 1, p yarn D to last 3 sts, k3 yarn A.
**Row 11** Knit 2 yarn A, sl 1, k1, psso, change to yarn D, k3, turn.
**Row 12** Sl 1, p2, change to yarn A, k3.
**Row 13** Knit 33 yarn A, k17 yarn D, k3 yarn A.
**Row 14** Knit 3 yarn A, p16 yarn D, turn.
**Row 15** Sl 1; \*k5 yarn D, k1 yarn C, rep from \* once; k2 yarn D, k2tog yarn A, k2.
**Row 16** Knit 3 yarn A; \*p1 yarn D, p1 yarn C, rep from \* once; p3 yarn D; p1 yarn C; p1 yarn D; p1 yarn C; p3 yarn D.
**Row 17** Sl 1, k3 yarn D, k1 yarn C, k5 yarn D, k1 yarn C, k1 yarn D, change to yarn A, k2tog, k2.
**Row 18** Knit 3 yarn A, p10 yarn D, turn.
**Row 19** Sl 1, k8 yarn D, change to yarn A, k2tog, k2.
**Row 20** Knit 3 yarn A, p3 yarn D, p1 yarn C, p3 yarn D, turn.
**Row 21** Sl 1; \*k1 yarn D, k1 yarn C, rep from \* once; k1 yarn D; change to yarn A, k2tog, k2.
**Row 22** Knit 3 yarn A, p2 yarn D, p1 yarn C, p1 yarn D, turn.
**Row 23** Sl 1, k2 yarn D, change to yarn A, k2tog, k2.
**Row 24** Purl across all 50 sts yarn A. Bind off.

## Finishing

Line center of earflaps to center back of hat and sew them onto the hat.

## SLIPPERS

### Yarn
Main yarn M *1oz* bulky Shetland (pink)
Yarn A scraps of bulky Shetland (green)
### Needles
1 pair no 9
Size I crochet hook (optional)
### Notions
½yd narrow elastic (optional)

### Measurements

To fit sizes 1–2, 3–4, 5–6

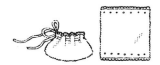

## Method

With yarn A cast on 15 (20, 25) sts. Change to yarn M and work 2 rows garter st. Make a row of eyelet holes: k1, \*yo, k2tog, rep from \* to end.
Work 18 (22, 26) rows garter st, then make another row of eyelet holes.
Work 2 rows garter st, change to yarn A and bind off on right side of work.
Work another slipper similarly.

## Finishing

Fold work in half and sew up end seams. If desired, crochet 2 × 60-chain cords using yarn A. Thread through eyelet holes and tie in bow over seam. Alternatively, thread shirring elastic through eyelet holes, pull up tight and sew ends together.

# Tassle Tops

A cosy overjacket, babybag or kimono can all be made following
this very simple pattern. Worked in garter stitch throughout it is
an ideal garment for beginners.

## OVERJACKET AND BABYBAG

**Yarn**
*Overjacket*
Main yarn M 6 (6, 8, 8, 8, 10)oz soft spun
Shetland
Yarn A Scraps contrasting yarn of any
thickness (green or red)
*Babybag and kimono*
Main yarn M 8 (8, 10, 12, 14, 16)oz soft spun
Shetland
Yarn A Scraps contrasting yarn of any
thickness (green or red)
**Needles**
1 pair no 9
**Notions**
Stitch holder
*Overjacket and kimono*
1 × ¾in button
*Babybag*
7 × ¾in buttons
**Stitch gauge**
16 sts and 26 rows to 4in over garter st on
no 9 needles (or size needed to obtain given
tension).

### Front

Cast on 36 (40, 46, 50, 56, 60) sts using yarn A.
Change to yarn M and, working in garter st
throughout, work without shaping until front
measures 7¾ (8¼, 8¾, 9, 9½, 10¼)in for overjacket,
or 13¾ (15¼, 17¾, 19¾, 21¾, 23¾)in for babybag
and kimono (or more or less as required),
ending with a wrong-side row. Then divide sts
for front neck opening: Knit 18 (20, 23, 25, 28,
30) sts, turn. Work 18 (20, 22, 24, 28, 30) rows
on these sts.
**Next row** Bind off 10 sts (for neck), k to end.
Break yarn and leave remaining 8 (10, 13, 15,
18, 20) sts on stitch holder or spare needle.
Work other side of front similarly working last
row as follows: Knit 8 (10, 13, 15, 18, 20) sts,
bind off remaining 10 sts.

### Back

With right side facing, k across sts on first side
of front, cast on 20 sts, k across second side of
front. Work down back until it is same length as
front, ending with a wrong-side row. Bind off on
right side using yarn A.

### Sleeves

With right side of work facing, and beginning
and ending 3¼ (3¾, 3¾, 4¼, 4¼, 5)in from
shoulder line on each side, pick up 25 (30, 30,
35, 35, 40) sts. Work 35 (41, 47, 53, 59, 65) rows
in garter st (or more or less as required). Bind
off in yarn A. Work another sleeve similarly.

### Hood

With right side of work facing, and beginning at
center front, knit up 30 (30, 35, 35, 40, 40) sts
around neck.
**Next row** Double sts by knitting into the front
   and back of every st – 60 (60, 70, 70, 80,
   80) sts.

Work 36 (40, 44, 48, 54, 60)
rows and bind off
on right side using yarn A.

### Flap – Babybag only

With yarn A, cast on same number of sts as
used formain body of garment. Change to
yarn M and work 3 rows in garter st.
**Next row** Make 3 evenly-spaced buttonholes
   by working: yfwd, k2tog.
Work 20 rows in garter st. Work 3 buttonholes
in next row.
Work 3 further rows in garter st. Change to
yarn A, bind off on right side of work. Sew
buttons onto main body of garment to
correspond with buttonholes.

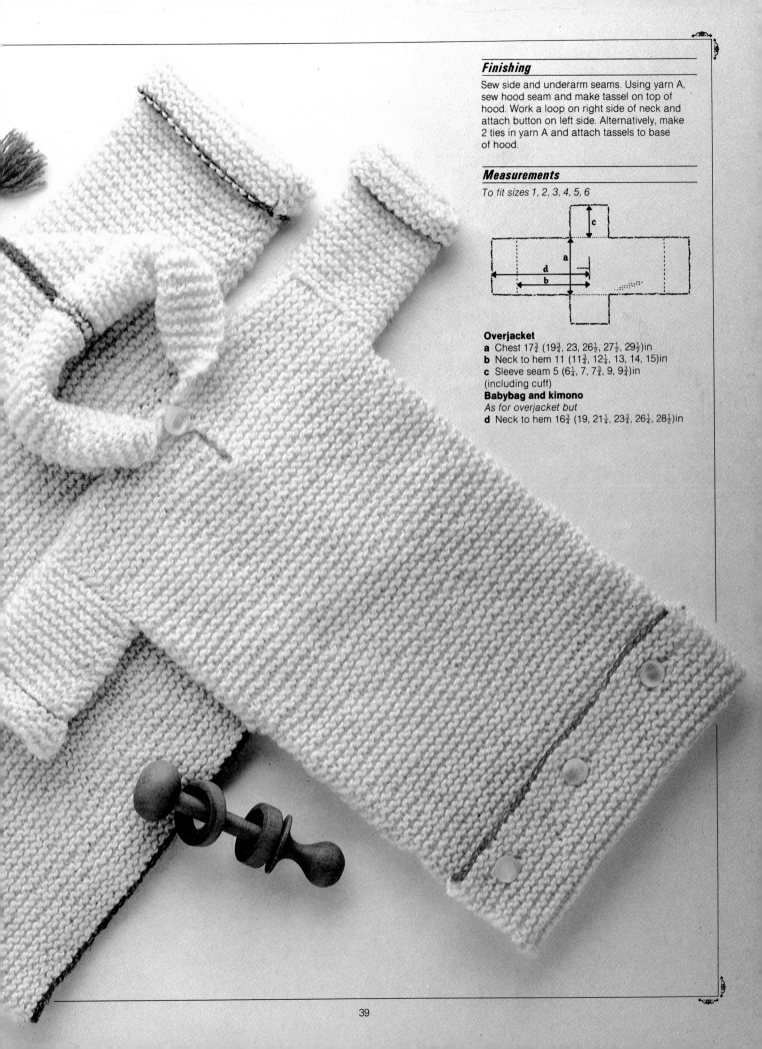

## Finishing

Sew side and underarm seams. Using yarn A, sew hood seam and make tassel on top of hood. Work a loop on right side of neck and attach button on left side. Alternatively, make 2 ties in yarn A and attach tassels to base of hood.

## Measurements

*To fit sizes 1, 2, 3, 4, 5, 6*

**Overjacket**
a Chest 17$\frac{3}{4}$ (19$\frac{3}{4}$, 23, 26$\frac{1}{2}$, 27$\frac{1}{2}$, 29$\frac{1}{2}$)in
b Neck to hem 11 (11$\frac{3}{4}$, 12$\frac{1}{4}$, 13, 14, 15)in
c Sleeve seam 5 (6$\frac{1}{4}$, 7, 7$\frac{3}{4}$, 9, 9$\frac{3}{4}$)in
(including cuff)
**Babybag and kimono**
*As for overjacket but*
d Neck to hem 16$\frac{3}{4}$ (19, 21$\frac{1}{4}$, 23$\frac{3}{4}$, 26$\frac{1}{4}$, 28$\frac{1}{2}$)in

# Winter Playtime

Bright stripy accessories show up clearly in the snow. Knitted in acrylic yarn they dry quickly and do not mat. The muffler can be worn in several ways and won't get caught in wheels or branches.

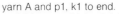

## HAT

### Yarn

Yarn A $\frac{1}{3}$oz knitting worsted (blue)
Yarn B $\frac{1}{3}$oz knitting worsted (green)
Yarn C $\frac{1}{3}$oz knitting worsted (yellow)
Yarn D $\frac{1}{3}$oz knitting worsted (red)

### Needles

1 pair no 4
1 pair no 6

### Stitch gauge

19 sts and 41 rows to 4in over garter st on no 6 needles (or size needed to obtain given tension).

### Method

With yarn A and no 4 needles cast on 72 (78) sts. Work k1, p1 rib for 6 rows. Change to no 6 needles and garter st, working stripes over 2 rows in following order: yarn B, yarn C, yarn D, yarn A. When 6 ($7\frac{3}{4}$)in have been worked from beginning, decrease by 6 sts every right-side row as follows: *K10 (11), k2tog, rep from * to end; then *k9 (10), k2tog, rep from * to end, and so on until 12 sts remain. Break yarn and thread through sts. Sew seam.

## MUFFLER

### Yarn

Yarn A $\frac{3}{4}$oz knitting worsted (blue)
Yarn B $\frac{1}{3}$oz knitting worsted (green)
Yarn C $\frac{1}{3}$oz knitting worsted (yellow)
Yarn D $\frac{1}{3}$oz knitting worsted (red)

### Needles

1 pair no 6

### Notions

3 × $\frac{1}{2}$in buttons

### Stitch gauge

As hat

### Method

With yarn A and no 6 needles, cast on 130 (160) sts. Work in garter st as follows:

**Row 1** Knit to last 3 sts in yarn A, p1, k1, p1.
**Row 2** With yarn A k1, p1, k1, p1, change to yarn B and k to end.
**Row 3** With yarn B k to last 5 sts, change to yarn A and p1, k1 to end.
**Row 4** With yarn A (k1, p1) 3 times, change to yarn C and k to end.
**Row 5** With yarn C k to last 7 sts, change to yarn A and p1, k1 to end.
**Row 6** With yarn A (k1, p1) 4 times, change to yarn D and k to end.
**Row 7** With yarn D k to last 9 sts, change to

yarn A and p1, k1 to end.
**Row 8** With yarn A k1, p1, k1, yfwd, k2tog, p1, k1, p1, k to end.
**Row 9** With yarn A k to last 9 sts, then p1, k1 to end.
**Row 10** With yarn A (k1, p1) 4 times, change to yarn B and k to end.
**Row 11** With yarn B k to last 7 sts, change to yarn A and p1, k1 to end.
**Row 12** With yarn A (k1, p1) 3 times, change to yarn C and k to end.
**Row 13** With yarn C k to last 5 sts, change to yarn A and p1, k1 to end.
**Row 14** With yarn A (k1, p1) twice, change to yarn D and k to end.
**Row 15** With yarn D k to last 3 sts, change to yarn A and p1, k1, p1.
**Row 16** With yarn A k1, p1, k to end.
Repeat these 16 rows twice, then bind off in yarn A.

### Finishing

Sew on buttons to correspond with buttonholes. This muffler can be worn in any of 4 ways: crossed over the neck and buttoned; crossed over the chest and buttoned center back; around the head over the ears and buttoned back neck; or knotted at the neck as an ordinary scarf.

## MITTENS

### Yarn

Yarn A $\frac{1}{3}$oz knitting worsted (blue)
Yarn B $\frac{1}{3}$oz knitting worsted (green)
Yarn C $\frac{1}{3}$oz knitting worsted (yellow)
Yarn D $\frac{1}{3}$oz knitting worsted (red)

### Needles

1 pair no 4
1 pair no 6

### Stitch gauge

As hat

### Method

Using no 4 needles and yarn A, cast on 24 sts. Work k1, p1 rib for 10 rows. Change to no 6 needles. Continue in garter st stripes over 2 rows in this order: yarn B, yarn C, yarn D, yarn A. Work 6 (10) rows.
*Small size mitten:*
**Next row** **Knit 9, slip next 6 sts onto stitch holder, cast on 4 sts, k to end**.
Continue in stripes until 12 stripes have been worked in all – 24 rows.
*Large size mitten:* On row 11 work as small mitten ** to **. Continue until 18 stripes have been worked in all – 36 rows.
*(Both sizes) Shape top:*
**Row 1** *K2tog, k7, k2tog, rep from *.
**Row 2** *K2tog, k5, k2tog, rep from *.
Bind off.
*Shape thumb:* Slip sts onto needle (from left to right). Using relevant yarn (A or C) cast on 2, k6, cast on 2. Work on 10 sts in stripes for 10 (14) rows.
**Next row** *K2tog, k1, k2tog, rep from * twice.
Bind off.

### Finishing

Sew up thumb seam and sew base of thumb to body of mitten. Sew up top and side seams. Work another mitten similarly. Sew them to ends of long crochet chain of yarn A, if desired.

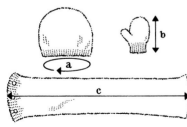

### Measurements

In 2 sizes to fit sizes 1–3, 4–6

**Hat**
**a** Circumference 15 ($16\frac{1}{4}$)in
**Mittens**
**b** Length $4\frac{3}{4}$ (6)in
**Muffler**
**c** Length $27\frac{1}{4}$ (33)in

# SNOWFLAKES

Swiss-styled classic winter jacket with matching hat and mittens
or gloves sports a traditional snowflake design.

## JACKET

**Yarn**
Main yarn M 3 (4, 5, 6, 7, 8)oz 2-ply Shetland
(grey)
Yarn A 1 (1, 2, 2, 3, 3)oz 2-ply Shetland
(natural)
Yarn B 1oz 2-ply Shetland (vermilion)

**Needles**
1 pair no 2
1 pair long no 4 (5, 6, 4, 5, 6)

**Notions**
6 buttons

**Stitch gauge**
24 sts and 32 rows to 4in over st st on no 4
needles; 22 sts and 30 rows to 4in over st st on
no 5 needles; 20 sts and 28 rows to 4in over
st st on no 6 needles (or size needed to
obtain given tension).

## Sleeves

With yarn M and no 2 needles, cast on 36 (36,
36, 46, 46, 46) sts. K1, p1 rib for 12 (12, 12, 20,
20, 20) rows. Change to no 4 (5, 6, 4, 5, 6)
needles and st st and work 3 rows without
shaping.
**Next row** Refer to graph and work in pattern.
Increase 1 st both ends of rows 7, 11 and 15
and then every 10th row.
**NB** When working yarn B, take 20in length for
each star and weave ends in carefully as work
prpgresses.
Continue until work measures 6¾ (7, 7½, 8¾, 9,
9¾)in from beginning (or more or less as
required), ending on a wrong-side row.
Increase 1 st at the beginning of the next 4
rows. Increase 1 st both ends of the next 3 (3, 3,
5, 5, 5) rows. Purl 1 row. Break yarn.

## Body

Keep pattern over sleeve sts, then with yarn M,
cast on 35 (40, 45, 50, 55, 60) sts and knit
across cast on and sleeve sts. Break yarn. Cast
on 35 (40, 45, 50, 55, 60) sts and purl across all
sts on needle.
Work in pattern until star motifs are completed,
working first and last 3 sts every row in garter
stitch. Work 3 row stripe following Graph A
across the whole width of work. Continue
pattern across all sts until work measures 3¼
(3½, 3½, 4, 4, 4¼)in from cast-on body sts ending
with a wrong-side row.
Count sts on needle. Halve this number and
subtract 4 (4, 4, 6, 6, 6). Knit this number of sts.

bind off 8 (8, 8, 12, 12, 12) and knit to end.
Work on this half of garment until it measures
5 (5½, 6, 6¼, 6½, 6¾)in from cast-on body sts,
ending with a wrong-side row. Change to
yarn A and bind off.
Complete other sts on needle to match.
Work another half garment similarly.

## Button-bands

Press both halves of work well. Join center
back seam using yarn A leaving a fine white
stripe. With right side facing and using yarn B,
knit up sts evenly right front edge, around
neck and down left front.
*Make buttonholes:* Knit 4 rows garter st,
working buttonholes in second row on right
front for girl and left front for boy. Calculate the
spacing as follows:
Count sts on front button-band (excluding neck
sts), deduct 6 (3 top, 3 bottom), deduct 12 (the
stitches required for making the holes), and
divide by 5 to get the number of sts between
buttonholes. At button-band: work k3; *yo,
k2tog, k number of required sts between
buttonholes, rep from * 5 times; yo, k2tog,  3.

## Finishing

Sew side and underarm seams and press
carefully. Sew on buttons to correspond with
holes.

## Measurements

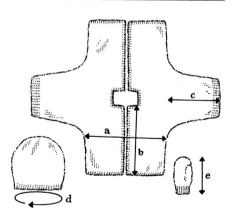

### Jacket
**a** Chest 20½ (22, 23¾, 25¼, 26, 26¾)in
**b** Neck to hem 10¼ (12¼, 14¼, 14¼, 16¼, 19)in
**c** Sleeve seam 7½ (7¾, 8¼, 9¾, 10¼, 11)in
### Hat
**d** Around head 13 (14¼, 15¾)in
### Mittens
**e** Length 5in (including 1¼in wrist band)

Traditional pewter or silver buttons make this jacket particularly appealing.

# SNOWFLAKES

**Graph A**

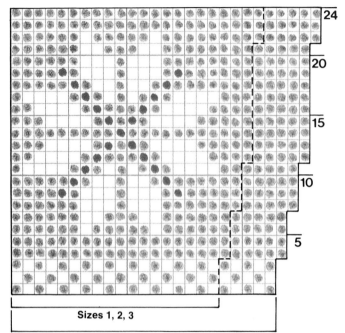

Sizes 1, 2, 3

Sizes 4, 5, 6

**Graph B**

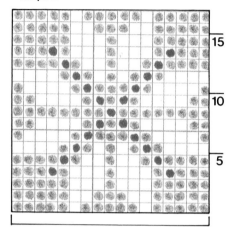

17 st repeat

## MITTENS

**NB** *These mittens are suitable for babies and toddlers, gloves may be better for older children (see opposite).*

### Yarn

Main yarn M *1oz* 2-ply Shetland (grey)
Scraps of yarns A and B (natural and vermilion)

### Needles

1 set no 2 double-pointed
1 set no 5 double-pointed

### Stitch gauge

22 sts and 30 rows over 4in over st st on no 5 needles (or size needed to obtain given tension).

## Method

With yarn M and no 2 needles, cast on 34 sts spaced 12, 12, 10 sts on 3 needles. Work k1, p1 rib for 12 rounds. Change to no 5 needles and work 3 rounds in st st without shaping.
*Commence pattern:*

**Round 1** Knit 1 yarn A, k1 yarn M across 16 sts of palm, k6 yarn M, k1 yarn A, k5 yarn M, k1 yarn A, k5 yarn M.

**Round 2** K1 yarn M, k1 yarn A across 16 sts of palm, k6 yarn M, k2 yarn A, k3 yarn M, k2 yarn A and k5 yarn M.

**NB** *Be careful to weave in lengths of yarn at back of work as you proceed or a child's fingers will become tangled.*

Continue alternating yarn A and yarn M across palm and follow Graph B for pattern on back of hand. Work 4 rounds in pattern, then slip first 6 sts (for thumb) onto stitch holder. Cast on 6 sts and continue in pattern.

**NB** *When working left mitten, k10 sts, then slip next 6 sts onto stitch holder (for thumb). Cast on 6 sts and continue.*

Work further 11 rounds without shaping.
*Commence shaping:*

**Round 1** *K2tog, k13, k2tog, rep from * once.
**Round 2** *K2tog, k11, k2tog, rep from * once.

**Round 3** *K2tog, k9, k2tog, rep from * once.
**Round 4** *K2tog, k7, k2tog, rep from * once.
Bind off.
*Shape thumb:* Knit up 4 sts from stitch holder on first needle, then 2 plus 2 picked up from cast-on edge on second needle, and 4 picked up from cast-on edge on third needle. Work 10 rounds st st then k2tog across all sts. Break yarn and thread through sts. Work another mitten similarly altering thumb position as indicated.

## Finishing

Sew seam at top of hand and finish top of thumb securely. Press st st sections well.

## Chain

If required, work a long chain of yarn M with crochet hook and sew to base of mittens.

## HAT

### Yarn

Main yarn M *2oz* 2-ply Shetland (grey)
Yarn A *1oz* 2-ply Shetland (natural)
Yarn B *½oz* 2-ply Shetland (vermilion)

### Needles

1 pair no 4 (5, 6)

### Stitch gauge

As for jacket

## Method

Cast on 80 sts using yarn M and work 6 rows k1, p1 rib. Change to st st and work 2 rows without shaping.

**Row 1** *Knit 9, increase by knitting into front and back next st, rep from * to end – 88 sts.

**Row 2** *and every alternate row:* Purl.

**Row 3** *Knit 10, increase by knitting into front and back of next st, rep from * to end – 96 sts.
Continue in this way until 136 sts on needle,

ending with a wrong-side row.
Refer to Graph B for pattern and work band of 8 adjoining stars over work without shaping.
*Shaping for crown:*

**Row 1** Decrease: *k15, k2tog, rep from * to end – 128 sts.

**Row 2** *and every alternate row:* Purl.

**Row 3** *Knit 14, k2tog, rep from * to end – 120 sts.

Continue in this way until 48 sts remain. Then continue to decrease but alternating 1st yarn M and 1st yarn A, until 16 sts remain. Break yarn and thread through sts.

## Finishing

Sew up back seam and neaten threads. Press st st section well from inside.

# FINGER FUN

One good basic glove pattern worked in the round on four needles can be used for a variety of effects. Work it in one yarn; with different colored fingers; in stripes; introduce your own patterns; or sew funny faces onto the fingers.

## GLOVES

### Yarn
*1oz* 2-ply Shetland

### Needles
1 set 4 double-pointed no 2
1 set 4 double-pointed no 5

### Stitch gauge
23 sts and 28 rows to 4in over st st on no 5 needles (or size needed to obtain given tension).

## Measurements

*To fit sizes 4–6*
Wrist to end longest finger 7½in (including wrist band).

## Right hand glove

With no 2 needles, cast on 34 sts spaced as follows: 12, 12, 10 sts over 3 needles. Work k1, p1 rib for 20 rounds. Change to no 5 needles and work 10 rounds without shaping.
*Shape thumb hole:* Slip first 7 sts onto stitch holder or spare thread (for thumb). Cast on 7 sts and continue to end of round. Work 11 rounds without shaping. Begin to work fingers.
**NB** *When working left glove k 7 sts then slip next 7 sts onto stitch holder (for thumb). Cast on 7 sts and continue.*

**Finger 1** Knit 5, slip 24 sts onto stitch holder, cast on 2, k5 – 12 sts. Work 12 rounds st st, then k2tog across all sts, break yarn and thread through sts. Secure thread firmly.
**Finger 2** Knit up 2 sts from base of first finger, pick up 4 from stitch holder, cast on 2, slip next 16 sts onto stitch holder, k remaining 4 sts – 12 sts. Work 15 rounds st st, then k2tog across all sts. Break yarn. Thread yarn through sts and secure firmly.
**Finger 3** As finger 2 but work 12 rounds st st.
**Finger 4** Pick up the 8 remaining sts from stitch holder, pick up 2 at base of 3rd finger – 10 sts. Work 10 rounds st st, then k2tog across all sts, break yarn, thread through sts and secure firmly.
**Thumb** Slip 4 sts from stitch holder onto one needle, slip the other 3 sts onto second needle plus 2 sts knitted up from cast-on edge, and knit up 5 sts onto third needle – 14 sts. Work 12 rounds then k2tog across all sts. Break yarn, thread through sts and secure firmly.

## Left hand glove

Work as right hand reversing shaping for thumb, as indicated.

**Finger 4** Knit up 4 sts from stitch holder, slip 26 sts onto stitch holder, cast on 2, knit 4. Work 10 rounds st st, then k2tog across all sts. Break yarn, thread through sts and secure firmly.
**Finger 3** Knit up 2 sts from base of finger 4, knit up 4 sts from stitch holder, cast on 2, leave next 18 sts on stitch holder, then knit up remaining 4 sts. Work 12 rounds st st, k2tog across all sts. Break yarn, thread through sts and secure firmly.
**Finger 2** As finger 3, but work 15 rounds st st.
**Finger 1** Pick up 2 sts at base of finger 2, and knit up remaining 10 sts. Work 12 rounds st st, then k2tog across all sts. Break yarn, thread through sts and secure firmly.

## Finishing

Press st st sections of gloves well.

## Chain

If required, crochet a long chain with a matching yarn and sew ends to the base of gloves.

## Measurements

*To fit sizes 1, 2, 3, 4, 5, 6*

**Dress**
**a** Chest very full
**b** Neck to hem 11¾ (14¼, 16½, 19, 21¼, 23¾)in
**c** Sleeve seam 6 (6¾, 7½, 8¾, 9½, 10¾)in
**Bonnet**
*To fit sizes 1, 2, 3 only*
**d** Around face 15 (16¼, 17)in

Glorious deep blue full coat-dress and matching frilled bonnet made of Shetland yarn with rich borders of red, pink and vermillion flowers, looks a treat on every little girl.

## DRESS

### Yarn

Main yarn M 3 (4, 4, 6, 8, 10)oz 2-ply Shetland (blue)

Yarn A 1 (1, 1, 1, 2, 2)oz 2-ply Shetland (green)

Scraps 2-ply Shetland (dark red, bright red, pink and yellow)

### Needles

1 pair long no 2 (3, 4, 2, 3, 4)in

Similar size circular (or set of 4 double-pointed)

### Notions

9 (9, 9, 10, 10, 10) tiny buttons

Stitch holder

### Stitch gauge

30 sts and 38 rows to 4in over st st on no 2 needles; 28 sts and 36 rows to 4in over st st on no 3 needles; 26 sts and 34 rows to 4in over st st on no 4 needles (or size needed to obtain given tension).

## Body

With yarn M and using 2-needle method, cast on 200 (200, 200, 300, 300, 300) sts. Work 3 rows st st then knit row 4 to make fold line for hem. Continue in st st.

**Row 7** Knit up hem by catching cast-on loops on needle.

Work 2 rows.

**Row 10** Following Graph A commence pattern. Continue until work measures $7\frac{3}{4}$ ($10\frac{1}{4}$, $12\frac{1}{4}$, $14\frac{1}{4}$, $16\frac{1}{4}$, 18)in (or more or less as required) from fold line ending with a purl row.

*Shape armholes:* Knit 45 (45, 45, 68, 68, 68), bind off 10 (10, 10, 14, 14, 14), k90 (90, 90, 136, 136, 136), bind off 10 (10, 10, 10, 14, 14, 14), k45 (45, 45, 68, 68, 68).

*Work left front:* Purl to last 2 sts, p2tog, turn. k2tog, k to end. Repeat these 2 rows once (once, once, twice, twice, twice) – 41 (41, 41, 62, 62, 62) sts. Then work 7 (7, 7, 11, 11, 11) rows. Then work as follows:

**Row 1** Knit 30 (30, 30, 50, 50, 50), turn.

**Row 2** *and every alternate row:* Sl 1, p to end.

**Row 3** Knit 26 (26, 26, 45, 45, 45), turn.

**Row 5** Knit 22 (22, 22, 40, 40, 40), turn.

**Row 7** Knit 18 (18, 18, 35, 35, 35), turn.

**Row 9** Knit 14 (14, 14, 30, 30, 30), turn.

**Row 11** Knit 10 (10, 10, 25, 25, 25), turn.

**Row 13** Knit 6 (6, 6, 20, 20, 20), turn.

*Larger 3 sizes:*

**Row 15** Knit 15, turn.

**Row 17** Knit 10, turn.

Break yarn. Slip all sts onto circular needle or stitch holder.

*Shape back:* With wrong side facing, p2tog, p to last 2 sts, p2tog. K2tog, k to last 2 sts, k2tog. Repeat last 2 rows once (once, once, twice, twice, twice) – 82 (82, 82, 124, 124, 124) sts.

*Right back:* Shape yoke as for left front. Then rejoin yarn at other end (left back) and repeat shaping but reading k for p and p for k.

*Shape right front:* Work as left front, reversing shaping.

## Sleeves

With yarn M, cast on 30 (30, 30, 45, 45, 45) sts.

# Blue Belle

Work 5 rows garter st, then double sts by knitting into front and back of every st – 60 (60, 60, 90, 90, 90) sts. Continue in st st. Work next 6 rows in pattern following Graph B. Continue until work measures 6 (6¾, 7½, 8¾, 9½, 10¾)in (or more or less as required) ending with a purl row.

*Commence shaping:* Bind off 5 (5, 5, 7, 7, 7) sts at beginning of next 2 rows.

**Row 1** K2tog, k to last 2 sts, k2tog.

**Row 2** P2tog, p to last 2 sts, p2tog.

Repeat these 2 rows once (once, once, twice, twice, twice) – 42 (42, 42, 64, 64, 64) sts. Work 21 (21, 21, 29, 29, 29) rows. Then work as follows:

**Row 1** Knit 36 (36, 36, 54, 54, 54), turn.

**Row 2** Sl 2, p26 (26, 26, 42, 42, 42), turn.

**Row 3** Sl 2, k21 (21, 21, 36, 36, 36), turn.

**Row 4** Sl 2, p16 (16, 16, 30, 30, 30), turn.

**Row 5** Sl 2, k11 (11, 11, 24, 24, 24), turn.

**Row 6** Sl 2, p6 (6  6, 18, 18, 18), turn.

*Larger three sizes.*

**Row 7** Sl 2, k12, turn.

**Row 8** Sl 2, p6, turn.

Knit to end. Break yarn. Slip all sts onto circular needle or stitch holder between front and back of skirt. Work another sleeve similarly.

## Yoke

248 (248, 248, 376, 376, 376) sts on circular needle. Work back and forth in rows starting from center front. With right side facing, k1, then k2tog to last st, k1 – 125 (125, 125, 189, 189, 189) sts. Purl 1 row. Change to yarn A and with right side facing, k 1 row. Knit 5 further rows. Change to yarn M, commence working st st. Refer to Graph C for pattern and shape as follows:

**Row 1** Knit 7 (7, 7, 3, 3, 3), *k2tog, k7, rep from * to last 10 (10, 10, 6, 6, 6) sts, k2tog, k8 (8, 8, 4, 4, 4).

**Row 5** Knit 3, *k2tog, k6, rep from * to last 5 sts, k2tog, k3.

**Row 9** Knit 2, *k2tog, k5, rep from * to last 5 sts, k2tog, k3.

**Row 13** Knit 2, *k2tog, k4, rep from * to last 4 sts, k2tog, k2 – 70 (70, 70, 105, 105, 105) sts.

*Larger sizes:*

**Row 19** Knit 1, *k2tog, k3, rep from * to last 4 sts, k2tog, k2 – 70 (70, 70, 84, 84, 84) sts.

Work 2 (2, 2, 1, 1, 1) more rows and leave work on needle.

## Edging

Pick up sts evenly from hem to neck using yarn A and circular needle (or 1st needle of set of 4). Knit across sts of neck and pick up sts down other front neck to hem (with further needles if using set of 4). Knit 3 rows garter st, increasing one st at neck corners on every row. Work 9 (9, 9, 10, 10, 10) evenly-spaced buttonholes on right edge of work by: yfwd, k2tog. Knit 3 rows garter st and bind off loosely.

## Finishing

Sew up underarm and armhole seams and press gently. Sew buttons in place to correspond with buttonholes.

## BONNET

### Yarn

Main yarn M *1oz* 2-ply Shetland (blue)
Yarn A *1oz* 2-ply Shetland (green)
Scraps 2-ply Shetland (dark red, bright red, pink and yellow)

### Needles

1 pair no 2 (3, 4)

### Stitch gauge

As for coat

## Frill

Using yarn A cast on 200 sts. Work 5 rows garter st. K2tog to end – 100 sts. Change to yarn M, and work 6 rows st st. Refer to Graph A and work 18 rows in pattern. Work 20 rows yarn M (or more or less as required).

**Graph A** (smaller 3 sizes)

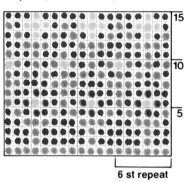

6 st repeat

**Graph B** (smaller 3 sizes)

6 st repeat

**Graph C** (smaller 3 sizes)

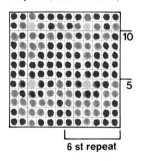

6 st repeat

*Decrease for crown:*

**Row 1** *Knit 8, k2tog, rep from * to end – 90 sts.

**Row 2** *and every alternate row:* Purl.

**Row 3** *Knit 7, k2tog, rep from * to end – 80 sts. Continue in this way until 10 sts remain. Break yarn and thread through remaining sts. Sew up back seam to row at which decreasing commenced.

## Neck band and ties

With yarn A, cast on 200 sts and work 5 rows garter st. Bind off.

## Finishing

Center band on bonnet and sew from back seam to both fronts. Press well.

**Graph A** (larger 3 sizes)

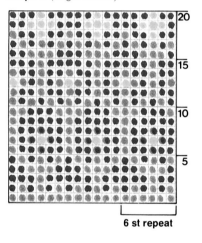

6 st repeat

**Graph B** (larger 3 sizes)

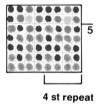

4 st repeat

**Graph C** (larger 3 sizes)

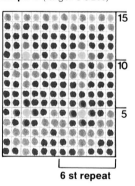

6 st repeat

# CHUNKY FAIR-ISLE

Worked in a matter of days, this glorious jacket and hat are ideal for beginners to Fair Isle work since there are few stitches, thick yarn and large needles.

**Graph A** (main photograph)

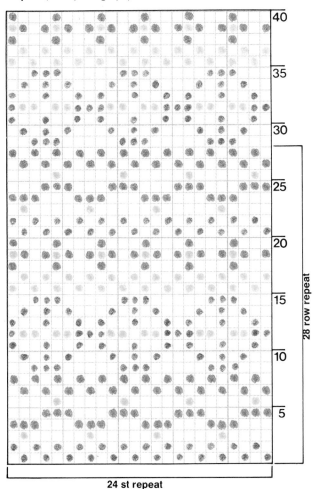

24 st repeat

28 row repeat

**Graph B**
(alternative colorway,
see inset overleaf)

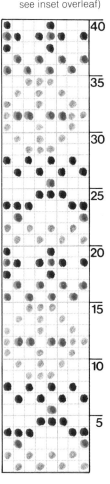

## JACKET

### Yarn
Main yarn M 8 (8, 10)oz soft-spun Shetland (natural)
Yarn A 3oz soft-spun Shetland (blue)
Yarn B 2oz soft-spun Shetland (red)
Yarn C 2oz soft-spun Shetland (green)

### Needles
1 pair no 5
1 pair no 9

### Notions
7 × ⅔in buttons

### Stitch gauge
19 sts and 19 rows to 4in over st st on no 9 needles (or size needed to obtain given tension).

## Body

Using yarn M and no 5 needles, cast on 106 (130, 154) sts. Work 2 (4, 4) rows k1, p1 rib.

**Next row** Make a buttonhole – yon, k2tog – on third st from beginning for girl, from end for boy.
Work further 3 (3, 5) rows k1, p1 rib. Slip first 5 sts onto safety pin.

**Next row** Change to no 9 needles and, working in st st, work in 1 row of pattern from graph to last 5 sts, slip last 5 sts on needle on to safety pin.
Turn and continue in pattern on remaining 96 (120, 144) sts. (Unless you prefer to use another method, leave threads loose across back of work. This is called *stranding*, see p. 124.)
Continue until work measures 9 (11¾, 15)in from beginning, ending with a wrong-side row.

**Next row** Knit 22 (27, 32) sts in pattern, bind off 4 (6, 8) sts, k44 (54, 64) in pattern, bind off 4 (6, 8), k22 (27, 32) in pattern.
*Shape left front:* Work on these last 22 (27, 32) sts following pattern from graph.

**Row 1** *and every alternate row:* Purl to last 3 sts, change to yarn M, p3.

**Row 2** *and every alternate row:* With yarn M, k1, sl 1, k1, psso, k to end following pattern.
Continue in this way decreasing one st every k row until 14 (18, 22) sts remain.
Bind off in yarn M.
*Shape back:* Rejoin yarn to wrong side at back 44 (54, 64) sts. Working first and last 3 sts in yarn M, work as follows:

**Row 1** *and every alternate row:* Purl in pattern without shaping.

**Row 2** *and every alternate row:* Knit 1, sl 1, k1, psso, k in pattern to last 3 sts, k2tog, k1.
Continue in this way decreasing 2 sts every k row until 28 (36, 44) sts remain.
Bind off in yarn M.
*Shape right front:* Rejoin yarn to right front.

**Row 1** *and every alternate row:* Purl first 3 sts in yarn M, work in pattern to end.

**Row 2** *and every alternate row:* Knit in pattern to last 3 sts, change to yarn M, k2tog, k1.
Continue in this way decreasing 1 st every k row until 14 (18, 22) sts remain.
Bind off in yarn M.

## Sleeves

Using yarn M and no 5 needles, cast on 30 (36, 42) sts. Work 15 (18, 21) rows k1, p1 rib, then change to no 9 needles and st st.
Knit into front and back every third st – 40 (48, 56) sts. Refer to graph and work rows in pattern as graph. Continue until work measures 10¼ (13¾, 17½)in, ending with same pattern row as body at armhole, then shape as follows:

# CHUNKY FAIR-ISLE

*Shape sleeve:* Bind off 2 (3, 4) sts beginning next 2 rows. Working first and last 3 sts in yarn M, work as follows:

**Row 1** *and every alternate row:* Knit 1, sl 1, k1, psso, k to last 3 sts, k2tog, k1.

**Row 2** *and every alternate row:* Purl without shaping.

Work in this way decreasing 2 sts every k row until 20 (24, 28) sts remain. Then continue working 8 (10, 12) rows without shaping using yarn M for first and last 3 sts each row. Bind off. Work another sleeve similarly.

Join raglan seams then sew straight rows at top of sleeves to first 7 (9, 11) sts of bound-off edge of back and front.

## Collar

Right side facing. Using yarn M and no 5 needles, pick up 62 (76, 90) sts evenly around neck. Work 12 (16, 20) rows k1, p1 rib and bind off in rib.

## Button-bands

Using no 5 needles and yarn M, pick up the 5 sts from hem of work. Work in k1, p1 rib, making buttonholes every 12th (14th, 16th) row on left front for boy and right front for girl. Work other band similarly without buttonholes.

## Finishing

Press stockinette stitch sections well. Sew front bands in place and sew buttons on to correspond with buttonholes. Join sleeve seams and fold back cuffs if desired.

## HAT

**Yarn**

Main yarn M *2oz* soft-spun Shetland (natural)
Yarn A ½oz soft-spun Shetland (blue)
Yarn B ½oz soft-spun Shetland (red)
Yarn C ½oz soft-spun Shetland (green)

**Needles**

1 pair no 7 (8, 9)

**Stitch gauge**

20 sts and 20 rows to 4in over st st on no 7 needles; 18 sts and 18 rows to 4in over st st on no 8 needles; 17 sts and 17 rows to 4in over st st on no 9 needles (or size needed to obtain given tension).

## Method

Using yarn M cast on 72 sts. Work 25 rows k1, p1 rib. Change to st st and work 20 rows in pattern as graph.

*Shape crown:*

**Row 1** *K2tog yarn M; (k1 yarn A, k1 yarn M) 4 times, k2tog yarn A, rep from * to end.

**Row 2** *Purl 1 yarn M, p1 yarn A, rep from * to end.

**Row 3** *K2tog yarn B; (k1 yarn M, k1 yarn B) 3 times, k2tog yarn M, (k1 yarn B, k1 yarn M) 3 times, rep from * to end.

**Row 4** *Purl 1 yarn B, p1 yarn M, rep from * to end.

**Row 5** *K2tog yarn M, (k1 yarn C, k1 yarn M) twice, k2tog yarn C, rep from * to end.

**Row 6** *Purl 1 yarn M, p1 yarn C, rep from * to end

Continue this way using yarns in rotation and decreasing 12 sts per k row until 12 sts remain. Break yarn and thread through sts. Sew up back seam and affix tassel.

## Measurements

*To fit sizes 2–3, 4–6 and up to 8 yrs*

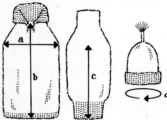

**Jacket**

**a** Chest 21¾ (26¾, 32)in
**b** Neck to hem 15 (17¾, 21)in
**c** Sleeve seam 10¼ (13¾, 17½)in (with cuff turned back)

**Hat**

**d** Around head 14¼ (15¾, 16½)in

Close up of alternative colorway achieved by working Graph B overleaf.

# Bobbly Aran

A large, cosy, chunky jacket with or without hood for midwinter warmth.

Detail of back

## JACKET

### Yarn
8 (9, 10, 11, 12, 13)oz thick Aran yarn
### Needles
1 pair no 7 (8, 9, 7, 8, 9)
Cable needle
### Notions
4 (5, 6, 7, 8, 9) leather or bone $\frac{1}{2}$in buttons
Stitch holder
### Stitch gauge
19 sts and 24 rows to 4in over pattern on no 7 needles; 17 sts and 22 rows to 4in over pattern on no 8 needles; 16 sts and 21 rows to 4in over pattern on no 9 needles (or size needed to obtain given tension).

## Measurements

*To fit sizes 1, 2, 3, 4, 5, 6*

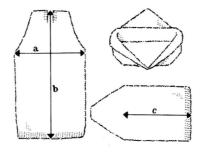

**a** Chest 20 (22, 23, 24, 26, 27$\frac{1}{4}$)in
**b** Back: neck to hem 9$\frac{3}{4}$ (11, 13, 13$\frac{3}{4}$, 15$\frac{3}{4}$, 17$\frac{1}{2}$)in
**c** Sleeve seam 6$\frac{3}{4}$ (7$\frac{1}{2}$, 8$\frac{3}{4}$, 9$\frac{1}{2}$, 10$\frac{3}{4}$, 11$\frac{3}{4}$)in

## Body

Cast on 99 (99, 99, 115, 115, 115) sts and work 5 rows in k1, p1 rib. Then work as follows:
*Sizes 1, 2 and 3*
**Row 1** Rib 5, p2, fc, p2, c4f, 8stpd, p7, fc, p2, c4b, 8stpd, fc, p3, k3, p3, fc, 8stpd, c4f, p2, fc, p7, 8stpd, c4b, p2, fc, p2, rib 5.
**Row 2** Rib 5, k2, p2tog, k2, p4, k3, p2, k3, k7, p2tog, k2, p4, k3, p2, k3, p2tog, k3, p3, k3, p2tog, k3, p2, k3, p4, k2, p2tog, k7, k3, p2, k3, p4, k2, p2tog, k2, rib 5.
*Sizes 4, 5 and 6*
**Row 1** Rib 5, p2, fc, p2, c4f, 8stpd, c4f, p5, fc, p2, c4b, 8stpd, c4b, p2, fc, p3, k3, p3, fc, p2, c4f, 8stpd, c4f, p2, fc, p5, c4b, 8stpd, c4b, p2, fc, p2, rib 5.
**Row 2** Rib 5, k2, p2tog, k2, p4, k3, p2, k3, p4, k5, p2tog, k2, p4, k3, p2, k3, p4, k2, p2tog, k3, p3, k3, p2tog, k2, p4, k3, p2, k3, p4, k2, p2tog, k5, p4, k3, p2, k3, p4, k2, p2tog, k2, rib 5.
*All sizes* Continue in pattern working bobble middle st row 3 and again every 6th row. Work buttonhole in row 3 and every following 12th row (yo, k2tog) in middle of right rib section for girl and left rib section for boy.
Continue in pattern until work measures 6 (7, 8$\frac{3}{4}$, 9$\frac{3}{4}$, 11$\frac{1}{2}$, 12$\frac{1}{2}$)in (or more or less as required) ending with a wrong-side row.
*Shape armhole:* Continuing in pattern work 24 (24, 24, 27, 27, 27) sts, bind off 6 (6, 6, 8, 8, 8),

**NB** *Techniques used in this pattern: fc (false cable), c4f (cable 4 forward), c4b (cable 4 back), 8stpd (8 stitch panel diamond) are described below.*

### False cable (fc)
**Row 1** Knit into front and back of st.
**Row 2** P2 tog.
Repeat these 2 rows to form pattern.

### Cable 4 forward (c4f)
**Row 1** Knit 4.
**Row 2** Purl 4.
**Row 3** Slip 2 sts onto cable needle, leave at front of work, k2, k2 sts on cable needle.
**Row 4** As row 2.
Repeat these 4 rows to form cable.

### Cable 4 back (c4b)
**Row 1** Knit 4.
**Row 2** Purl 4.
**Row 3** Slip 2 sts onto cable needle, leave at back of work, k2, k2 sts on cable needle.
**Row 4** As row 2.
Repeat these 4 rows to form cable.

### 8 stitch panel diamond (8stpd)
**Row 1** Purl 3, k2, p3.
**Row 2** Knit 3, p2, k3.
**Row 3** Purl 2, slip next st onto cable needle and leave at back of work, k1, p st on cable needle, slip next st onto cable needle and leave at front of work, k1, k st on cable needle, p2.
**Row 4** Knit 2, p1, k1, p2, k2.
**Row 5** Purl 1, slip next st onto cable needle and leave at back of work, k1, p st on cable needle, k1, p1, slip next st onto cable needle and leave at front of work, k1, k st on cable needle, p1.
**Row 6** Knit 1, p1, k1, p1, k1, p2, k1.
**Row 7** Purl 1, slip next st onto cable needle and leave at front of work, p1, k st on cable needle, p1, k1, slip next st onto cable needle and leave at back of work, k1, p st on cable needle, p1.
**Row 8** As row 4.
**Row 9** Purl 2, slip next st onto cable needle and leave at front of work, p1, k st on cable needle, slip next st onto cable needle and leave at back of work, k1, p st on cable needle, p2.
**Row 10** As row 2.
**Row 11** Purl 3, slip next st onto cable needle and leave at front of work, k1, k st on cable needle, p3.
**Row 12** As row 2.
Repeat rows 3 to 12 to form pattern.

### Bobble
**Row 1** Knit into front, back, front, back of next st, turn.
**Row 2** Knit 4, turn.
**Row 3** Purl 4, turn.
**Row 4** As row 2.
**Row 5** P4tog.

work 39 (39, 39, 45, 45, 45), bind off 6 (6, 6, 8, 8, 8), work 24 (24, 24, 27, 27, 27). Continue on last 24 (24, 24, 27, 27, 27) sts only.

*Shape left front:* Knit 1, p1, k1, k2tog at armhole edge at the beginning of every alternate row until 12 (12, 12, 14, 14, 14) sts remain. Slip these sts onto holder.

*Shape back:* With wrong side facing, rejoin yarn to middle 39 (39, 39, 45, 45, 45) sts. Work 1 row in pattern.

**Next row** Knit 1, p1, k1, k2tog, work in pattern to last 5 sts, sl 1, k1, psso, k1, p1, k1.

Work every alternate row in this way, until 15 (15, 15, 19, 19, 19) sts remain on needle. Slip all sts onto holder.

*Shape right front:* With wrong side facing, rejoin yarn to last set sts and work in pattern to end. Then, work in pattern to last 5 sts, sl 1, k1, psso, k1, p1, k1. Continue until 12 (12, 12, 14, 14, 14) sts remain and slip onto holder.

## Sleeves

Cast on 35 (35, 35, 45, 45, 45) sts and work 5 rows k1, p1 rib.

**Row 1** Purl 1 (1, 1, 6, 6, 6), c4b, p2, fc, p2, c4b, p2, k3, p2, c4f, p2, fc, p2, c4f, p1 (1, 1, 6, 6, 6).

Continue in pattern, making bobble on middle st on row 3 and again every 6th row until work measures $6\frac{3}{4}$ ($7\frac{1}{2}$, $8\frac{3}{4}$, $9\frac{1}{2}$, $10\frac{3}{4}$, $11\frac{3}{4}$)in (or more or less as desired), ending with a wrong-side row.

*Shape sleeve head:* Bind off 3 (3, 3, 4, 4, 4) sts at the beginning of the next 2 rows.

**Next row** Knit 1, p1, k1, k2tog, work in pattern to last 5 sts, sl 1, k1, psso, k1, p1, k1.

Work 3 rows in pattern. Repeat last 4 rows twice. Work similarly both ends of next and following alternate rows until 11 sts remain on needle. Work another sleeve similarly.

**Neck**

Join raglan sleeve. With right side of work facing, work across front, sleeve, back, sleeve and other front sts – 61 (61, 61, 69, 69, 69) sts. Lose 8 sts as follows: rib 5, k2tog twice, k11 (11, 11, 13, 13, 13), k2tog, k6 (6, 6, 8, 8, 8), k2tog, k1, k2tog, k6 (6, 6, 8, 8, 8), k2tog, k11 (11, 11, 13, 13, 13), k2tog twice, rib 5. Work 5 rows in k1, p1 rib.If no hood required, bind off loosely in rib.

## Hood

With wrong side of work facing, rib 5, k1 (1, 1, 2, 2, 2), *k2, k into the front and back of next st, rep from * to last 5 (5, 5, 6, 6, 6) sts, k1 (1, 1, 2, 2, 2), rib 5 – 68 (68, 68, 78, 78, 78) sts.

*Commence pattern:* Rib 5, p2, fc, p2, c4f, p2, fc, p34 (34, 34, 44, 44, 44) sts, fc, p2, c4b, p2, fc, p2, rib 5. Continue in pattern until hood measures $4\frac{3}{4}$ (5, $5\frac{1}{2}$, $6\frac{1}{4}$, $6\frac{3}{4}$, 7)in from neck.

*Shape hood:* Work middle 2 sts together for the next 10 rows – 58 (58, 58, 68, 68, 68) sts. With wrong side of work facing, k29 (29, 29, 34, 34, 34) sts and fold right sides of hood together. Taking another needle, knit through first st on each needle, knitting the two sts together. Repeat with next 2 sts and bind off first st. Continue binding off in this way to end.

## Finishing

Sew underarm and sleeve seams. Sew buttons on front to correspond with buttonholes.

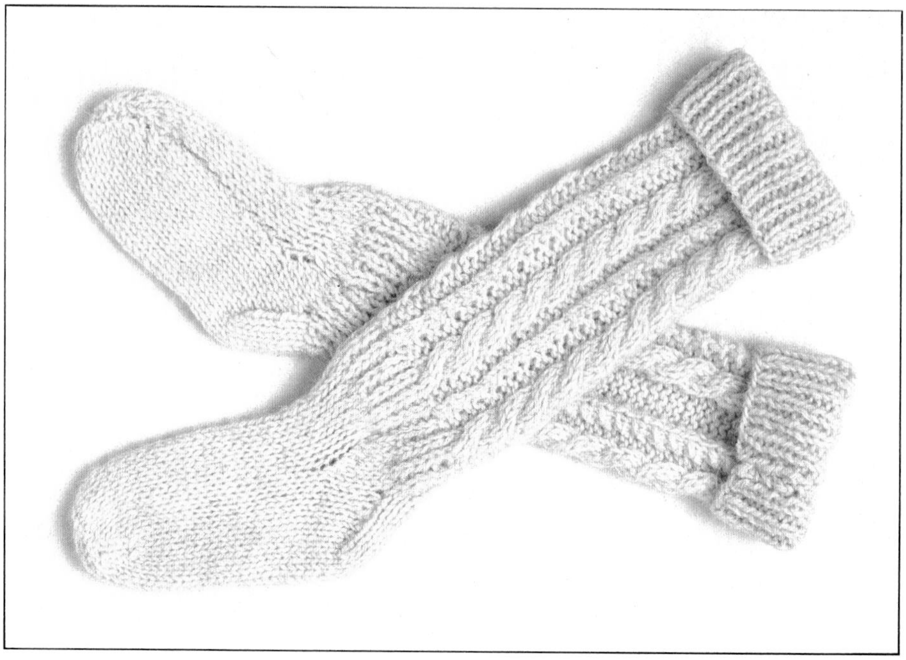

## SOCKS

**Yarn**

*2 (2, 3, 3, 4, 4)oz thick Aran yarn*

**Needles**

1 pair no 7 (8, 9, 7, 8, 9)

Cable needle

**Stitch gauge**

19 sts and 24 rows to 4in over pattern on no 7 needles; 17 sts and 22 rows to 4in over pattern on no 8 needles; 16 sts and 21 rows to 4in over pattern on no 9 needles (or size needed to obtain given tension).

## Measurements

*To fit sizes 1, 2, 3, 4, 5, 6*

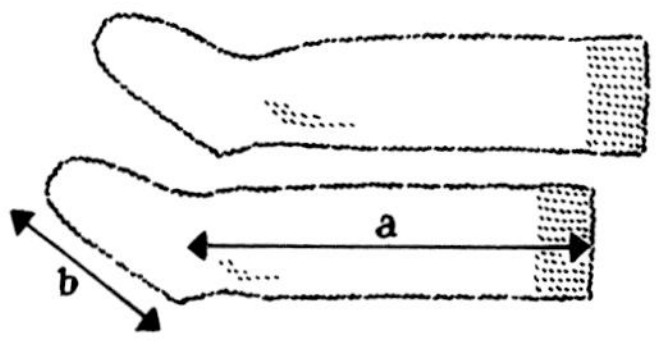


**a** Length: top to ankle $7\frac{3}{4}$ (9, $10\frac{3}{4}$, $11\frac{1}{2}$, 13, $14\frac{1}{2}$)in

**b** Heel to toe 4 ($4\frac{1}{4}$, 5, $5\frac{1}{2}$, 6, $6\frac{3}{4}$)in

**NB** *Techniques used in socks pattern are described below.*

**Cable 4 forward (c4f)**

**Row 1** Slip 2 sts onto cable needle and leave at front of work, k2, k2 sts on cable needle.

**Row 2** Purl 4.

**Row 3** Knit 4.

**Row 4** As row 2.

Repeat these 4 rows to form cable.

**False cable (fc)**

*See jacket, p. 53.*

## Method

Cast on 30 (30, 30, 40, 40, 40) sts and work 10 rows k1, p1 rib. Then work as follows:

**Row 1** Purl 1; *fc, p2, c4f, p2, rep from * to last 2 (2, 2, 3, 3, 3) sts; p2 (2, 2, 3, 3, 3).

**Row 2** Knit 2 (2, 2, 3, 3, 3); *k2, p4, k2, p2tog, rep from * to last st; k1.

Continue in pattern until work measures $5\frac{1}{2}$ ($6\frac{3}{4}$, $7\frac{3}{4}$, 9, $10\frac{3}{4}$, $11\frac{3}{4}$)in from beginning, ending with a wrong-side row. Work 5 rows k1, p1 rib.

**Next row** Purl 16 (16, 16, 18, 18, 18), p2tog 6 (6, 6, 10, 10, 10) times, p2 – 24 (24, 24, 30, 30, 30) sts.

Knit 1 row.

*Shape heel:* Purl 14 (14, 14, 20, 20, 20) sts, turn. Work 6 (6, 6, 8, 8, 8) rows st st on these sts, then work as follows:

**Row 1** Knit 8 (8, 8, 12, 12, 12), k2tog, turn.

**Row 2** Work 4 (4, 4, 6, 6, 6) sts, work 2tog, turn.

Repeat row 2 until all heel sts are on one needle – 5 (5, 5, 7, 7, 7) sts. Break yarn.

Pick up 4 (4, 4, 6, 6, 6) sts purlwise from side of heel; p across 5 (5, 5, 7, 7, 7) sts on needle; pick up 4 (4, 4, 6, 6, 6) sts purlwise from other side of heel. Break yarn. Slip other 10 sts onto right-hand needle.

*Commence foot:* Knit across all sts – 23 (23, 23, 29, 29, 29) sts, then work as follows:

**Row 1** P2tog, p9 (9, 9, 15, 15, 15), p2tog, p10.

**Row 2** Knit 10, k2tog, k7 (7, 7, 13, 13, 13), k2tog.

*Larger 3 sizes only:*

**Row 3** P2tog, p11, p2tog, p10.

Work these 19 (19, 19, 23, 23, 23) sts in st st without shaping until foot measures $3\frac{1}{4}$ ($3\frac{1}{2}$, $4\frac{1}{4}$, $4\frac{3}{4}$, 5, 6)in (or more or less as required), ending with a purl row.

*Shape toe:*

**Row 1** K2tog, k5 (5, 5, 7, 7, 7), k2tog twice, k6 (6, 6, 8, 8, 8), k2tog.

**Row 2** Purl.

**Row 3** K2tog, k3 (3, 3, 5, 5, 5), k2tog twice, k4 (4, 4, 6, 6, 6), k2tog – 11 (11, 11, 15, 15, 15) sts. Bind off.

Work other sock similarly to end of rib at ankle, then p2, p2tog 6 (6, 6, 10, 10, 10) times, p16 (16, 16, 18, 18, 18). Knit 1 row. Purl 1 row.

*Shape heel:* Work as other sock, reading p for k and k for p.

## Finishing

Sew up leg and toe seam on the inside. Press gently.

# Classic Coat

Worked in washable acrylic and cotton chenille, this tailored coat can be worn by both sexes. Little girls can sport the hat and muff.

## COAT

### Yarn
Main yarn M 8¾ (12¼)oz knitting worsted
Yarn A 1¾oz super chenille

### Needles
1 pair no 6 (7)

### Notions
7 × ¾in buttons
1 (1½)yd lining material to match main yarn

### Stitch gauge
18 sts and 29 rows to 4in over moss st on no 6 needles using knitting worsted yarn; 16 sts and 27 rows to 4in over moss st on no 7 needles using knitting worsted yarn (or size needed to obtain given tension).

## Pockets

Using yarn M, cast on 20 sts and work 20 rows st st. Change to yarn A and work 4 rows garter st, for pocket flap. Bind off.
Make another similarly.

## Front

Cast on 40 sts. Work 7¾ (13¾)in moss st, ending on a right-side row.
*Make buttonholes:* (If coat is for a boy, work buttonholes into left front.) Work 25 sts moss st, bind off 2, work 8 moss st, bind off 2, work 3 moss st.
**Next row** Work 3 moss st, cast on 2 sts, work 8 moss st, cast on 2 sts, work 25 moss st.
Work 2 rows moss st.
*Pick up pocket:* Work 4 sts moss st, bind off 20. With chenille flap of pocket lining folded away from you, pick up 20 sts from last row yarn M. Work to end in moss st.
Work 15 rows moss st, then, make 2 buttonholes in next row. Work further 18 rows moss st. Then make 2 buttonholes as before in next row.
*Shape armhole:* Bind off 6 sts, work moss st to end. Decrease 1 st armhole edge beginning next 2 alternate rows – 32 sts.
Continue in moss st until work measures 17 (23¼)in from hem fold ending with a wrong-side row.
*Shape neck:* Bind off 16 sts, work moss st to end – 16 sts.
**Row 1** Work 1 row without shaping.
**Row 2** K2tog, work moss st to end.
**Row 3** Bind off 5 sts, work moss st to end.
**Row 4** Work 1 row without shaping.
**R w 5** Bind off 5 sts, work moss st to end.
Bind off.
Work left front similarly, reversing shaping and omitting buttonholes.

## Back

Using yarn M cast on 80 sts. Work six vertical stripes for back pleats as follows:
**Row 1** *and every odd-numbered row:* (K1, p1) 8 times; k1; *k1, (p1, k1) 4 times, rep from * 4 times; k1; (p1, k1) 8 times; p1.
**Row 2** *and every even-numbered row:* Work 17 moss st; *p1, work 8 moss st, rep from * 4 times; p1; work 17 moss st.
Repeat these 2 rows until work measures same as front to beginning of armhole shaping then:
**Row 1** Bind off 6 sts; work 11 moss st (include st remaining on needle after binding off); k1; *bind off 7, slip st from right needle onto left, k2tog, work 8 moss st, rep from * twice; continue in moss st to end.
**Row 2** Bind off 6 sts; work 10 moss st (including st remaining on needle after binding off); *change to yarn A, p4, change to yarn M, work 6 moss st, rep from * twice; continue in moss st to end.
**Row 3** K2tog; work 9 moss st; *change to yarn A, k2, change to yarn M, work 8 moss st, rep from * twice; work to end in moss st.
**Row 4** K2tog, work 9 moss st; *change to yarn A, p2tog, change to yarn M, work 8 moss st, rep from * twice; work to end in moss st.
Break yarn A and tie ends together over each triangle at back of work.
**Row 5** K2tog, work 8 moss st; *k into front and back of chenille st, work 8 moss st, rep from * twice; work 2 moss st.
**Row 6** K2tog, work to end in moss st – 40 sts.
Work without shaping until armholes measure same as fronts, then bind off 5 sts beginning next 4 rows. Bind off.

## Sleeves

Using yarn M cast on 40 sts. Work in moss st, increasing 1 st both ends of rows 20 and 40. Continue until work measures 9 (11)in from beginning (or more or less as required), then bind off 6 sts at the beginning of the next 2 rows. K2tog beginning next 4 rows, then work 6 rows without shaping. K2tog beginning next 10 rows. K2tog both ends next 6 rows. Bind off.
Work another sleeve similarly.

## Making up

Press pieces *carefully.*
### Lining
Lay knitted sections out flat on lining material and cut out lining ¾in larger all round. Taking ¾in turnings, sew. Sew shoulder and side seams and set sleeves into armholes.
### Make up knitted sections
Fold pleats centered either side of vertical stripes and catch tops to back of garment. Sew shoulder seams. Sew down pocket linings.

## Collar

Starting halfway along front lapel, right side work facing, using chenille, pick up 35 (40) sts. Work 10 rows garter st and bind off.

## Finishing

Sew side and sleeve seams. Set sleeves into armholes. Fix buttons to correspond with buttonholes.
On front section with buttonholes, make loop buttonhole on corner of lapel and attach corresponding button to other section under collar. Fit lining inside garment, fold under at wrist, neck, front edges and hem and catch to garment. Snip through lining behind each buttonhole and catch carefully on inside of buttonhole.

## BERET

### Yarn
3½oz super chenille
### Needles
1 pair no 5
### Stitch gauge
14 sts and 28 rows to 4in over garter st on no 5 needles.

## Method

Cast on 60 sts using 2-needle method and work in garter st throughout. Knit 3 rows.
*Increase row:* *Knit into front and back of next st, k8, k into front and back of next st, rep from * 5 times – 72 sts.
*Next and every alternate row:* Knit without shaping.
*Increase row:* *Knit into front and back of next st, k10, k into front and back of next st, rep from * 5 times – 84 sts.
Continue in this way increasing 12 sts every alternate row until there are 120 sts on needle. Knit 6 rows without shaping.
*Shape crown:* *Knit 18, k2tog, rep from * to end.
*Next and every alternate row:* Knit without shaping.
*Decrease row:* *Knit 17, k2tog, rep from * to end.
Continue in this way decreasing 6 sts every alternate row until there are 48 sts on needle. Knit 1 row without shaping. Then, *k1, k2tog, rep from * to end – 32 sts.
**Next row** Knit without shaping.
Then, k2tog to end – 16 sts. K2tog to end – 8 sts.

## Finishing

Break yarn leaving 19¾in length yarn, and thread through remaining sts. Draw up and secure end. Using sewing needle, work 4 chains at this point (stalk), then thread yarn back through chains and sew up seam.

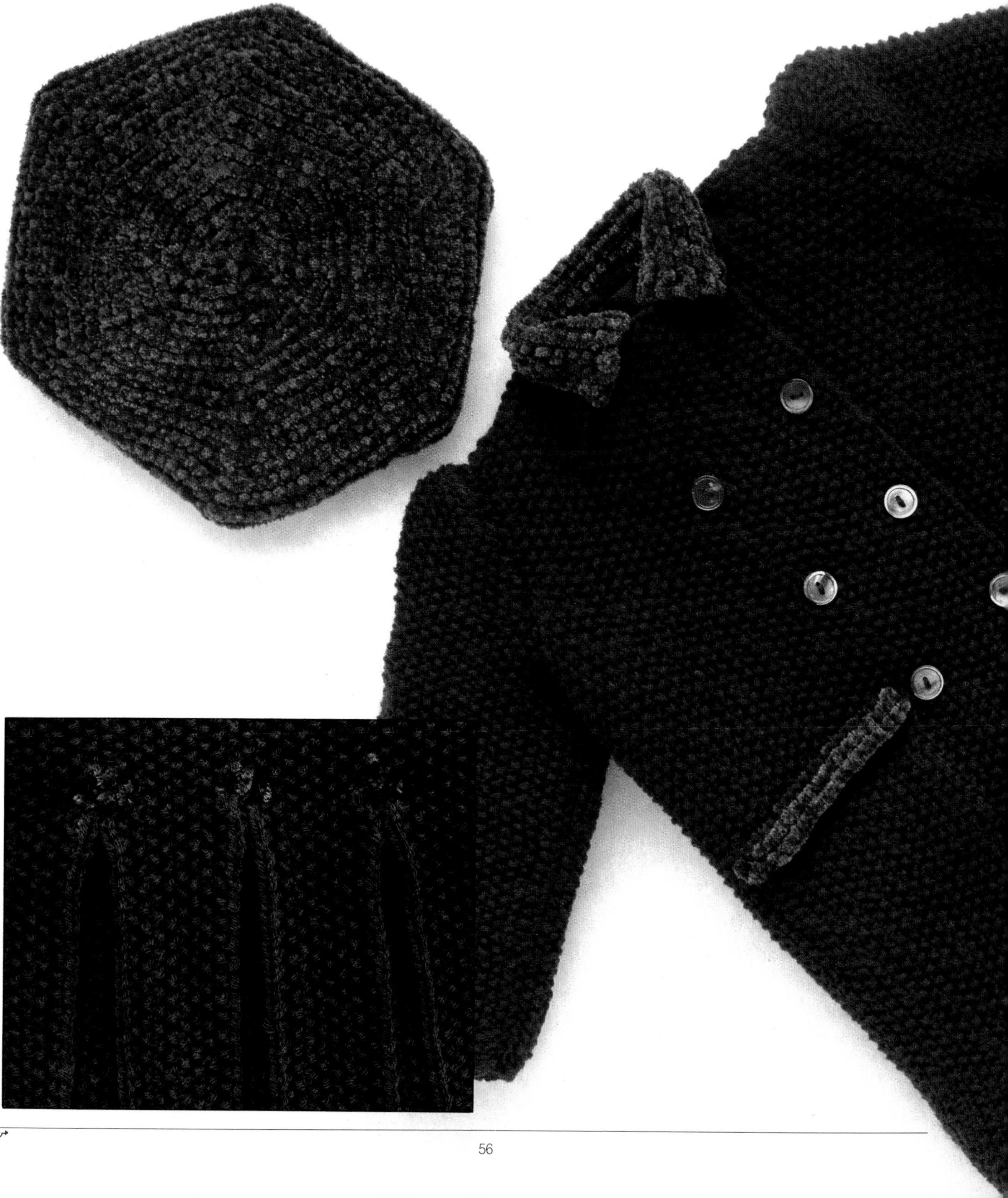

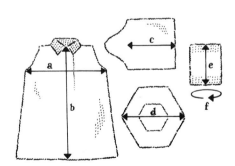

### Neck cord

Make long neck cord by taking 8yd chenille. Fold yarn in half and knot end. Put loop over cupboard or door handle. Insert pencil through knotted end and twist yarn very tightly. Unloop cord from handle and fold in half. The yarn will twist back on itself and make a thick neck cord.

### Finishing

Lay work onto lining fabric. Cut out lining, allowing ¾in all round. Fold over seam allowance on long sides of work and sew to muff just inside on *wrong* side of work. Sew up seam of knitted work, turn inside out and sew seam of lining. Attach neck cord to inside of muff.

### Measurements

### MUFF

**Yarn**
Main yarn M ¾oz knitting worsted
Yarn A ¾oz super chenille
**Needles**
1 pair no 9
**Notions**
¼yd lining material to match main yarn
**Stitch gauge**
14 sts and 26 rows to 4in over moss st on no 9 needles using knitting worsted yarn

### Method

Using yarn A cast on 40 sts. Work 7 rows garter st. Change to yarn M and k 1 row. Work 21 rows moss st. Change back to yarn A and work 7 rows garter st. Bind off.

**Coat**
*To fit sizes 3–4, 5–6*
**a** Chest up to 23¾ (26¾)in
**b** Neck to hem 17½ (23¾)in
**c** Sleeve seam 9 (11)in
**Beret**
*To fit any child up to 6 years*
**d** Diameter of top 9¾in
**Muff**
**e** Width 6in
**f** Circumference 10¼in

# Summer Snowdrops

A delightful cotton dress with matching socks and panties is easy to work and makes a lovely cool outfit suitable for any summer occasion.

## DRESS

### Yarn
Main yarn M 4½ (5½, 6¼, 7, 8¾, 10½)oz medium-weight cotton (white)
Yarn A 1 (1, 1, 1, 1, 1)oz medium-weight cotton (green)
Yarn B ¾ (¾, ¾, ¾, ¾, ¾)oz medium-weight cotton (blue or pink)
Scraps medium-weight cotton (yellow)

### Needles
1 size no 2 (3, 4, 2, 3, 4) circular

### Notions
3 small buttons
Stitch holder

### Stitch gauge
28 sts and 36 rows over 4in on no 2 needles; 26 sts and 34 rows over 4in on no 3 needles; 24 sts and 32 rows over 4in on no 4 needles (or size needed to obtain given tension).

## Front

Using yarn M, cast on 80 (80, 80, 100, 100, 100) sts. Working back and forth in rows, work 9 rows st st, but knit row 4 instead of purling to form fold line for nem and pick up cast-on loops into row 9. Following pattern on Graph A work 8 rows. Work 10 rows plain then work 3 little flowers across next 5 rows following pattern on Graph B. (This is easier if you break off about 11¾in of yarns A and B and work each flower individually, knotting ends when finished. Alternatively, flowers can be embroidered on afterwards.)
*Space the flowers as follows:* Knit 10 yarn M, k1 yarn A, k25 (25, 25, 35, 35, 35) yarn M, k1 yarn A, k25 (25, 25, 35, 35, 35) yarn M, k1 yarn A, k17 yarn M. Work flowers up from this base line. Work 11 rows yarn M, then work 2 little flowers across next 5 rows following pattern on Graph C.
*Space flowers as follows:* Knit 24 (24, 24, 29, 29, 29) yarn M, k1 yarn A, k25 (25, 25, 35, 35, 35) yarn M, k1 yarn A, k29 (29, 29, 34, 34, 34) yarn M.
*Sizes 2 and 3:* Work another row of 3 flowers, as first row.
*Size 4:* Work another 2 rows of flowers, as above.
*Size 5:* Work another 3 rows of flowers.
*Size 6:* Work another 4 rows of flowers.
*All sizes:* Work 11 rows without shaping and check length before shaping armholes.
*Shape armholes:* Bind off 5 sts at the beginning of the next 2 rows. K2tog at the beginning of the next 4 rows – 66 (66, 66, 86, 86, 86) sts. Work 6 rows without shaping.
*Larger 3 sizes only:*
**Next row** Knit 30, turn.
Purl one row.
*All sizes:*
**Row 1** Knit 26, turn.
**Row 2** and every alternate row: Purl.
**Row 3** Knit 22, turn.
**Row 5** Knit 18, turn.
**Row 7** Knit 14, turn.
**Row 9** Knit 10, turn.

**Row 11** Knit 6, turn.
Break thread and slip all stitches onto flexible part of needle.
*Shape right armhole:* Use the same method, reading p for k and k for p, starting from p26 (26, 26, 30, 30, 30) and ending with p6. Slip all sts onto stitch holder.
Work back similarly.

## Sleeves

Using 2-needle method and yarn A, cast on 50 (50, 50, 60, 60, 60) sts. Change to yarn M and work 4 rows garter st. Change to yarn A, k2tog to end – 25 (25, 25, 30, 30, 30) sts. Knit one row. Change to yarn M and double sts: k into front and back of each st. Purl one row. Work a further 4 rows in st st.
*Shape armhole:* Bind off 5 sts at the beginning of the next 2 rows. Continue in st st, but k2tog at the beginning of the next 4 rows – 36 (36, 36, 46, 46, 46) sts. Work 10 (10, 10, 12, 12, 12) rows without shaping.
*Sizes 1, 2 and 3 only:* Knit 26, turn. Sl 2, p16, turn. Sl 2, k11, turn. Sl 2, p6.
*Sizes 4, 5 and 6 only:* Knit 36, turn. Sl 2, p26, turn. Sl 2, k21, turn. Sl 2, p16, turn. Sl 2, k11, turn. Sl 2, p6.
*All sizes:* Break yarn and slip all sts onto stitch holder, between front and back of body sections. Work another sleeve similarly.

## Yoke

Slip all sts onto circular needle – 204 (204, 204, 264, 264, 264) sts.
Move sts around so that points of needle are at center back. Using yarn A, k2tog across all sts – 102 (102, 102, 132, 132, 132) sts. Working back and forth in rows, k5 rows garter st. Refering to Graph D for pattern and working in st st:
**Row 1** With yarn A, cast on 3 sts (button-band), change to yarn M and work in pattern, *k2tog, k4, rep from * to end.
**Row 2** With yarn A, cast on 3 sts, change to yarn M and work in pattern to last 3 sts, k3 yarn A.

Continue in pattern working first and last three sts in yarn A garter st. Make buttonholes at end of rows 5, 11 and 17 – k to last three sts, k2tog, yfwd, k1. On rows 7, 13, 15 work as follows:
**Row 7** Knit 3 yarn A; *k2tog, k3, rep from * to last 3 sts; k3 yarn A.
**Row 13** Knit 3 yarn A; *k2tog, k2, rep from * to last 3 sts; k3 yarn A.
**Row 15** Change to yarn A and work 3 rows garter st.
Bind off.

## Finishing

Sew in sleeves. Join side and sleeve seams. Sew buttons to correspond with buttonholes and stitch the two sets of 3 sts yarn A (base of button-bands) together. Press work well.

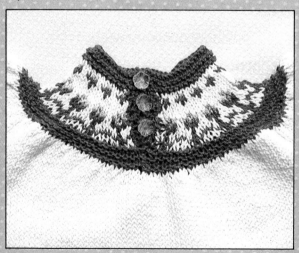

Detail showing back of yoke

58

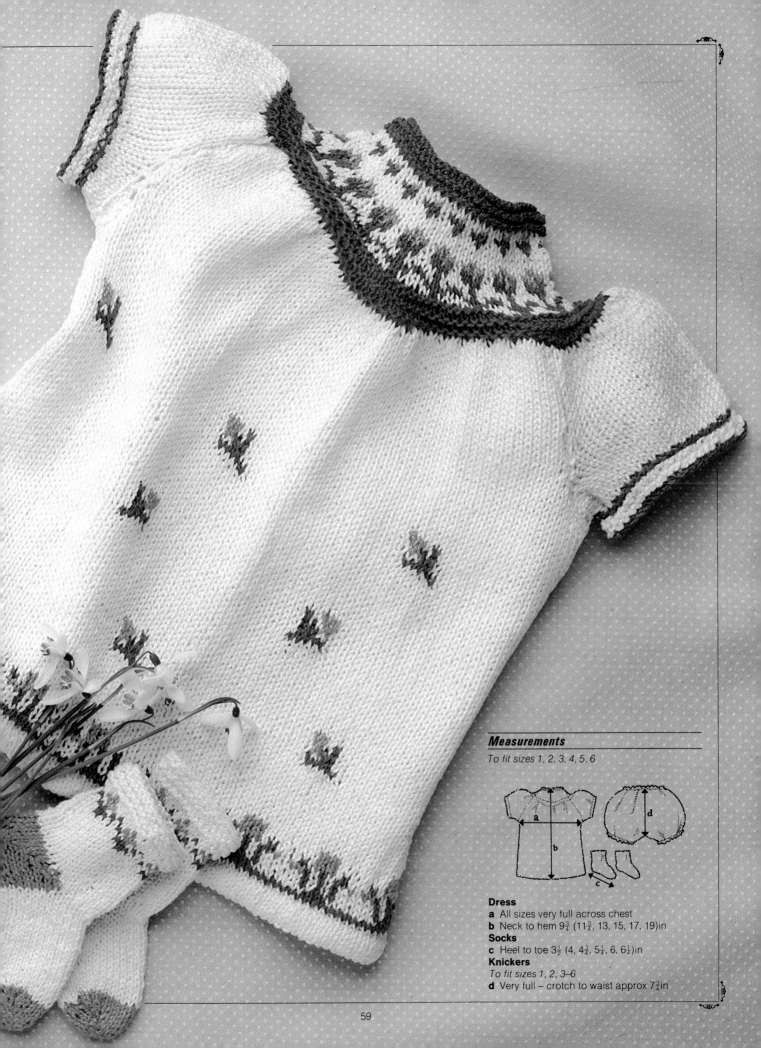

## Measurements

*To fit sizes 1, 2, 3, 4, 5, 6*

**Dress**
**a** All sizes very full across chest
**b** Neck to hem 9¾ (11¾, 13, 15, 17, 19)in
**Socks**
**c** Heel to toe 3½ (4, 4¾, 5¼, 6, 6½)in
**Knickers**
*To fit sizes 1, 2, 3–6*
**d** Very full – crotch to waist approx 7¾in

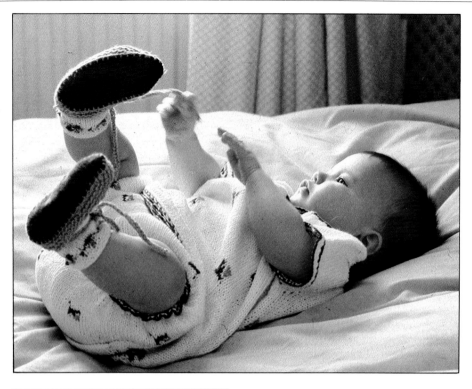

## PANTIES

**Yarn**
Yarn M 2¾ (2¾, 3½)oz medium-weight cotton (white)
Yarn A 1oz medium-weight cotton (green)
Yarn B ¾oz medium-weight cotton (blue or pink)
**Needles**
1 pair no 2 (3, 4) circular
**Notions**
2yd × ¼in soft elastic
**Stitch gauge**
As for dress

### Legs

With yarn A cast on 80 (80, 100) sts. Change to yarn M working back and forth in rows, and work 4 rows garter st.
**Next row** Change to yarn A and k2tog to end – 40 (40, 50) sts.
Knit one row. Then work as follows:
**Row 1** With yarn M, double sts on needle: k into front and back of each st.
**Row 2** and every alternate row: Purl.
**Row 3** Knit 5, turn.
**Row 5** Knit 10, turn.
Continue increasing by k5 every knit row until knitting 30.
**Row 15** Knit without shaping.
**Row 16** Purl 5, turn.
**Row 17** and every alternate row: Knit.
Continue in this way increasing by p5 every purl row until purling 30. Break yarn, push sts onto flexible part of needle.
Work another leg similarly but do not break yarn.

### Main section

With right sides facing, knit 3 rounds st st.
**Round 4** **Commence foundation row of little flowers: Knit 10 (10, 12) yarn M; k1 yarn A; *k19 (19, 24) yarn M, k1 yarn A, rep from * to last 9 (9, 12) sts; k9 (9, 12) yarn M.**
Follow Graph B for pattern, then continue in

rounds yarn M.
**Round 19** Commence second row of flowers following Graph C working as follows: K2 yarn M; k1 yarn A; *k19 (19, 24) yarn M, k1 yarn A, rep from * to last 17 (17, 22) sts; k17 (17, 22) yarn M.
Continue in pattern.
**Round 34** Work another row of flowers as Round 4 from ** to **.
Work further 17 rounds st st yarn M.
*Shape waist:* With yarn A, k2tog across all sts. Knit one round yarn A. With yarn M, double sts: k into front and back of each st. Knit 3 rounds garter st. Bind off in yarn A.

### Finishing

Sew crotch seam. Thread sufficient elastic to fit comfortably around child's thighs and waist through small holes between sts of yarn A. Sew ends together.

## SOCKS

**Yarn**
Main yarn M 1¾oz medium-weight cotton (white)
Yarn A scraps medium-weight cotton (green)
Yarn B scraps medium-weight cotton (blue or pink)
Scraps medium-weight cotton (yellow)
**Needles**
Set of 4 double-pointed no 2 (3, 4, 2, 3, 4)
**Stitch gauge**
As for dress

### Method

Using yarn M cast on 30 (30, 30, 42, 42, 42) sts evenly over 3 needles. *Knit one round. Purl one round. Repeat from * twice. Continue in yarn M working in knit rounds (incorporating pattern from Graph E over next 5 rounds) until 14 (14, 16, 18, 20, 22) rounds have been worked

from beginning for ankle socks, or 30 (35, 40, 45, 50, 55) rounds have been worked from the beginning for knee socks.
*Shape heel:* Change to yarn B. Knit 16 (16, 16, 20, 20, 20) sts, turn. Purl 15 (15, 15, 19, 19, 19) sts, turn. Continue in this way until purling 7, then turn and k8. Turn, p9. Continue in this way until purling 15 (15, 15, 19, 19, 19). Break yarn and change to yarn M. Knit 16 (16, 16, 20, 20, 20) sts; (k2tog, k1) 4 (4, 4, 7, 7, 7) times; k2 (2, 2, 1, 1, 1) – 26 (26, 26, 35, 35, 35) sts.
Work without shaping until foot measures 3¼ (3½, 4¼, 4¾, 5½, 6)in from heel (or more or less as required), turn. Break yarn.
**Round 1** Change to yarn B, k2tog, k9 (9, 9, 14, 14, 14), k2tog, k2tog, k9 (9, 9, 13, 13, 13), k2tog.
**Round 2** *and every alternate round:* Knit without shaping.
**Round 3** K2tog, k7 (7, 7, 12, 12, 12), k2tog, k2tog, k7 (7, 7, 11, 11, 11), k2tog.
**Round 5** K2tog, k5 (5, 5, 10, 10, 10), k2tog, k2tog, k5 (5, 5, 9, 9, 9), k2tog.
*Larger 3 sizes only:*
**Round 7** K2tog, k8, k2tog, k2tog, k7, k2tog.
**Round 9** K2tog, k6, k2tog, k2tog, k5, k2tog.
*All sizes:* Knit one round. Bind off.
Work another sock similarly.

### Finishing

Sew up seam and neaten odd strands of yarn on inside of work.

**Graph A**

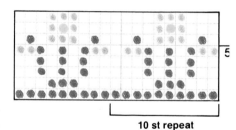

**10 st repeat**

**Graph B**

**5 st repeat**

**Graph C**

**5 st repeat**

**Graph D**

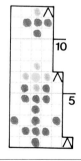

**Graph E**

**6 st repeat**

# PARTY PUMPS

With this one simple pattern you can make little shoes with suede
soles, espadrilles with long criss-cross lacing or ballet slippers.
These pumps make ideal presents for new babies and toddlers alike.

## SHOES

### Yarn
*1oz medium-weight cotton*

### Needles
1 pair no 2 (3, 4, 2, 3, 4)

### Notions
*All optional*
2 mother-of-pearl buttons
2yd shiny ribbon for espadrilles or ballet
slippers
Square of soft suede for soles

### Stitch gauge
24 sts to 4in over garter st on no 2 needles;
21 sts to 4in over garter st on no 3 needles;
18 sts to 4in over garter st on no 4 needles (or
size needed to obtain given tension).

### Measurements

Sole 3½ (4¼, 4¾, 5¼, 6, 6¼)in
**Shape of slipper before assembly**

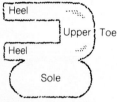

## Method

Cast on 14 (14, 14, 21, 21, 21) sts. Work in
garter st throughout. Increase one st at the
beginning of every row until there are 22 (22,
22, 33, 33, 33) sts on needle. Then k2tog at the
beginning of every row until 14 (14, 14, 21, 21,
21) sts remain. Using 2-needle method, cast on
5 (5, 5, 8, 8, 8) sts at beginning of next row – 19
(19, 19, 29, 29, 29) sts. Keeping this (heel) edge
straight, increase one st at the beginning next
and every alternate row until there are 23 (23,
23, 35, 35, 35) sts on needle – ending at heel.
Bind off 13 (13, 13, 20, 20, 20) sts beginning
next row. Continue working on these 10 (10, 10,
15, 15, 15) sts for 13 (13, 13, 15, 15, 15) rows.
**Next row** Cast on 13 (13, 13, 20, 20, 20) sts, k
  to end.
Then decrease one st at the beginning of next
and every following alternate row (toe edge).
Bind off.
Make another slipper similarly.

## Finishing

Sew heel and sole seams, easing in fullness
at toe.

### Button strap
Cast on 10 (10, 10, 12, 12, 12) sts, pick up 10
sts from back of heel, cast on 10 (10, 10, 12, 12,
12) sts.
**Next row** Knit to last 3 sts, *make buttonhole:*
  *yfwd, k2tog, k1.*
Bind off. Attach button to other end of strap, to
correspond with buttonhole.

### Long strap
*(For bow, ballet slippers and criss-cross
espadrille lacing)* Cast on 50 (50, 50, 70, 70, 70)
sts, pick up 10 sts from back of heel, cast on 50
(50, 50, 70, 70, 70) sts. Bind off.
**NB** *As an alternative you can sew lengths of
ribbon onto the slipper.*

### Suede soles
Place finished slipper on child's foot. Stand
child on square of suede and draw around the
foot. Cut suede along this line. If possible, make
holes ¼in from edge using a domestic sewing
machine without thread and longest stitch size.
Attach using blanket or oversewing stitch.
Make another sole similarly.

# Seaside Sally

Smart cool beachwear set of pretty sleeveless top and frilly mob-cap to keep the sun off, and a pair of swimming trunks. The trunks will fit both sexes but a bit of femininity can be added by tying bows over the side seams.

## VEST

**Yarn**

Main yarn M 3½ (3½, 3½, 5¼, 5¼, 7)oz medium-weight cotton (white)
Yarn A Scraps medium-weight cotton (dark red)

**Needles**

1 pair no 4 (5, 6, 4, 5, 6)

**Notions**

½yd shiny ribbon (dark red)

**Stitch gauge**

26 sts and 36 rows to 4in over st st on no 4 needles; 24 sts and 34 rows to 4in over st st on no 5 needles; 22 sts and 32 rows to 4in over st st on no 6 needles (or size needed to obtain given tension).

### Body

Cast on 140 (140, 140, 175, 175, 175) sts. Work 4 rows garter st, then continue in st st. Work 10 rows, then decrease as follows: *K2tog, k31, k2tog, rep from * to end – 132 (132, 132, 165, 165, 165) sts.
Work 11 rows st st without shaping.
**Next row** *K2tog, k29, k2tog, rep from * to end – 124 (124, 124, 155, 155, 155) sts. Continue without shaping until work measures 4¾ (6, 7, 8¼, 9½, 10¾)in (or more or less as required), ending with a wrong-side row.
*Divide for armholes:* Knit 26 (26, 26, 33, 33, 33) sts, bind off 10 (10, 10, 12, 12, 12), k52 (52, 52, 65, 65, 65), bind off 10 (10, 10, 12, 12, 12), k26 (26, 26, 33, 33, 33).
*Right back:* Working on the last 26 (26, 26, 33, 33, 33) sts. Bind off 5 (5, 5, 6, 6, 6) sts, p to end – 21 (21, 21, 27, 27, 27) sts.
* *K2tog beginning next 10 rows – 11 (11, 11, 17, 17, 17) sts. Work without shaping until vest measures 7¾ (9¾, 11¾, 13½, 15, 16¼)in (or more or less as required) and bind off. * *
Rejoin yarn to wrong side of front and p to end. Knit 21 (21, 21, 27, 27, 27) sts, bind off 10 (10, 10, 11, 11, 11), k21 (21 21, 27, 27, 27).
*Right front:* Work on the last 21 (21, 21, 27, 27, 27) sts as back from * * to * *.
Finish other shoulders similarly.
Right side facing, using yarn A, knit up 36 (36, 36, 45, 45, 45) sts evenly around armhole. Knit 2 rows and bind off.
Finish other armhole similarly.

### Finishing

Sew shoulder seams together. Pick up 72 (72, 72, 90, 90, 90) sts round neck edge using yarn A, k 2 rows and bind off. Sew body seam leaving 2in opening at neck edge on smaller sizes. Press well and tie bow across center front.

## MOB CAP

**Yarn**

Main yarn M 1¾oz medium-weight cotton (white)
Yarn A Scraps medium-weight cotton (dark red)

**Needles**

1 pair no 3

**Notions**

1yd narrow elastic
1½yd ribbon to match yarn A

### Method

With yarn A cast on 200 sts using 2-needle method.
Change to yarn M then work as follows:
**Row 1** *and every alternate row:* Knit without shaping.
**Row 2** *Knit 1, p1, rep from * to end.
**Row 4** *Purl 1, k1, rep from * to end.
Work 16 rows st st.
*Make holes for elastic* as follows:
**Row 1** Change to yarn A and k2tog to end – 100 sts.
**Row 2** *Yfwd, k2tog, rep from * to end.
**Row 3** Change to yarn M and *k1, k into front and back next st, rep from * to end – 150 sts.
Work 31 more rows st st ending with a wrong-side row.
*Shape crown:*
**Row 1** *Knit 13, k2tog, rep from * to end – 140 sts.
**Row 2** *and every alternate row:* Purl.
**Row 3** *Knit 12, k2tog, rep from * to end -- 130 sts.
Continue this way until 10 sts remain on needle. Break yarn and thread through these sts.

### Finishing

Sew up seam and thread elastic through eyelet holes and secure ends. Press work well. Thread ribbon through eyelet holes over elastic and tie bow center front.

## SWIMMING TRUNKS

**Yarn**

Main yarn M 1oz medium-weight cotton (white)
Yarn A 1¾oz medium-weight cotton (dark red)

**Needles**

1pair no 5

**Notions**

1½yd narrow elastic

**Stitch gauge**

24 sts and 36 rows to 4in over st st on no 5 needles (or size needed to obtain given tension).

### Front

With yarn A cast on 60 (70, 80) sts using 2-needle method. Work 10 rows st st then knit up cast-on edge into next row to make casing for elastic. Purl 1 row. Change to yarn M, work 2 row stripe. Continue in st st working 4 rows yarn A, 2 rows yarn M throughout.
*Shape front:* Beginning of second stripe, yarn M, bind off 10 (15, 20) sts using yarn A, k39 yarn M, bind off 10 (15, 20) using scrap yarn A.
**Next row** Purl to end in yarn M.
K2tog beginning every row until 16 sts remain on needle.
Work 11 (15, 21) rows without shaping ending with wrong side of work facing. Bind off.

### Measurements

**Mob-cap**
*One size to fit sizes 1–6*
**Vest**
*To fit sizes 1, 2, 3, 4, 5, 6*
**a** Chest 19 (20½, 22, 23¾, 25¾, 25¾)in
**b** Length: neck to hem 7¾ (9¾, 11¾, 13½, 15, 16¼)in
**Swimming trunks**
*To fit sizes 1–2, 3–4, 5–6*
**c** Hip stretches to 19¾ (23, 26)in

### Back

Work as for front until beginning of second stripe of yarn M, then work as follows:
**Row 1** Bind off 4 (7, 10) using yarn A, k51 (55, 59) yarn M, bind off 4 (7, 10) sts using scrap yarn A.
**Row 2** Purl to end in yarn M.
K2tog beginning every row until 16 sts remain on needle. Work 3 rows and, with wrong side facing, bind off.

### Leg bands

Sew side seams. Right side facing, using yarn A, pick up about 60 (80, 100) sts around leg hole. Work 6 rows st st and bind off. Work other leg band similarly.

### Bows

With yarn A, cast on 30 sts. Work in garter st throughout. K2tog beginning every row until 6 sts on needle. Work 16 (20, 24) rows without shaping, then increase 1 st at beginning every row until 30 sts on needle. Bind off.

### Finishing

Cut 2 pieces of elastic to fit around legs, sew ends together. Sew leg bands down to inside of main body of work enclosing length of elastic. Sew up crotch seam. Thread elastic through waistband and sew ends together. Tie bows around narrowest part of work over side seams if desired.

Bows can be worked in yarn A and tied over side seams of bikini.

# RED ROBIN

Cotton T-shirt and matching shorts are attractive enough for a party, and comfortably cool even when it is really hot. Surprise your tot with this musical ball.

## T-SHIRT

**Yarn**
Main yarn M 3½ (3½, 5¼, 5¼, 7, 7)oz medium-weight cotton (red)
Yarn A 1¾oz medium-weight cotton (white)
**Needles**
1 pair no 3 (4, 5, 3, 4, 5)
**Notions**
3 small buttons
**Stitch gauge**
28 sts and 38 rows to 4in over st st using no 3 needles; 26 sts and 36 rows to 4in over st st using no 4 needles; 24 sts and 34 rows to 4in over st st using no 5 needles (or size needed to obtain given tension).

## Measurements

To fit sizes 1, 2, 3, 4, 5, 6

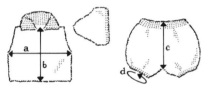

**T-shirt**
**a** Chest 18½ (20, 21¾, 23¾, 25¼, 27¼)in
**b** Neck to hem 8¼ (9½, 11, 12½, 14¼, 15¾)in
**Shorts**
**c** Waist to crotch 6¼ (6¾, 7, 6¼, 6¾, 7)in
**d** Circumference of leg 5 (5½, 6, 6¼, 6¾, 7, 7½)in

## Front

Cast on 66 (66, 66, 83, 83, 83) sts using 2-needle method and yarn M. Working in st st throughout, work 8 rows, then knit up cast-on row for hem.
Continue without shaping until work measures 4¾ (6, 7, 8¼, 9, 9¾)in (or more or less as required) from hem fold, ending with wrong-side row.
*Shape armhole:* Bind off 4 (4, 4, 8, 8, 8) sts, k27 (27, 27, 31, 31, 31), bind off 4 (4, 4, 5, 5, 5) k27 (27, 27, 31, 31, 31), bind off 4 (4, 4, 8, 8, 8).
Break yarn, and keeping right side work facing, rejoin yarn to first 27 (27, 27, 31, 31, 31) sts on needle. **K2tog beginning next 3 k rows.
Continue without shaping until work measures 8¼ (9½, 11, 12½, 14¼, 15¾)in from hem (or more or less as required).
*Shape neck:* Bind off 5 (5, 5, 6, 6, 6) sts at neck edge, p to end. Work 2 (2, 2, 4, 4, 4) further rows without shaping and bind off.
Complete other side of front similarly, reversing shaping, from **.

## Back

Cast on 66 (66, 66, 83, 83, 83) sts and work as front until shaping armholes.
*Shape armholes:* Bind off 4 (4, 4, 8, 8, 8) sts, k58 (58, 58, 67, 67, 67), bind off 4 (4, 4, 8, 8, 8).
Then work as follows:
**Next row** P2tog, p to end.

Work k2tog beginning next 5 rows, then work without shaping until work measures 8¾ (10¼, 11½, 13½, 15, 16½)in (i.e., until it measures same as front from hem to shoulders). Bind off.

## Sleeves

Using yarn A, cast on 40 (40, 40, 50, 50, 50) sts. Work 5 rows k1, p1 rib. Change to yarn M and st st and increase by knitting into front and back every 5th st – 48 (48, 48, 60, 60, 60). Work 9 (9, 9, 15, 15, 15) rows st st.
*Shape armhole:* Bind off 3 (3, 3, 5, 5, 5) sts beginning of next 2 rows. Decrease 1 st beginning of every row until 6 sts remain. Bind off knitting 2 tog.
Work another sleeve similarly.

## Button-bands

Right side work facing, and using yarn A, knit up sts evenly from sides of center front slit.
*Button-band:* Work 5 rows k1, p1 rib and bind off in rib.
*Buttonhole band:* Work as button-band but incorporate 3 evenly-spaced buttonholes on 3rd row: k1, yo, k2tog.

## Collar

Right side work facing, knit up sts evenly around neck. Double sts by knitting into front and back each st. Work 15 (15, 15, 20, 20, 20) rows k1, p1 rib and bind off in rib.

## Finishing

Sew base of button-bands to bound-off edge in center front. Sew side and shoulder seams. Sew sleeve seam and set sleeve into armhole. Press work well and attach buttons.

## SHORTS

**Yarn**
Main yarn M 2¾ (2¾, 3½, 3½, 3½, 3½)oz medium-weight cotton (red)
Yarn A 1¾oz medium-weight cotton (white)
**Needles**
1 no 2 (3, 4, 2, 3, 4) circular
**Notions**
½yd soft elastic
**Stitch gauge**
30 sts and 40 rows to 4in over st st using no 2 needles; 28 sts and 38 rows to 4in over st st using no 3 needles; 26 sts and 36 rows to 4in over st st on no 3 needles (or size needed to obtain given tension).

## Method

With yarn A cast on 40 (40, 40, 50, 50, 50) sts using 2-needle method. Working back and forth in rows, work 10 rows k1, p1 rib. Change to yarn M and knit up sts on cast-on row alternating 1 st from needle with 1 loop from cast-on edge – 80 (80, 80, 100, 100, 100) sts.
*Shape crotch:* Knit one row then,

**Row 2** *and every alternate row:* Purl without shaping.
**Row 3** Knit 5, turn.
**Row 5** Knit 10, turn.
Continue in this way until knitting 30 sts, then turn.
**Row 15** Knit to end of row.
**Row 16** Purl 5, turn.
**Row 17** *and every alternate row:* Knit without shaping.
**Row 18** Purl 10, turn.
**Row 20** Purl 15, turn.
Continue in this way until purling 30. Break yarn and push sts onto flexible part of needle. Work another leg similarly but do not break the yarn.
*Shape body:* Right side work facing, work 55 rounds st st over all 160 (160, 160, 200, 200, 200) sts (or more or less as required).
*Shape waist:* Change to yarn A. Work 20 rounds k1, p1 rib and bind off.

## Finishing

Fold waist back and catch it to inside of work. Thread elastic through casing. Sew crotch and leg seams.

## MUSICAL BALL

### Yarn

$1\frac{3}{4}$oz 2-ply Shetland or medium-weight cotton or $1\frac{3}{4}$oz 4-ply acrylic

### Needles

1 pair no 4

### Notions

Quantity of washable stuffing
Waterproof plastic containers (plastic photographic film canisters are ideal) containing beads, buttons, rice and/or bells

## Measurements

Approx $7\frac{3}{4}$in in diameter

## Panels

Cast on one st. Work 20 rows st st increasing one st at the beginning of every row – 21 sts. Work 15 rows without shaping, knit a further 20 rows decreasing one st at the beginning of every row. Break yarn and thread through last st.
Make another 5 complete sections in the same way.

## Finishing

Stitch 6 sections together using contrasting yarn and large blanket or oversewing sts leaving a small gap for stuffing. Fill ball with stuffing and place waterproof cannister in the middle. Sew up seam.

# Cotton Charmers

Cute cotton cardigan with slightly puffed sleeve tops can be made with a zipper or button fastening. It is shown here in a blue, white and red combination, or white, pink and green yarn, see overleaf.

## CARDIGAN

**Yarn**
Main yarn M *1¾ (1¾, 2¾, 2¾, 2¾, 3½)oz* medium-weight cotton (royal blue)
Yarn A *1¾ (1¾, 1¾, 1¾, 2¾, 2¾)oz* soft medium-weight cotton (red)
Yarn B *1¾ (1¾, 1¾, 1¾, 2¾, 2¾)oz* soft medium-weight cotton (white)
**Needles**
1 pair no 2 (3, 4, 2, 3, 4)
**Notions**
Open end zipper same color as main yarn
*or*
10 tiny buttons
Stitch holder or safety pin
**Stitch gauge**
30 sts and 40 rows to 4in over st st on no 2 needles; 28 sts and 38 rows to 4in over st st on no 3 needles; 24 sts and 36 rows to 4in over st st on no 4 needles (or size needed to obtain given tension)

## Measurements

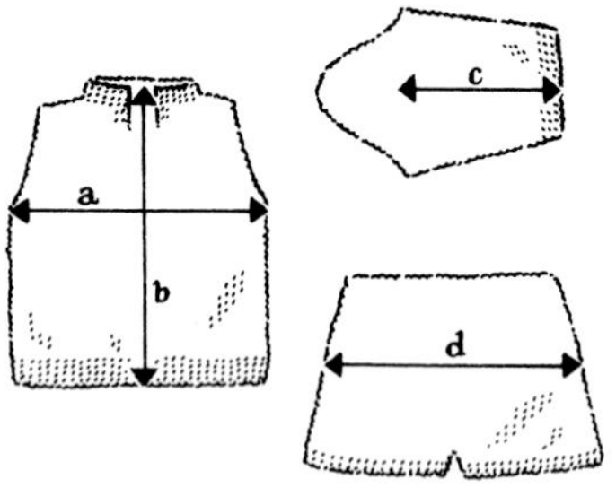


**Cardigan**
*To fit sizes 1, 2, 3, 4, 5, 6*
**a** Chest 20 (21, 22, 23, 24, 25¼)in
**b** Neck to hem 9 (9¾, 11, 11¾, 13, 14¼)in
**c** Sleeve seam 7 (7¾, 8¾, 9½, 10¾, 11¾)in
**Shorts**
*To fit sizes 1–2, 3–4, 5–6*
**d** Hip 17¾ (19¼, 21¼)in
**e** Length 7¾in

## Body

With yarn M cast on 150 (150, 150, 170, 170, 170) sts. Work 7 rows k1, p1 rib. Slip first and last 5 sts on needle onto stitch holder or safety pin. Work center 140 (140, 140, 160, 160, 160) sts in pattern as follows:
**Row 1** With yarn A *k3, sl 1, rep from * to end.
**Row 2** With yarn A *sl 1, p3, rep from * to end.
**Row 3** With yarn B k1; *sl 1, k3, rep from * to last 3 sts; sl 1, k2.
**Row 4** With yarn B p2; *sl 1, p3, rep from * to last 2 sts; sl 1, p1.
**Row 5** With yarn M work as row 1.
**Row 6** With yarn M work as row 2.
**Row 7** With yarn A work as row 3.
**Row 8** With yarn A work as row 4.
**Row 9** With yarn B work as row 1.
**Row 10** With yarn B work as row 2.
**Row 11** With yarn M work as row 3.
**Row 12** With yarn M work as row 4.

Repeat these 12 rows until work measures 5½ (6¼, 7½, 7¾, 8¼, 8¾)in from beginning, ending with a wrong-side row.
*Divide for armholes:* Pattern 30 (30, 30, 35, 35, 35) sts; bind off 10; pattern 60 (60, 60, 70, 70, 70); bind off 10; pattern 30 (30, 30, 35, 35, 35).
*Work right front:* Working on the last 30 (30, 30, 35, 35, 35) sts, k2tog beginning of next 3 alternate rows (armhole edge). Continue without shaping until work measures 8¾ (9½, 10¾, 11½, 12½, 13¾)in from beginning.
*Shape neck:* Bind off 10 (10, 10, 13, 13, 13) sts at neck edge. Continue in pattern, k one row, then k2tog beginning next row at neck edge. Work 5 more rows in pattern. Bind off.
*Work back:* Rejoin yarn to right side of 60 (60, 60, 70, 70, 70) sts divided for back. K2tog beginning of next 6 rows. Continue without shaping until work measures 9 (9¾, 11, 11¾, 13, 14¼)in from beginning. Bind off.
*Work left front:* Rejoin yarn to right side of remaining 30 (30, 30, 35, 35, 35) sts. K2tog beginning next 3 alternate rows (armhole edge). Continue shaping as for right front.

## Sleeves

With yarn M cast on 36 (36, 36, 48, 48, 48) sts. Work 7 rows k1, p1 rib. Commence pattern (Rows 1–12 as above) *but* increase 1 st both ends first row yarn A in every pattern sequence until there are 56 (56, 56, 68, 68, 68) sts on needle. Continue until sleeve measures 7 (7¾, 8¾, 9½, 10¾, 11¾)in from beginning (or more or less as required). Bind off 5 sts beginning of next 2 rows and working in pattern, k2tog beginning every row until 12 sts remain. Bind off knitting 2tog along row.
Work another sleeve similarly.
Press all 3 sections well. Sew shoulder seams.

## Front bands

Knit up 5 sts on stitch holders in k1, p1 rib to required length to make front bands.
*If using buttons:* Work buttonholes into row 3 and again every 12 rows of right or left band as follows: right side facing, k1, k2tog, yfwd, p1, k1.
*All cardigans:* Do not bind off last 5 sts but leave on holder while other band is completed. Attach both bands to work.
*Shape collar:* Right side work facing, using yarn M, knit across sts on holder to right side of work, pick up 50 (50, 50, 60, 60, 60) sts around neck and pick up 5 sts from other holder. Work 5 rows k1, p1 rib, making buttonhole in row 3 if required. Bind off in rib.

## Finishing

Sew sleeve seams and fit sleeves into armholes easing in fullness at shoulder. Attach zip fastener or sew on buttons to correspond with buttonholes.

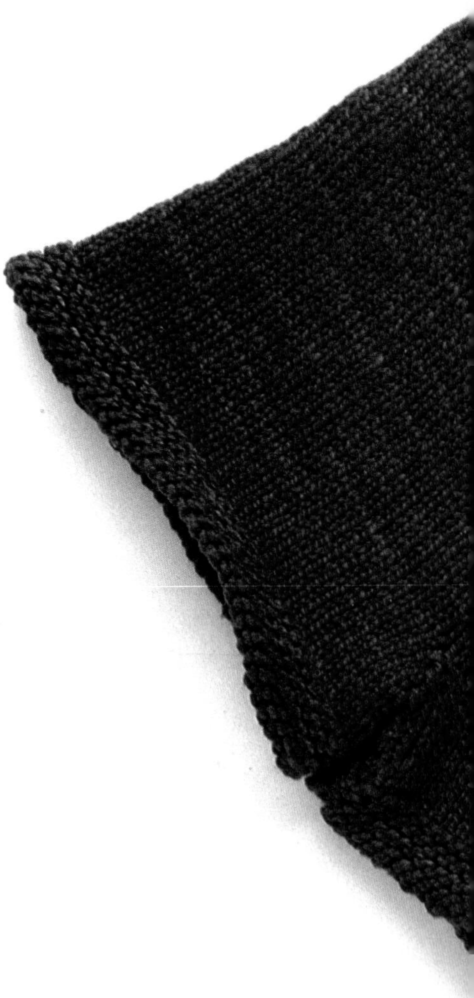

## SHORTS

**Yarn**
3½oz medium-weight cotton (blue)
**Needles**
1 no 4 (2, 3) circular
**Notions**
½yd ¼in elastic
**Stitch gauge**
28 sts and 36 rows to 4in over st st on no 2
needles; 26 sts and 34 rows to 4in over st st
on no 3 needles; 24 sts and 32 rows to 4in
over st st on no 4 needles (or size needed to
obtain given tension).

### Legs

Cast on 55 (70, 70) sts using 2-needle method.
Working back and forth in rows, work 7 rows
garter st. Break yarn and push all sts onto
flexible part of needle.
Work another leg similarly.
Knit across sts of 2nd leg, cast on 7 sts for
crotch, work across sts of 1st leg, cast on a
further 7 sts – 124 (154, 154) sts. Change to
st st and begin to work in rounds.
*Begin to shape crotch:*
**Round 1** Knit 53 (68, 68), k2tog, k5, k2tog, k53
(68, 68), k2tog, k5, k2tog.
**Round 2** Knit without shaping.
**Round 3** *and every alternate round:* Continue
decreasing as Round 1 until all crotch sts are
decreased.
Then, work sl 1, k2tog, psso on center sts until
100 (130, 130) sts remain. Work 60 rounds
without shaping.
*Work waistband:*
**Round 1** *and following 2 alternate rounds:*
 Purl.
**Rounds 2 and 4** Knit.
**Round 6** Knit 30 (40, 40), bind off 40 (50, 50),
k30 (40, 40).
*Shape flap for elastic:* Continue working back
and forth in rows on remaining 60 (80, 80) sts,
work 5 rows st st. Bind off.

### Finishing

Sew crotch seam. Fold over flap and sew hem
to inside of work encasing required length of
elastic.

### Alternative colorway

This cardigan was made following the pattern
overleaf but using white cotton as main yarn,
green cotton as yarn A and pink cotton as yarn
B. Finish off the cardigan by adding matching
buttons.

# SHIPS AHOY

Edwardian-style sailor outfits comprising long shorts, shirt and hat for a boy and a dress, socks and hat for a girl, are what the well-dressed child should have in his or her summer wardrobe.

## *SAILOR SHIRT*

**Yarn**
Main yarn M $4\frac{1}{2}$ *($5\frac{1}{4}$, $6\frac{1}{4}$, $6\frac{1}{4}$, 7, 8)*oz medium-weight cotton (blue)
Yarn A $1\frac{3}{4}$ *($1\frac{3}{4}$, $1\frac{3}{4}$, $1\frac{3}{4}$, $1\frac{3}{4}$, $1\frac{3}{4}$)*oz medium-weight cotton (white)
**Needles**
1 pair no 2 (3, 4, 2, 3, 4)
Similar size circular (or set of 4 double-pointed)
**Notions**
1yd satin ribbon (red)
2 mother-of-pearl buttons
**Stitch gauge**
28 sts and 36 rows to 4in over st st on no 2 needles; 26 sts and 34 rows to 4in over st st on no 3 needles; 24 sts and 32 rows to 4in over st st on no 4 needles (or size needed to obtain given tension).

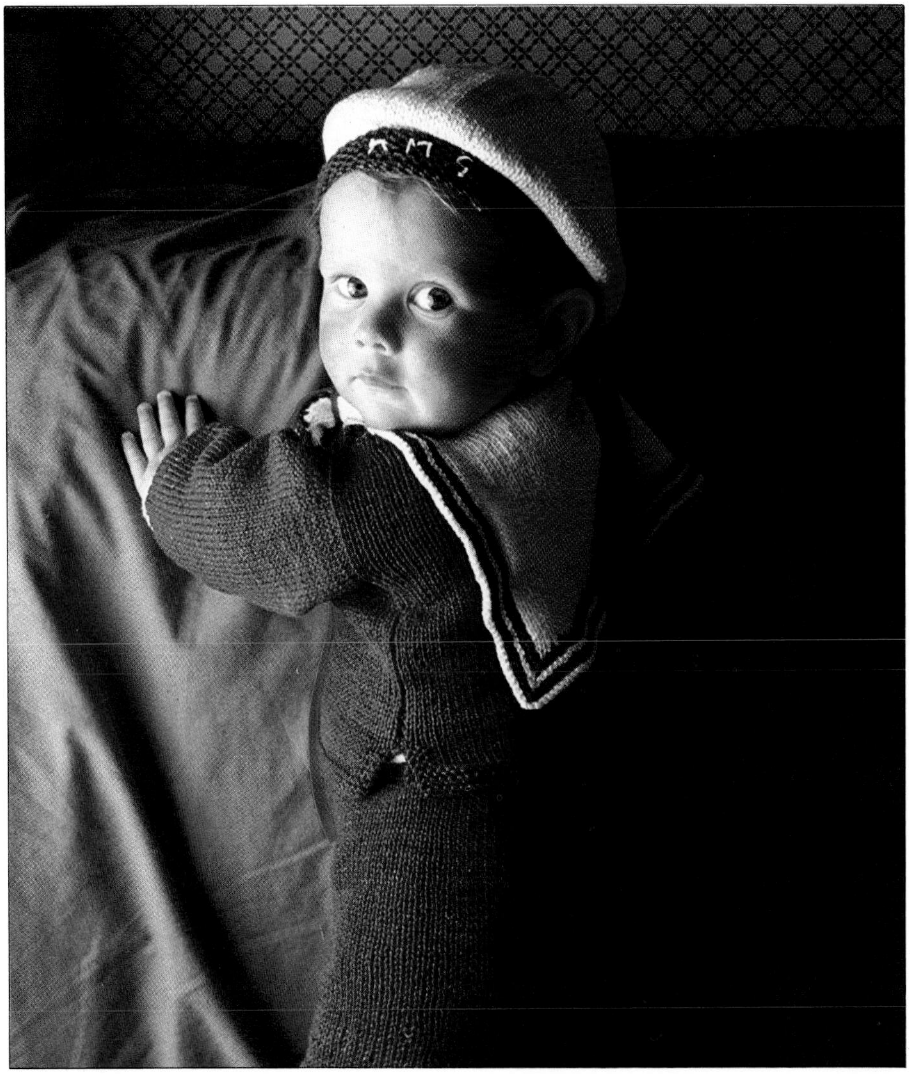

### *Body*

With yarn M cast on 60 (60, 60, 80, 80, 80) sts. *Work front:* Knit 8 rows garter st. Continue in st st first and last 3 sts of next 6 rows garter st (side-slit edging). Work until $8\frac{3}{4}$ ($10\frac{3}{4}$, $10\frac{3}{4}$, $11\frac{1}{2}$, $12\frac{1}{2}$, $13\frac{1}{2}$)in have been worked from beginning (or more or less as required) ending with a knit row.
**Next row** Purl 7 (7, 7, 12, 12, 12), k46 (46, 46, 56, 56, 56), p7 (7, 7, 12, 12, 12).
Knit 1 row. Repeat these 2 rows once.
*Shape neck:* Work as follows:
**Row 1** Purl 7 (7, 7, 12, 12, 12) sts, k3, bind off 40 (40, 40, 50, 50, 50), k3, p7 (7, 7, 12, 12, 12).
**Row 2** Knit 10 (10, 10, 15, 15, 15) sts, cast on 40 (40, 40, 50, 50, 50) sts for back neck, k10 (10, 10, 15, 15, 15).
**Row 3** *and next 2 purl rows:* Purl 7 (7, 7, 12, 12, 12) sts; k46 (46, 46, 56, 56, 56); p7 (7, 7, 12, 12, 12).
*Work back:* Continue on st st until back measures same as front to top of garter st edging for side slit ending with a k row. Work first and last 3 sts next 6 rows garter st. Work 8 rows garter st and bind off with wrong side facing.

### *Sleeves*

With right side facing and yarn M, pick up 30 (30, 30, 40, 40, 40) sts either side of center shoulder – 60 (60, 60, 80, 80, 80) sts. Work 55 (55, 55, 75, 75, 75) rows (or more or less as required) ending on a p row.
**Row 1** Change to yarn A, k2tog to end – 30 (30, 30, 40, 40, 40) sts.
**Row 2** Knit.
**Row 3** Change to yarn M, knit.
**Row 4** Knit.
**Row 5** Change to yarn A, knit.
**Row 6** Knit.
**Row 7** Change to yarn M, knit.
Bind off.

### *Collar*

With yarn A cast on 50 sts. Work 45 rows in st st.
**Next row** Knit 12, bind off 26, k12.
*Shape point:* Work 45 rows on these last 12 sts, then bind off 1 st every row on *outside* edge until 1 st remains, thread yarn through st to finish off. Rejoin yarn to remaining 12 sts and work other half similarly but reverse shaping.
*Work trim:* With right side facing and using circular needle (or first needle of set of 4) and yarn M, pick up stitches evenly all around outside of collar. Work 6 rows in garter st as follows: 1 row yarn M, 2 rows yarn A, 2 rows yarn M, 1 row yarn A, increasing one st at beginning and end of every row and at collar corners by knitting into the front and back of stitch. Bind off in yarn A.

### *Finishing*

Press both sections of garment well, sew underarm and side seams leaving small slit at hem on both sides. Sew right side of collar to inside back neck. Make 2 big loops either side of front edge of neck and attach buttons to correspond. Tie ribbon around points of collar.

### *Measurements*

*To fit sizes 1, 2, 3, 4, 5, 6*

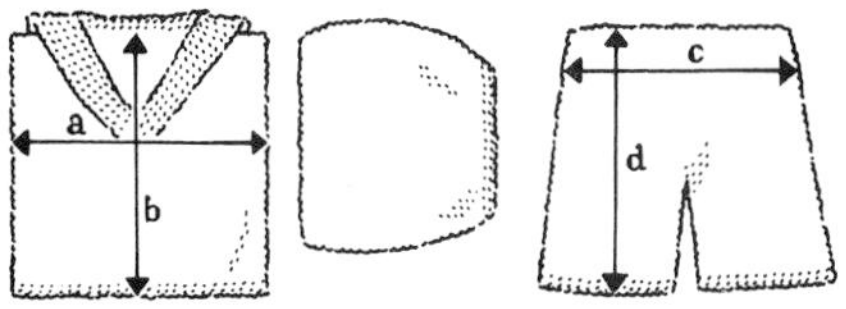


**Shirt**
**a** Chest 18 ($19\frac{3}{4}$, 21, 23, $24\frac{3}{4}$, 26)in
**b** Neck to hem 9 (11, 11, $11\frac{3}{4}$, 13, $13\frac{3}{4}$)in
**Shorts**
**c** Around hip $17\frac{3}{4}$ ($17\frac{3}{4}$, $19\frac{1}{4}$, $19\frac{1}{4}$, $21\frac{1}{4}$, $21\frac{1}{4}$)in
**d** Length $10\frac{1}{4}$ (11, $11\frac{3}{4}$, $14\frac{1}{2}$, $15\frac{1}{4}$, $16\frac{1}{4}$)in
**Hat**
*One size only – hat band is for adjusting to different sizes*
**e** Around head $23\frac{3}{4}$in

## SHORTS

**Yarn**
Main yarn M 3½ (3½, 3½, 5¼, 5¼, 7)oz medium-weight cotton (blue)

**Needles**
No 4 (4, 2, 2, 3, 3) circular (23¾in long)

**Notions**
4 mother-of-pearl buttons
½yd soft ¼in elastic

**Stitch gauge**
*As for shirt.*

### Legs

With yarn M cast on 27 (27, 35, 35, 35, 35) sts using 2-needle method. Working back and forth in rows, work 8 rows garter st. Break yarn and move sts to flexible part of needle. Work another cuff similarly, but do not break yarn. Change to st st and commence working across leg.

**Row 1** Knit 24 (24, 32, 32, 32, 32), p6, k24 (24, 32, 32, 32, 32).

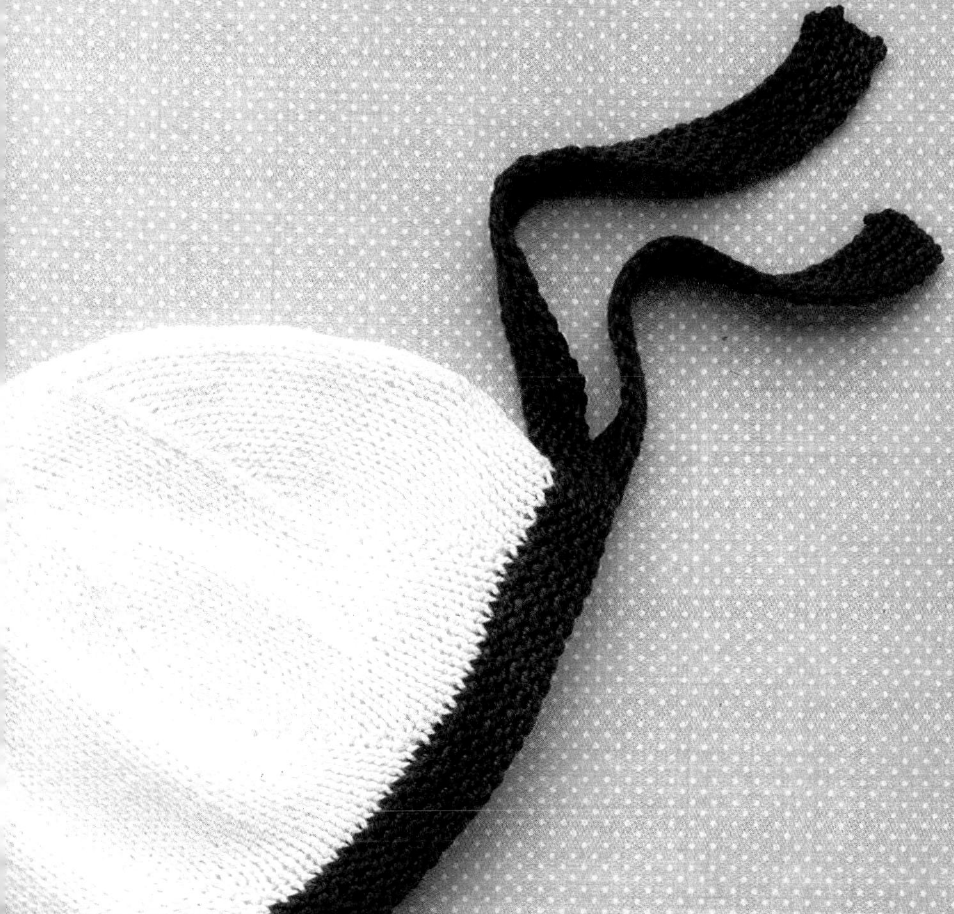

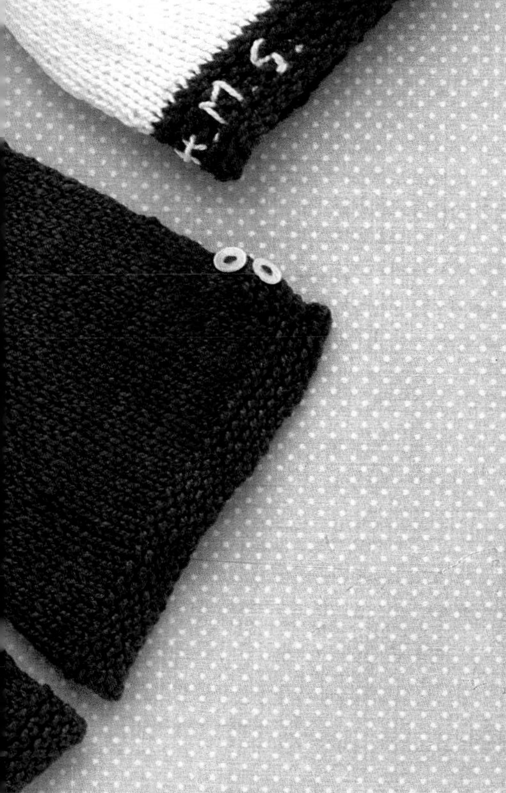

**Row 2** Purl.
Repeat these two rows twice. Continue in st st until work measures 2¼ (3¼, 4, 4¾, 5½, 6¼)in from beginning (or more or less as required). Break yarn and leave sts on needle. Work another piece similarly, but do not break yarn.
*Join pieces:*
**Row 1** Cast on 6, k across sts of first leg, cast on 6, k across sts of second leg.
**Row 2** *and every alternate row:* Purl.
**Row 3** *Sl 1, k1, psso, k4, k2tog, k52 (52, 68, 68, 68, 68), rep from * to end.
**Row 5** *Sl 1, k1, psso, k2, k2tog, k52 (52, 68, 68, 68, 68), rep from * to end.
**Row 7** *Sl 1, k1, psso, k2tog, k52 (52, 68, 68, 68, 68), rep from * to end.
**Row 8** Purl. Break yarn.

## Body

With 108 (108, 140, 140, 140, 140) sts on needle, continue in rounds working as follows: sl 1, k2tog, psso in center front and back until 100 (100, 130, 130, 130, 130) sts remain. Continue in st st until work measures 7¾ (7¾, 9¾, 9¾, 9¾)in from crotch (or more or less as required). Work 6 rounds garter st.
*Shape front:* Knit 30 (30, 40, 40, 40, 40) sts, bind off 40 (40, 50, 50, 50), k30 (30, 40, 40, 40, 40). Work 4 rows st st on remaining 60 (60, 80, 80, 80, 80) sts. Bind off.

## Finishing

Join leg and crotch seams and attach hem of flap to inside of work (back) over required length of elastic. Sew 2 buttons, one above the other, over the side slit on outside of legs.

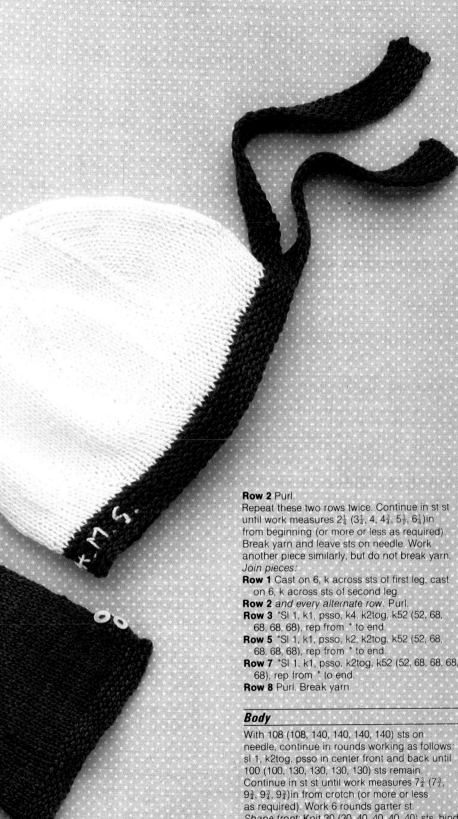

## HAT

**Yarn**
Main yarn M *1oz* medium-weight cotton (blue)
Yarn A *1¾oz* medium-weight cotton (white)
**Needles**
1 pair no 5
**Stitch gauge**
22 sts and 30 rows to 4in over st st (or size needed to obtain given tension).

## Method

With yarn M cast on 140 sts. Work 8 rows in garter st. Bind off 35, k70, bind off 35. Change to yarn A and work 2 rows st st.
**Row 3** *Knit 9, increase into next st, rep from * to end.
**Row 4** *and every alternate row:* Purl without shaping.
**Row 5** *Knit 10, increase into next st, rep from * to end.
Continue this way until there are 119 sts on needle. Work 9 rows without shaping.
*Shape crown*
**Row 1** *Knit 15, k2tog, rep from * to end.
**Row 3** *Knit 14, k2tog, rep from * to end.
Continue this way until 28 sts remain. Break yarn. Thread yarn through remaining sts and secure end.

## Finishing

Sew up seam over white sts and tie blue ends in a double knot when on child's head. Embroider H.M.S. and the child's name in yarn A on headband if desired.

## SAILOR DRESS

**Yarn**
Main yarn M 7 *(7, 7, 8¾, 10½, 11½)oz* medium-weight cotton (white)
Yarn A *1¾ (1¾, 1¾, 1¾, 1¾, 1¾)oz* soft medium-weight cotton (blue)
**Needles**
1 pair no 2 (3, 4, 2, 3, 4)
Similar size circular (or set of 4 double-pointed)
**Notions**
1yd red satin ribbon
2 mother-of-pearl buttons
**Stitch gauge**
28 sts and 36 rows to 4in over st st on no 2 needles; 26 sts and 34 rows to 4in over st st on no 3 needles; 24 sts and 32 rows to 4in over st st on no 4 needles (or size needed to obtain given tension).

## Body

With yarn M cast on 60 (60, 60, 80, 80, 80) sts.
*Work front:* Working back and forth in rows, k 8 rows garter st. Continue in st st working first and last 3 sts of next 6 rows garter st (side-slit edging). Then continue until work measures 11¾ (13½, 13½, 15¼, 16½, 17½)in from beginning (or more or less as required) ending with a knit row.
**Next row** Purl 7 (7, 7, 12, 12, 12) sts; k46 (46, 46, 56, 56, 56); p7 (7, 7, 12, 12, 12) sts.
Knit 1 row. Repeat these 2 rows once.
*Shape neck:* Work as follows:
**Row 1** Purl 7 (7, 7, 12, 12, 12), k3, bind off 40 (40, 40, 50, 50, 50), k3, p7 (7, 7, 12, 12, 12).
**Row 2** Knit 10 (10, 10, 15, 15, 15) sts, cast on 40 (40, 40, 50, 50, 50) sts for back neck, k10 (10, 10, 15, 15, 15).
**Row 1** Purl 7 (7, 7, 12, 12, 12), k3, bind off 40

12, 12), k46 (46, 46, 56, 56, 56), p7 (7, 7, 12, 12, 12).
*Work back:* Continue in st st until back measures the same as front to top of garter st edging for side slit, ending with a k row. Knit first and last 3 sts next 6 rows garter st. Work 8 rows garter st and bind off with wrong side facing.

## Sleeves

With the right side facing and yarn M, pick up 30 (30, 30, 40, 40, 40) sts either side of center shoulder – 60 (60, 60, 80, 80, 80) sts. Work 20 (20, 20, 25, 25, 25) rows st st (or more or less as required) ending on a p row.
**Row 1** Change to yarn A, k2tog to end – 30 (30, 30, 40, 40, 40) sts.
**Row 2** Knit.
**Row 3** Change to yarn M, knit.
**Row 4** Knit.
**Row 5** Change to yarn A, knit.
**Row 6** Knit.
**Row 7** Change to yarn M, knit.
Bind off.

## Collar

With yarn A cast on 50 sts. Work 45 rows in st st.
**Next row** Knit 12 sts, bind off 26, k12.
*Shape point:* Work 45 rows on these last 12 sts. Then bind off 1 st every row on *outside* edge until 1 st remains, thread yarn through st to finish off. Rejoin yarn to remaining 12 sts and work other half similarly but reverse shaping.
*Work trim:* With right side facing and using circular needle or first needle of set of 4 and yarn M, pick up stitches evenly all around outside of collar. Work 6 rows in garter st as follows: 1 row yarn M, 2 rows yarn A, 2 rows yarn M, 1 row yarn A, increasing one st at beginning and end of every row and at collar corners by knitting into the front and back of stitch. Bind off in yarn A.

## Finishing

Press both sections of garment well, sew underarm and side seams, leaving small split at hem on both sides. Sew right side of collar to inside back neck. Make 2 loops either side of front edge of neck and attach buttons to correspond. Tie ribbon in bow around both points of collar.

## SUN HAT

**Yarn**
1½oz medium-weight cotton (white)
**Needles**
1 pair no 2
**Stitch gauge**
28 sts and 38 rows to 4in over st st on no 2 needles (or size needed to obtain given tension)

## Base

Cast on 132 sts. Work 9 rows garter st.
**Next row** *Knit 9, k2tog, rep from * to end – 120 sts.
Work a further 9 rows in garter st.
**Next row** *Knit 8, k2tog, rep from * to end – 108 sts.
Change to st st and work 25 (35, 45) rows.

*Decrease for crown:*
**Row 1** *Sl 1, k1, psso, k14, k2tog, rep from * to end – 96 sts.
**Row 2** *and every alternate row:* Purl.
**Rows 3 and 5** Knit.
**Row 7** *Sl 1, k1, psso, k12, k2tog, rep from * to end – 84 sts.
**Rows 9 and 11** Knit.
**Row 13** *Sl 1, k1, psso, k10, k2tog, rep from * to end – 72 sts.
**Row 15** Knit.
**Row 17** *Sl 1, k1, psso, k8, k2tog, rep from * to end – 60 sts.
**Row 19** Knit.
**Row 21** *Sl 1, k1, psso, k6, k2tog, rep from * to end – 48 sts.
**Row 23** *Sl 1, k1, psso, k4, k2tog, rep from * to end – 36 sts.
**Row 25** *Sl 1, k1, psso, k2, k2tog, rep from * to end – 24 sts.
**Row 27** K2tog across all sts – 12 sts.
Break yarn and thread through all sts.

## Finishing

Sew up seam. Fold brim over and affix at center back with one or two small sts. If desired, attach ribbons to base of brim rows about 4in from center back on each side and tie under chin.

## ANKLE SOCKS

**Yarn**
Main yarn M 1½oz medium-weight cotton (white)
Yarn A scraps medium-weight cotton (blue)
1 set 4 double-pointed no 2 (3, 4, 2, 3, 4)in
**Stitch gauge**
*As for dress.*

## Method

With yarn M, cast on 30 (30, 30, 42, 42, 42) sts evenly over 3 needles. Knit 1 round, p 1 round. Change to yarn A, k 1 round, p 1 round. Change back to yarn M, k 1 round, p 1 round. Work another stripe in yarn A as before. Continue in yarn M until 14 (14, 16, 18, 20, 22) rounds have been worked from beginning (or more or less as required).
*Shape heel:* Change to yarn A. Knit 16 (16, 16, 16, 16, 20, 20, 20) sts, turn. Purl 15 (15, 15, 19, 19, 19), turn. Continue in this way until purling 7, turn and k8. Turn, p9. Continue in this way until purling 15 (15, 15, 19, 19, 19). Break yarn and change to yarn M.
*Work foot:* Knit 16 (16, 16, 20, 20, 20); *k2tog, k1, rep from * 4 (4, 4, 7, 7, 7) times; k2 (2, 2, 1, 1, 1) – 26 (26, 26, 35, 35, 35) sts. Work 14 (16, 18, 20, 22, 24) rounds (or more or less as required). Break yarn.
*Shape toe:* Using yarn A, work as follows:
**Round 1** K2tog, k9 (9, 9, 14, 14, 14), k2tog twice, k9 (9, 9, 13, 13, 13), k2tog.
**Round 2** *and every alternate round:* Knit.
**Round 3** K2tog, k7 (7, 7, 12, 12, 12), k2tog twice, k7 (7, 7, 11, 11, 11), k2tog.
**Round 5** K2tog, k5 (5, 5, 10, 10, 10), k2tog twice, k5 (5, 5, 9, 9, 9), k2tog.
*Larger 3 sizes only:*
**Round 7** K2tog, k8, k2tog twice, k7, k2tog.
**Round 8** K2tog, k6, k2tog twice, k5, k2tog.
*All sizes:* Knit one round.
Bind off.
Sew up toe seam.
Work another sock similarly.

## Measurements

*To fit sizes 1, 2, 3, 4, 5, 6*

**Dress**
**a** Chest 18 (19¾, 21, 23, 24½, 26)in
**b** Neck to hem 12½ (13¾, 15, 15¾, 17, 17¾)in
**Socks**
**c** Heel to toe 3½ (4, 4¾, 5¼, 6, 6¼)in
**Sun hat**
*To fit sizes 1–2, 3–4, 5–6*
**d** Around head 16½in
**e** Crown to brim 7 (8½, 9)in

# CHRISTENING SET

For that special day, this beautiful tiered gown, bonnet and pretty little bootees is bound to be cherished as a family heirloom. Extra tiers can be added to the dress to make it as long and full as you like. The delicate cobweb shawl (see overleaf) completes the set.

## Measurements

*In 2 sizes to fit babies 0–5 months, 5–8 months*

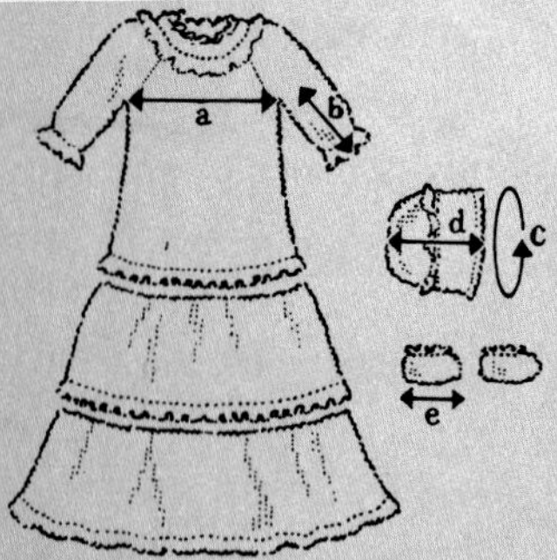

**Dress**
a  Chest 15¾ (18½)in
b  Arm seam 5 (7½)in

**Bonnet**
c  Around face 12½ (15¾)in
d  Face to crown 5½ (6¾)in

**Bootees**
e  Heel to toe 3½ (4¼)in

## GOWN

### Yarn

*Cotton*

Dress to first frill 2¾oz fine cotton
First tier 1¾oz fine cotton
Second tier 2¾oz fine cotton
Increase amount by *1oz* for each subsequent tier (eg 3½oz for third tier etc.)

*Silk*

Dress to first frill 3½oz 4-ply silk
First tier 1¾oz 4-ply silk
Second tier 3½oz 4-ply silk
Increase amount by 1¾oz for each subsequent tier (eg 5¼oz for third tier etc.)

### Needles

1 pair no 1 (3) or similar size circular

### Notions

About 3yd fine ribbon
2 tiny mother-of-pearl buttons

### Stitch gauge

34 sts and 42 rows to 4in over st st on no 1 needles; 28 sts and 34 rows to 4in over st st on no 3 needles (or size needed to obtain given tension).

### Robe

Start at frill. Cast on 300 sts.
**Row 1** *and every odd-numbered row* (unless otherwise instructed): Knit.
**Row 2** Knit 1; *yfwd, k2tog, rep from * to last st, k1.
**Row 4** Knit 2; *yfwd, k2tog, rep from * to end.
**Row 6** Knit 1; *k2, ppso, rep from * to last st; k1 – 151 sts.
**Rows 8, 10 and 12** Purl.
**Row 13** Knit 1; *yfwd, k2tog, rep from * to end.
**Row 14** Purl.
**Rows 15, 16 and 17** Knit
**Row 18** Purl.
**Rows 19, 20 and 21** Knit.
**Row 22** Purl.
**Rows 23, 24 and 25** Knit.
Continue in st st until work measures 8¼ (11)in from beginning, ending on a purl row, but:
**Row 49** *K11, k2tog, rep from * to last 8 sts; k8.
**Row 75** *K10, k2tog, rep from * to last 8 sts; k8 – 129 sts.
*Shape armholes:* Knit 30, bind off 5, k59, bind off 5, k30.
*Shape right back:* K2tog at the beginning of the next 3 k rows (arm edge) – 27 sts. Work 9 rows st st on these sts, then as follows:
**Row 1** Knit 18, turn.
**Row 2** Sl 1, p17.
**Row 3** Knit 15, turn.
  **Row 4** Sl 1, p14.
  **Row 5** Knit 12, turn.
    **Row 6** Sl 1, p11.
    **Row 7** Knit 9, turn.
      **Row 8** Sl 1, p8.
      **Row 9** Knit 6, turn.
        **Row 10** Sl 1, p5.
        **Row 11** Knit 3, turn.
        **Row 12** Sl 1, p2.

Break yarn and slip all sts onto holder.
*Shape right front:* Purl across all sts of front. Decrease one st at both ends of first 3 k rows, continue 9 rows st st.
*Shape right front:* Work yoke as right back. Break yarn and slip sts onto holder.
*Left back:* Continue across sts of left back, decrease one st at arm edge on the first 3 purl rows. Work 9 rows st st then shape for yoke as right back, but reading purl for knit and vice versa. Shape left front yoke similarly. Slip all sts onto holder.

### Sleeves

Cast on 50 sts.

**Row 1** *and every alternate row* (unless otherwise instructed): Knit.
**Row 2** Knit 1; *yfwd, k2tog, rep from * to last st; k1.
**Row 4** Knit 2; *yfwd, k2tog, rep from * to end.
**Row 6** Knit 1; *k2, ppso, rep from * to last st; k1 – 26 sts.
**Row 8** Purl.
**Row 9** Knit 1; *yfwd, k2tog, rep from * to end; k1.
**Row 10** Purl.
**Row 11** *K1, increase by knitting into front and back of next st, rep from * to end – 39 sts.
**Rows 12 and 13** Knit.
**Row 14** Purl.
**Rows 15, 16 and 17** Knit.
**Row 18** Purl.
**Rows 19, 20 and 21** Knit.
Continue in st st increasing one st both ends of rows 36 and 52, until work measures 5 (7½)in from beginning – 43 sts.
*Shape sleeve head:* Bind off 2 sts at the beginning of the next 2 rows, then one st at the beginning of the next 6 rows – 33 sts. Work 21 rows without shaping, then continue as follows:
**Row 1** Knit 28, turn.
**Row 2** Sl 1, p22, turn.
**Row 3** Sl 1, k19, turn.
**Row 4** Sl 1, p16, turn.
**Row 5** Sl 1, k13, turn.
**Row 6** Sl 1, p10, turn.
**Row 7** Sl 1, k7, turn.
Break yarn and slip all sts onto holder between front and back skirt sts. Work another sleeve similarly.

### Yoke

With right sides facing, knit across all sts on holder in following order: left back, sleeve, front, sleeve, right back – 173 sts.
**Row 1** *Knit 1, k2tog, rep from * to last 2 sts; k2 – 116 sts.
**Rows 2, 3 and 4** Knit.
**Row 5** Purl.
**Row 6** Knit 1; (yfwd, k2tog) 3 times; *yfwd, k3tog, (yfwd, k2tog) 3 times, rep from * to last st; k1 – 102 sts.
**Row 7** Purl.
**Rows 8 and 9** Knit.
**Row 10** *Knit 7, k2tog, rep from * to last 5 sts; k5 – 93 sts.
**Row 11** Purl.
**Rows 12 and 13** Knit.
**Row 14** *Knit 6, k2tog, rep from * to last 5 sts; k5 – 82 sts.
**Row 15** Purl.
**Rows 16, 17 and 18** Knit.
**Row 19** Purl.
**Row 20** Knit 1; (yfwd, k2tog) twice; *yfwd, k3tog, (yfwd, k2tog) twice, rep from * to end – 71 sts.
**Row 21** Purl.
**Row 22** Double sts for neck frill by knitting into front and back of all sts – 142 sts.
**Row 23** Knit.
**Row 24** Knit 1; *yfwd, k2tog, rep from * to last st; k1. Bind off.
*Work yoke frill:* With right side of work facing and neck of work towards you, knit up all sts through loops of first row of garter st at shoulder.
**Row 1** Knit 1; *yfwd, k1, rep from * to end – 231 sts.
**Rows 2 and 4** Knit.
**Row 3** Knit 1; *yfwd, k2tog, rep from * to end. Bind off.

# CHRISTENING SET

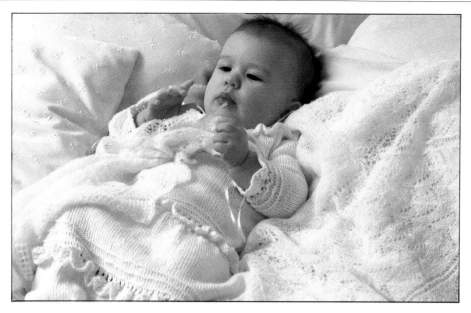

## Tiers

**NB** *Stitches for tiers are estimated by adding half as many again to amount used in previous layer. Thus, if you cast on 300 sts for base frill of skirt, cast on 450 sts for next tier and 675 sts for second tier.*
Starting at base of frill cast on 450 sts.
**Row 1** *and every odd-numbered row:* Knit.
**Row 2** Knit 1; *yfwd, k2tog, rep from * to last st; k1.
**Row 4** Knit 2; *yfwd, k2tog, rep from * to end.
**Row 6** Knit 1; *k2, ppso, rep from * to last st, k1 – 226 sts.
**Row 8** Purl.
**Row 9** Knit 1; *yfwd, k2tog, rep from * to last st, k1.
**Row 10** Purl.
**Rows 11, 12 and 13** Knit.
**Row 14** Purl.
**Rows 15, 16 and 17** Knit.
**Row 18** Purl.
**Rows 19, 20 and 21** Knit.
Continue in st st until work measures 6in from beginning ending on a purl row.
**Next row** *Knit 1, k2tog, rep from * to last st, k1.
Bind off. Sew this bound-off edge to main body of robe leaving frill at front of work.
Make further tiers as required.

### Finishing

Sew up underarm and shoulder seams. Sew up back seam, working from hem to 4 (6)in from neck edge. Roll edges of neck opening and sew neatly to work. Thread fine ribbon through wrists and both rows of eyelets on yoke if desired, tie bows at front and attach ends center back. Place two small buttons on left back at eyelet rows and use first eyelet as buttonhole. Press well.

### BONNET

**Yarn**
*1oz* fine cotton or 4-ply silk
**Needles**
1 pair no 1 (3)
**Notions**
1yd × 2in wide satin ribbon
**Stitch gauge**
34 sts and 42 rows to 4in over st st on no 1

needles; 28 sts and 34 rows to 4in over st st on no 3 needles (or size needed to obtain given tension).

### Method

Cast on 80 sts using 2-needle method.
**Row 1** Knit.
**Row 2** *and every even-numbered row:* Purl.
**Row 3** Knit 1; *yfwd, k2tog, rep from * to last st; k1.
**Row 5** (*hem*) Needle through st k wise, pick up cast-on loop and knit the 2tog.
**Row 7** Knit 1; *yfwd, k2tog, rep from * to last st, k1.
**Row 9** Knit 1; *yfwd, k2tog, k2, rep from * to last st, k1.
**Row 11** Knit 2; *yfwd, k3tog, yfwd, k1, rep from * to end.
**Row 13** Knit 3; *yfwd, k2tog, k2, rep from * to last st; k1.
Continue in st st, but knitting rows 26, 30 and 34 until work measures 3¼ (3½)in from edge. Then work as follows:
**Row 1** Knit 1; *yfwd, k2tog, rep from * to last st; k1.
**Row 2** Purl.
**Row 3** Knit.
**Row 4** Knit. Work 6 rows in st st.
**Row 11** Cast on 8, knit across all sts – 88 sts.
**Row 12** Purl.
**Row 13** *Knit 9, k2tog, rep from * to end – 80 sts.
**Row 17** *Knit 8, k2tog, rep from * to end – 72 sts.
**Row 25** *Knit 6, k3tog, rep from * to end – 56 sts.
**Row 26** Knit.
**Row 27** *Knit 4, k3tog, rep from * to end – 40 sts.
**Row 28** Knit.
**Row 29** *Knit 2, k3tog, rep from * to end – 24 sts.
**Row 30** Knit.
**Row 31** K2tog across all sts – 12 sts.
Break yarn and thread through sts.

### Frill

With right side of work facing and front towards you, pick up 80 sts from last row of garter st and work as follows:
**Row 1** Knit 1; *yfwd, k1, rep from * to end.

**Row 2** Knit.
**Row 3** Knit 1; *yfwd, k2tog, rep from * to end.
**Row 4** Bind off.

### Finishing

Sew up back seam leaving a small hole center crown where sts are gathered. Pick up 53 sts evenly around neck.
*Work row of eyelets:* Knit 1; *yfwd, k2tog, rep from * to end. Bind off. Press face edge carefully and attach lengths of wide satin ribbon to corners. This ribbon is intended to hang freely – do not tie.

### BOOTEES

**Yarn**
About ⅓oz fine cotton or 4-ply silk
**Needles**
1 pair no 1 (3)
**Notions**
1yd fine ribbon

### Method

Cast on 20 sts. Work in garter st, increase one st at the beginning of every row until 28 sts on needle, then decrease one st at the beginning of every row until 20 sts remain.
**Next row** Cast on 5 sts for heel and k to end. Change to st st.
**Next row** Increase one st and purl to end. Knit next 3 alternate rows without shaping. Continue to increase one st at toe edge every purl row until 29 sts on needle.
**Next row** Bind off 10 sts, knit to end.
Then, purl 17 sts, p2tog, turn. K2tog, k16, turn. Purl 15, p2tog. Work 6 rows without shaping. Increase one st at the beginning of the next row, k16. Then p17, increase 1, turn. Increase 1, k18, turn. Purl 19. Cast on 10 sts at the beginning of the next row and knit to end. Continue decreasing one st at toe edge at the beginning of every purl row until 25 sts remain. Bind off. With right side of work facing, pick up 30 sts around edge and work as follows:
**Row 1** Knit 1; *yfwd, k1, rep from * to end – 59 sts
**Row 2** Knit.
**Row 3** Knit 1; *yfwd, k2tog, rep from * to end. Bind off.
Work another slipper similarly reversing shaping.

### Finishing

Sew up sole and heel seams and thread ribbon through first row of eyelets at base of frill. Tie into large bow when on baby's foot.

### COBWEB SHAWL

**Yarn**
*3oz* 1-ply Shetland
**Needles**
1 pair no 3 long
1 pair no 3 short for edging
1 pair no 5

### Measurements

39½in square

## Center

Cast on 120 sts using 2-needle method and no 3 long needles. Work 240 rows in garter st, commencing each row with yfwd, k2tog, to make large loops along the edges.
**Work a row of eyelets – yfwd, k2tog – and p 1 row.

## Borders

Work a small border of hearts for the first section as follows:
**Row 1** Yfwd, k1; *yfwd, k2tog, k7, rep from * to last 2 sts; yfwd, k2tog.
**Row 2** *and every even-numbered row:* Yrn, p to end.
**Row 3** Yfwd, k1; *yfwd, sl 1, k2tog, psso, yfwd, k6, rep from * to last 4 sts; yfwd, sl 1, k2tog; psso, yfwd, k1.
**Row 5** Yfwd, k1; *yfwd, sl 1, k1, psso, k1, k2tog, yfwd, k4, rep from * to last 6 sts; yfwd, sl 1, k1, psso, k1; k2tog; yfwd, k1.
**Row 7** Yfwd, k1; *yfwd, sl 1, k1, psso, k3, k2tog, yfwd, k2, rep from * to last 8 sts; yfwd, sl 1, k1, psso, k3, k2tog, yfwd, k1.
**Row 9** Yfwd, k2; *yfwd, sl 1, k1, psso, k1, yfwd, k2tog twice, yfwd, k2, rep from * to end.
**Row 11** Yfwd, k2; *k2tog, yfwd, k2tog, yfwd, k1, yfwd, sl 1, k1, psso, yfwd, sl 1, k1, psso, rep from * to last 2 sts; k2.
**Row 13** Yfwd, k to end.
**Row 15** K2tog; *yfwd, k2tog, rep from * to end.
**NB** *Check that you have 133 sts on needle before commencing next border. If not, increase at beginning of next row.*
**Row 16** Yrn, p2tog, p to end row, increasing by knitting into front and back of 7th and every following 13th st – 143 sts.
Commence a border of horseshoes for the second section.
**Row 17** Yfwd, k2tog; *yfwd, k3, sl 1, k2tog, psso, k3, yfwd, k1, rep from * to last st; k1.
**Rows 18 and 20** Yrn, p2tog, p to end row.
**Row 19** As row 17.
**Row 21** Yrn, p2tog; *k1, yfwd, k2, sl 1, k2tog, psso, k2, yo, k1, p1, rep from * to last st; k1.
**Rows 22 and 24** Yfwd, k2tog; *p9, k1, rep from * to last st; k1.

**Row 23** Yfwd, p2tog; *k2, yfwd, k1, sl 1, k2tog, psso, k1, yfwd, k2, p1, rep from * to last st; k1.
**Row 25** Yrn, p2tog; *k3, yfwd, sl 1, k2tog, psso, yfwd, k3, p1, rep from * to last st; k1.
**Rows 26 to 33** Repeat rows 18 to 25.
**Rows 34 and 36** As row 18.
**Row 35** Yfwd, k2tog; *yfwd, k1, yfwd, k2, sl 1, k2tog, psso, k2, yfwd, k1, yfwd, k1, rep from * to last st; k1.
**Row 37** Yfwd, k2tog; *k1, yfwd, k3, sl 1, k2tog, psso, k3, yfwd, k1, p1, rep from * to last st; k1.
**Row 38** Yfwd, k2tog; *p11, k1, rep from * to last st; k1.
**Row 39** Yfwd, k2tog; *k2, yfwd, k2, sl 1, k2tog, psso, k2, yfwd, k2, p1, rep from * to last st; k1.
**Row 40** As row 38.
**Row 41** Yfwd, k2tog; *k3, yfwd, k1, sl 1, k2tog, psso, k1, yfwd, k3, p1, rep from * to last st; k1.
**Row 42** As row 38.
**Row 43** Yfwd, k2tog; *k4, yfwd, sl 1, k2tog, psso, yfwd, k4, p1, rep from * to last st; k1.
**Row 44** As row 18.
**Row 45** Yfwd, k2tog; yfwd, k4, sl 1, k2tog, psso, k4, yfwd, k1, rep from * to last st; k1.
**Row 46 to 53** Repeat rows 36 to 43.
**Rows 54 and 56** As row 18.
**Row 55** Yfwd, k2tog; *yfwd, k1, yfwd, k3, sl 1, k2tog, psso, k3, yfwd, k1, yfwd, k1, rep from * to last st; k1.
**Row 57** Yfwd, k2tog; *k1, yfwd, k4, sl 1, k2tog, psso, k4, yfwd, k1, p1, rep from * to last st; k1.
**Row 58** Yfwd, k2tog; *p13, k1, rep from * to last st; k1.
**Row 59** Yfwd, k2tog; *k2, yfwd, k3, sl 1, k2tog, psso, k3, yfwd, k2, p1, rep from * to last st; k1.
**Rows 60, 62 and 64** As row 58.
**Row 61** Yfwd, k2tog; *k3, yfwd, k2, sl 1, k2tog, psso, k2, yfwd, k3, p1, rep from * to last st; k1.
**Row 63** Yfwd, k2tog; *k4, yfwd, k1, sl 1, k2tog, psso, k1, yfwd, k4, p1, rep from * to last st; k1.
**Row 65** Yfwd, k2tog; *k5, yfwd, sl 1, k2tog, psso, yfwd, k5, p1, rep from * to last st; k1.
**Row 66** As row 18.
**Row 67** Yfwd, k2tog; *yfwd, k5, sl 1, k2tog, psso, k5, yfwd, k1, rep from * to last st; k1.
**Rows 68 to 77** As rows 56 to 65.
**Row 78** As row 18.
**Row 79** Yfwd, k2tog; *yfwd, k1, yfwd, k4, sl 1, k2tog, psso, k4, yfwd, k1, yfwd, k1, rep from *

to last st; k1.
**Row 80** As row 18.
**Row 81** Yfwd, k2tog; *k1, yfwd, k5, sl 1, k2tog, psso, k5, yfwd, k1, p1, rep from * to last st; k1.
**Row 82** Yfwd, k2tog; *p15, k1, rep from * to last st; k1.
**Row 83** Yfwd, k2tog; *k2, yfwd, k4, sl 1, k2tog, psso, k4, yfwd, k2, p1, rep from * to last st; k1.
**Row 84** As row 82.
**Row 85** Yfwd, k2tog; *k3, yfwd, k3, sl 1, k2tog, psso, k3, yfwd, k3, p1, rep from * to last st; k1.
**Rows 86 and 88** As row 82.
**Row 87** Yfwd, k2tog; *k4, yfwd, k2, sl 1, k2tog, psso, k2, yfwd, k4, p1, rep from * to last st; k1.
**Row 89** Yfwd, k2tog; *k5, yfwd, k1, sl 1, k2tog, psso, k1, yfwd, k5, p1, rep from * to last st; k1.
**Row 91** Yfwd, k2tog; *k6, yfwd, sl 1, k2tog, psso, yfwd, k6, p1, rep from * to last st; k1.
**Row 92** Purl without shaping – 227 sts.
Bind off very loosely using no 5 needle.
Pick up 120 sts from cast-on edge (opposite edge) of central square and p 1 row. Repeat from **
Work another 2 sides in the same way, picking up every alternate loop and omitting the row of eyelets.

## Edging

***Cast on 14 sts, using shorter no 3 needles. Starting at one corner and working in an anticlockwise direction, pick up one loop from bound-off edge (making 15 sts), turn, and work as follows:
**Row 1** *K2tog, yfwd, rep from * once, k2tog, k8, yfwd, k1.
**Row 2** *and every even-numbered row:* Knit to end, pick up loop from bound-off edge.
**Row 3** *K2tog, yfwd, rep from * once; k2tog; k7; yfwd, k2tog; yfwd, k1.
**Row 5** *K2tog, yfwd, rep from * once; k2tog; k6; **yfwd, k2tog, rep from ** once; yfwd; k1.
**Row 7** *K2tog, yfwd, rep from * once; k2tog; k5; **yfwd, k2tog, rep from ** twice; yfwd, k1.
**Row 9** *K2tog, yfwd, rep from * once; k2tog; k4; **yfwd, k2tog, rep from ** 3 times; yfwd, k1.
**Row 11** *K2tog, yfwd, rep from * once; k2tog; k3; **yfwd, k2tog, rep from ** 4 times; yfwd, k1.
**Row 13** *K2tog, yfwd, rep from * once; k2tog; k2; **yfwd, k2tog, rep from ** 5 times; yfwd, k1.
**Row 15** *K2tog, yfwd, rep from * once; k2tog; k1; **yfwd, k2tog, rep from ** 6 times; yfwd, k1.
**Row 17** *K2tog, yfwd, rep from * once; k2tog; k2; **yfwd, k2tog, rep from ** 4 times; yfwd, sl 1, k3tog; psso, yfwd, k1.
**Row 19** *K2tog, yfwd, rep from * once; k2tog; k3; **yfwd, k2tog, rep from ** 3 times; yfwd, sl 1; k3tog; psso; yfwd, k1.
**Row 21** *K2tog, yfwd, rep from * once; k2tog; k4; **yfwd, k2tog, rep from ** twice; yfwd, sl 1, k3tog; psso; yfwd, k1.
**Row 23** *K2tog, yfwd, rep from * once; k2tog; k5; **yfwd, k2tog, rep from ** once; yfwd, sl 1, k3tog; psso, yfwd, k1.
**Row 25** *K2tog, yfwd, rep from * once; k2tog; k6; yfwd, k2tog; yfwd, sl 1, k3tog; psso, yfwd, k1.
**Row 27** *K2tog, yfwd, rep from * once, k2tog; k7; yfwd, sl 1, k3tog; psso, yfwd, k1.
**Row 29** *K2tog, yfwd, rep from * once; k2tog; k6; sl 1, k3tog; psso, yfwd, k1.
**Row 30** As row 2.
Repeat from *** working 2 points at the corners until the whole of the edge has been worked. Bind off and graft seams very carefully.

# Summer Frills

This pretty white cotton pinafore can be worn on its own in hot weather or over a simple dress for a party look, see overleaf. Complete the outfit with a frilly cotton bonnet.

## PINAFORE

### Yarn
5¼ (7, 7, 8¾, 10½, 12¼)oz medium-weight cotton (white)

### Needles
1 pair no 2 (3, 4, 2, 3, 4)

### Stitch gauge
28 sts and 36 rows to 4in over st st on no 2 needles; 26 sts and 34 rows to 4in over st st on no 3 needles; 24 sts and 32 rows to 4in over st on no 4 needles (or size needed to obtain given tension).

## Front

Cast on 169 (169, 169, 209, 209, 209) sts using 2-needle method.

**Row 1** Knit.

**Row 2** Work row of eyelets: k1, *yfwd, k2tog, rep from * to end.

**Row 3** Knit.

Work further 13 rows garter st, making an eyelet on 3rd st at beginning every row: k2, yfwd, k2tog.

**Row 17** Knit 2; yfwd; k2tog; k6; k2tog 20 (20, 20, 30, 30, 30) times; *k1, k2tog, rep from * 23 times; k2tog 20 (20, 20, 30, 30, 30) times; k10 – 106 (106, 106, 126, 126, 126) sts.

*Commence apron:* Work first 10 sts every row in garter st, making eyelet in 3rd st; work central 86 (86, 86, 106, 106, 106) sts st st, starting with a purl (wrong side) row; work last 10 sts every row in garter st.

Work 30 (40, 50, 60, 70, 80) rows.

*Decrease for outside frill of apron:*

**Row 1** Knit 2, yfwd, k2tog, k4, k2tog, p86 (86, 86, 106, 106, 106), k10.

**Row 2** Knit 2, yfwd, k2tog, k4, k2tog, k86 (86, 86, 106, 106, 106), k9.

Continue in this way decreasing 1 st per row until 94 (94, 94, 114, 114, 114) sts remain.

*Shape waistband:* K2tog across all sts – 47 (47, 47, 57, 57, 57) sts.

*Make ties:*

**Next row** Cast on 50, k to end.

Repeat this row – 147 (147, 147, 157, 157, 157) sts.

**Next row** Bind off 55, k to end.

Repeat this row – 37 (37, 37, 47, 47, 47) sts.

*Work bodice:* Continue in st st without shaping until work measures ¾ (1½, 2¼, 3¼, 4, 4¾)in from waist (or more or less as required).

*Shape neck:* Knit 10; *yfwd, k2tog, rep from * 7 (7, 7, 12, 12, 12) times; yfwd; k3tog; yfwd; k10. P12, bind off 12 (12, 12, 22, 22, 22), p12.

*Shape right shoulder:*

**Row 1** Knit 7, k3tog, yo, k2tog.

**Row 2** *and every alternate row:* Purl.

**Row 3** Knit 6, k2tog, yo, k2.

Repeat rows 2 and 3 until work measures 2¾ (2¾, 3¼, 4, 4, 4)in from neck shaping.

**Next row** *K2tog, yfwd, rep from * 4 times, k2. Bind off.

*Shape left shoulder:* Rejoin yarn to right side of work, then work as follows:

**Row 1** Knit 2, yfwd, k3tog, k to end.

**Row 2** *and every alternate row:* Purl.

**Row 3** Knit 2, yfwd, k2tog, k to end.

## Measurements

Shoulder to hem 11¾ (13¾, 17, 18, 21, 23¾)in

Repeat rows 2 and 3 and work as for right shoulder.
Work back similarly.

## Bodice frills

Sew shoulder seams together and press work. Right side of work facing and omitting bound-off sections, pick up 50 (60, 70, 80, 90, 100) sts evenly from waist over shoulder to back waist. Turn and double sts: knit into front and back of each st.
Work 2 rows garter st without shaping, then work as follows:
**Row 1** Knit to last 10 sts, turn.
Repeat row.
**Row 3** Knit to last 20 sts, turn.
Repeat last row.
Continue in this way knitting 10 less sts every row until knitting 10 sts, then turn, slip 1, k to end.
Work 4 rows garter st without shaping across all sts and bind off loosely.

## Finishing

Press work well over st st sections. Sew end of bodice frill to bound-off sections of apron.

## SUN BONNET

**Yarn**
1¾oz medium-weight cotton (white)
**Needles**
1 pair no 2 (3, 4)
**Stitch gauge**
28 sts and 36 rows to 4in over st st on no 2 needles; 26 sts and 34 rows to 4in over st st on no 3 needles; 24 sts and 32 rows to 4in over st st on no 4 needles (or size needed to obtain given tension).

## Measurements

*To fit sizes 1, 2, 3*

**a** Around face 12¼ (13, 14¼)in
**b** Front to back 4¼ (4¾, 5½)in

## Main section

Cast on 120 sts.
**Row 1** Knit 1; *yfwd, k2tog, rep from * to last st, k1.
**Row 2** *and every even-numbered row:* Knit.
**Row 3** Knit 2; *yfwd, k2tog, yfwd, k2tog, k2, rep from * to last 4 sts; k4.
**Row 5** Knit 5; *yfwd, k2tog, yfwd, k2tog, k2, rep from * to last st; k1.
**Row 7** Knit 6; *yfwd, k2tog, k4, rep from * to end.
**Row 9** K2tog to end – 60 sts.
**Row 10** *and every even-numbered row:* Purl.
**Row 11** Knit 1; *yfwd, k2tog, rep from * to last st; k1.
**Row 13** Knit 2; *yfwd, k2tog, k1, k2tog, yfwd, k3, rep from * to last 2 sts; k2.
**Row 15** K2tog; yfwd; k1; *yfwd, k2tog, rep from * to last st; k1.
**Row 17** Knit 4; *yfwd, k2tog, k2, rep from * to end.

**Row 19** Knit 8; *yfwd, k2tog, k6, rep from * to last 4 sts; yfwd; k2tog; k2.
**Row 21** As row 19.
**Row 23** Knit 1; *yfwd, k2tog, k3, k2tog, yfwd, k1, rep from * to last 3 sts; k3.
**Row 25** Knit 2; *yfwd, k2tog, k1, k2tog, yfwd, k3, rep from * to last 2 sts; k2.
**Row 27** *K2tog, yfwd, rep from * to last 4 sts; k4.
**Row 29** As row 17.
**Rows 31 and 33** As row 19.
**Row 35** As row 23.
**Row 37** As row 25.
**Row 39** As row 27.
**Row 41** As row 17.
**Rows 43 and 45** As row 19.
**Row 47** As row 23.
**Row 49** As row 25.
**Row 51** *Knit 3, yfwd, k2tog, k1, yfwd, k2tog, rep from * to last 4 sts; k4.
**Row 53** Knit 5; *yfwd, k2tog, k6, rep from * to last 7 sts; yfwd; k2tog; k5.
**Rows 55 and 57** Knit.
**Row 59** *Knit 2, yfwd, k2tog, k1, k2tog, yfwd, k1, k2tog, rep from * to end – 54 sts.
**Row 61** Knit 1; *(yfwd, k2tog) 3 times, yfwd, k3tog, rep from * to last 8 sts; (yfwd, k2tog) 4 times – 49 sts.
**Row 62** P2tog, p to end – 48 sts.
**Row 63** *Knit 1, yfwd, k2tog, k1, k2tog, yfwd, k2tog, rep from * to end – 42 sts.
**Row 65** Knit 1; *yfwd, k2tog, k3, k2tog, rep from * to last 6 sts; yfwd; k2tog; k2; k2tog – 36 sts.
**Row 67** Knit 2; *yfwd, k2tog, k1, k2tog, k1, rep from * to last 4 sts; yfwd; k2tog; k2tog – 30 sts.
**Row 69** *K2tog, k1, yfwd, k2tog, rep from * to end – 24 sts.
**Row 71** Knit 1; *k2tog, yfwd, rep from * to last st; k1.
**Row 72** Purl.
Break yarn and thread through remaining sts.

## Trimming

Right side of work facing, neck edge towards you, knit up 61 sts through small loops at fold line where work starts to decrease for crown.
**Row 1** Knit 1, k into front and back of every st – 121 sts.
**Row 2** Knit 1; *yfwd, k2tog, k3, rep from * to end.
**Row 3** *and every odd-numbered row:* Knit.
**Row 4** Knit 2; *yfwd, k2tog, k1, k2tog, yfwd, k1, rep from * to last 3 sts; yfwd, k2tog, k1.
**Row 6** Knit 1; *yfwd, k2tog, rep from * to end.
**Row 8** Bind off.

## Finishing

Sew up back seam (including trim).
*Make ties:* Cast on 250 sts. Bind off. Find center of the chain and sew on to neck working from back seam to both front corners. Press frills well.

# Winter Frills

Adorable and warm, this is a wool dress with frills around the shoulders. It looks great by itself or add a touch of elegance with a white collar, see overleaf, or the white pinafore, below.

## DRESS

### Yarn
5 (6, 7, 8, 9, 10)oz 2-ply Shetland

### Needles
1 pair no 2 (3, 4, 2, 3, 4)

### Notions
3 (4, 5, 6, 7, 8) mother-of-pearl buttons

### Stitch gauge
28 sts and 36 rows to 4in over st st on no 2 needles; 26 sts and 34 rows to 4in over st st on no 3 needles; 24 sts and 32 rows to 4in over st st on no 4 needles (or size needed to obtain given tension).

## Measurements

*To fit sizes 1, 2, 3, 4, 5, 6*

**a** Chest $18\frac{1}{2}$ ($20\frac{1}{2}$, $21\frac{1}{4}$, $22\frac{1}{2}$, $24\frac{1}{2}$, $25\frac{3}{4}$)in
**b** Neck to hem $12\frac{1}{2}$ ($15\frac{3}{4}$, 18, 21, $23\frac{3}{4}$, $25\frac{1}{4}$)in
**c** Sleeve seam $5\frac{1}{2}$ ($6\frac{3}{4}$, $7\frac{3}{4}$, $8\frac{3}{4}$, $9\frac{1}{2}$, $10\frac{1}{4}$)in

## Front

Cast on 150 (150, 150, 195, 195, 195) sts. Work 17 rows in garter st.
**Next row** *K1, k2tog, rep from * to end – 100 (100, 100, 130, 130, 130) sts.
Purl the next row and continue in st st without shaping until work measures $9\frac{3}{4}$ (11, $11\frac{3}{4}$, 13, $14\frac{1}{4}$, 15)in from beginning, ending with a wrong-side row.
*Shape bodice:* *K1, k2tog, rep from * to last st; k1 – 67 (67, 67, 87, 87, 87) sts. Then bind off 5 (5, 5, 10, 10, 10) sts at beginning of next 2 rows. Work across all sts in k1, p1 rib until work measures $3\frac{1}{4}$ ($4\frac{1}{4}$, 6, $7\frac{1}{2}$, 9, $9\frac{3}{4}$)in from waist (or more or less as required), ending with a wrong-side row.
*Shape neck:* Work 19 (19, 19, 21, 21, 21) sts; bind off 19 (19, 19, 25, 25, 25) sts; work 19 (19, 19, 21, 21, 21). Work one row across last 19 (19, 19, 21, 21, 21) sts.
*Shape right shoulder:* Bind off one st at the beginning of the next and following alternate rows (neck edge), work 2 further rows without shaping and bind off.
Finish other left shoulder similarly, reversing shaping.

## Back

Work as for front to beginning of bodice.
**Row 1** *K1, k2tog, rep from * to last st; k1 – 67 (67, 67, 87, 87, 87)sts.
**Row 2** Bind off 5 (5, 5, 10, 10, 10) sts, purl to end.
**Row 3** Bind off 5 (5, 5, 10, 10, 10) sts; *k1, p1, rep from * 14 (14, 14, 16, 16, 16) times; k1 (1, 1, 2, 2, 2) sts, turn.
*Shape button-bands:* Make 2 (2, 2, 3, 3, 3) sts

in first st, then knit first 4 (4, 4, 7, 7, 7) sts and continue in k1, p1 rib to end. Continue in k1, p1 rib, working 4 (4, 4, 7, 7, 7) sts at inside edge in garter st.
*Buttonholes:* Make buttonhole in 3rd (3rd, 3rd, 4th, 4th, 4th) st (yo, k2tog) of row 5 and again every 8th row.
Continue until work measures $3\frac{1}{2}$ ($4\frac{3}{4}$, $6\frac{1}{4}$, $7\frac{3}{4}$, $9\frac{1}{2}$, $10\frac{1}{4}$)in (or more or less as required), from waist, ending on a right-side row.
*Shape neck:* Bind off 12 (12, 12, 15, 15, 15) sts then work in k1, p1 rib to end. Work one row without shaping. Bind off one st at the beginning of the next and alternate row at the neck edge. Work one row without shaping in k1, p1 rib. Bind off.
Work other side of back similarly, reversing shaping and omitting buttonholes.

## Frill

Sew shoulder seams and press. With right side of work facing, pick up about 56 (72, 80, 110, 130, 130) sts evenly from waist over shoulder to back waist (omitting bound-off sections). Turn and double the number of sts: k into the front and back of each st. Work 2 rows garter st without shaping, then work as follows:
**Row 1** Knit to within last 10 sts, turn.
Repeat last row.
**Row 3** Knit to within last 20 sts, turn.
Repeat last row.
Continue in this way knitting 10 less sts and repeating the row until knitting 10 sts. Then turn, sl 1, k to end. Work 4 rows garter st without shaping across all sts and bind off loosely. Work other frill similarly.

## Sleeves

Right side facing, fold frill back towards you and pick up about 56 (72, 80, 110, 130, 130) sts from base of frill. Work 8 (8, 8, 18, 18, 18) rows st st without shaping, then bind off 3 (5, 7, 10, 12, 12) sts at the beginning of the next 2 rows. Bind off one st at the beginning of the next 4 (10, 10, 16, 20, 20) rows and continue without shaping until work measures $5\frac{1}{2}$ ($6\frac{3}{4}$, $7\frac{3}{4}$, $8\frac{3}{4}$, $9\frac{1}{2}$, $10\frac{1}{4}$)in from underarm shaping (or more or less as required), ending with a wrong-side row. K2tog across all sts and work 5 rows garter st. Bind off.
Work other sleeve similarly.

## Neck

Right side facing, pick up sts evenly around neck. Double sts by knitting into front and back each st. Work 6 rows garter st. Bind off.

## Finishing

Press work lightly over st st sections but omitting bodice. Sew straight edge at base of sleeve underarm to the bound-off edge of all 4 skirt sections then sew up skirt and arm seams. Catch bases of button-bands together and bases of frills to bodice. Sew on buttons to correspond with buttonholes.

## CIRCULAR COLLAR

**Yarn**
*1oz* medium-weight cotton
**Needles**
1 pair no 4
**Notions**
1yd narrow satin ribbon

## Method

Cast on 66 sts.
**Row 1** Sl 1, k to last but one st, turn.
**Row 2** Sl 1 – 2 sts on right needle – *yfwd, k2tog, rep from * to last 2 sts, turn.
**Row 3** Sl 1 – 3 sts on right needle – p to last 3 sts, turn.
**Row 4** Sl 1 – 4 sts on right needle – k1; *yfwd, k2tog, rep from * to last 5 sts; k1, turn.
**Row 5** Sl 1 – 5 sts on right needle – p to last 5 sts, turn.
**Row 6** Sl 1 – 6 sts on right needle – *yfwd, k2tog, rep from * to last 6 sts; turn.
**Row 7** Purl 54, p2tog, turn.
**Row 8** Knit 55, k2tog, turn.
**Row 9** Purl 56, p2tog, turn.
**Row 10** Knit 57, k2tog, turn.
**Row 11** Purl 58, p2tog, turn.
**Row 12** Knit 59, k2tog, turn.
**Row 13** Yfwd, k2tog, yfwd, k2tog, p to end.
**Row 14** Yfwd, k2tog, yfwd, k2tog, k to end.
**Row 15** Knit across all sts.
**Row 16** *Yfwd, k2tog, yfwd, sl 1, k2tog, psso, rep from * to end.
Bind off loosely.

## Finishing

Press wrong side of collar well and attach $\frac{1}{2}$yd ribbon to each corner to make neck fastening.

## POINTED COLLAR

**Yarn**
*1oz* medium-weight cotton
**Needles**
1 pair no 4
**Notions**
1yd narrow satin ribbon

## Method

Cast on 60 sts, then work as follows:
**Row 1** Yfwd; k1; *yfwd, k2tog, rep from * to last st; yfwd; k1.
**Row 2** *and every even-numbered row:* Purl.
**Row 3** Yfwd; k1; *yfwd, k2tog, rep from * to last st; yfwd, k1.
**Row 5** K2tog, yfwd, k2tog, k2tog, yfwd, k2tog, turn.
**Row 7** K2tog, yfwd, k2tog, yfwd, k2tog.
**Row 9** K2tog, k1, k2tog.
**Row 11** K3tog.
Break yarn and thread through loop. Darn end back through work. Rejoin yarn to work and continue from Row 5 making another point. Continue in this way until all sts have been worked and 8 points are complete.

## Finishing

Press collar well from wrong side. Attach $\frac{1}{2}$yd ribbon to each corner to make neck fastenings.

## Measurements

*One size only – adjust size with ribbon.*
**a** Around neck $8\frac{3}{4}$in
**b** Around neck $11\frac{3}{4}$in

Detail showing pointed collar tied around neck.

# BALLERINA

Just the thing for the budding ballerina. Worked in mohair yarn, this pretty little wrap-around bolero with its matching legwarmers and headband will make her look really professional.

## BOLERO

**Yarn**
$1\frac{3}{4}$ ($2\frac{3}{4}$, $2\frac{3}{4}$, $3\frac{1}{2}$, $3\frac{1}{2}$, $4\frac{1}{2}$)oz mohair (pink)
**Needles**
1 pair no 7
**Stitch gauge**
16 sts and 21 rows to 4in over st st.

### Back

Cast on 36 (38, 40, 45, 47, 50) sts. Work 3 rows garter st, then work in st st until back measures $3\frac{1}{4}$ (4, 5, 6, $6\frac{3}{4}$, 7)in from beginning. Bind off 3 sts beginning next 2 rows, then k2tog beginning next 4 rows. Continue without shaping until work measures 6 (7, 9, $10\frac{1}{4}$, $11\frac{1}{2}$, $11\frac{3}{4}$)in from beginning (or more or less as required), ending with a wrong-side row.
*Shape neck as follows:*
**Row 1** Knit.
**Row 2** Purl 6 (7, 8, 9, 10, 11), k14 (14, 14, 17, 17, 18), p6 (7, 8, 9, 10, 11).
Repeat these 2 rows.
**Row 5** Knit 8 (9, 10, 11, 12, 13), bind off 10 (10, 10, 13, 13, 14), k8 (9, 10, 11, 12, 13).
Purl 1 row on these last sts and bind off.
Break yarn.
Rejoin yarn to remaining sts, purl 1 row and bind off.

### Front

*Left front:* Cast on 100 (100, 100, 150, 150, 150) sts. Work 2 rows garter st. Bind off 64 (62, 60, 105, 103, 100) sts and k to end.
Knit next row without shaping.*
**Row 1** Knit 3, p2tog, p to end.
**Row 2** Knit to last 5 sts, k2tog, k3.
Repeat these 2 rows until 16 (17, 18, 19, 20, 21) sts remain.
Decrease 1 st on next 3 alternate rows, working other rows without shaping and always working 3 sts garter st as before.
**Continue without shaping until work measures the same as back, then bind off 3 sts at arm edge. K2tog beginning next 2 k rows and continue without shaping until work measures $6\frac{1}{4}$ ($7\frac{1}{2}$, $9\frac{1}{2}$, $10\frac{3}{4}$, $11\frac{3}{4}$, $12\frac{1}{4}$)in from beginning and bind off.
*Right front:* Work as left front to *.
**Row 1** Purl to last 5 sts, p2tog tbl, k3.
**Row 2** Knit 3, k2tog tbl, k to end.
Repeat these 2 rows until 16 (17, 18, 19, 20, 21) sts remain. Decrease 1 st on next 3 alternate rows, working other rows without shaping and always working 3 sts garter st as before.
Continue as left front from **, reversing shaping where necessary.

### Sleeves

Cast on 30 (35, 40, 45, 45, 50) sts. Work 3 rows garter st. Work 4 (4, 4, 8, 8, 10) rows st st. Bind off 3 sts beginning next 2 rows. K2tog beginning every row until 16 (18, 20, 20, 20, 20) sts remain. K2tog across all sts and bind off.

### Finishing

Sew side seams leaving $\frac{3}{4}$in hole above garter st section at hem (to thread tie). Sew shoulder seams and underarm seams. Set arms in armholes.

## LEGWARMERS

**Yarn**
1 ($1\frac{1}{4}$, $1\frac{3}{4}$, $2\frac{1}{4}$, $2\frac{3}{4}$, $3\frac{1}{2}$)oz mohair (pink)
**Needles**
1 pair no 7
**Notions**
1yd shirring elastic
**Stitch gauge**
16 sts and 21 rows to 4in over st st.

### Method

Cast on 30 (35, 40, 45, 45, 50) sts. Work 5 rows k1, p1 rib. Work 3 rows garter st, then work $4\frac{3}{4}$ ($5\frac{1}{2}$, 7, $7\frac{3}{4}$, $8\frac{3}{4}$, $9\frac{1}{2}$)in st st (or more or less as required). Work 3 rows garter st and bind off. Work another leg similarly.

### Finishing

Sew seams. Thread matching shirring elastic through ends if necessary.

## HEADBAND

**Yarn**
1oz mohair (pink)
**Needles**
1 pair no 7
**Notions**
$\frac{1}{2}$yd length elastic

### Method

Cast on 72 sts and work 12 rows st st, knitting row 6 instead of purling to make fold line.

### Finishing

Fold bandeau over required length of elastic and sew down side. Sew ends of elastic together securely and sew ends of bandeau together.

## Measurements

*To fit sizes 1, 2, 3, 4, 5, 6*

**Bolero**
**a** Chest 18½ (19¾, 20½, 22½, 23¼, 24½)in
**b** Shoulder to hem 6 (7, 8¾, 10¼, 11½, 11¾)in
**Legwarmers**
**c** Length 6¾ (7½, 9, 9¾, 10¾, 11½)in
**Headband**
*One size only*
**d** Circumference 16½in

## Measurements

*To fit sizes 1, 2, 3, 4, 5, 6*

**a** Chest 21$\frac{1}{4}$ (23, 24$\frac{1}{2}$, 25$\frac{1}{4}$, 26$\frac{1}{2}$, 28$\frac{1}{2}$)in
**b** Shoulder to hem 12$\frac{1}{2}$ (15$\frac{1}{4}$, 17$\frac{3}{4}$, 20$\frac{1}{2}$, 22$\frac{1}{2}$, 25$\frac{1}{4}$)in
**c** Skirt length 7$\frac{3}{4}$ (9$\frac{3}{4}$, 11$\frac{3}{4}$, 13$\frac{3}{4}$, 15$\frac{3}{4}$, 17$\frac{3}{4}$)in

Elegant pure silk party dress with beautiful satin ribbon bow at the waist locks striking on any girl. This classic style will never date, so it can be put away for the next generation when outgrown.

## Front

With yarn A cast on 181 (181, 181, 211, 211, 211) sts. Break yarn. Change to yarn M and work as follows:

**Row 1** *Sl 1, k5, turn, p5, turn, k2tog, k1, k2tog, rep from * to last st, sl 1 – 121 (121, 121, 141, 141, 141) sts.

**Row 2** *and every alternate row:* Purl.
Continue in st st, but:

**Row 5** Knit 2 yarn M; *k1 yarn B, k3 yarn M, rep from * to last 3 sts; k1 yarn B; k2 yarn M.

**Row 9** Knit 4 yarn M; *k1 yarn B, k3 yarn M, rep from * to last st, k1 yarn M.
Incorporate yarn B every following 4th row by working rows 5 and 9 alternately. Continue until work measures 7¾ (9¾, 11¾, 13¾, 15¾, 17¾)in from beginning (or more or less as required), ending with a wrong-side row.
*Shape bodice:*

**Row 1** *Knit 1, p2tog, rep from * to end. (*Smaller 3 sizes only,* work to last 4 sts, k1, p3tog) – 80 (80, 80, 94, 94, 94) sts.

**Row 2** Using yarn B, *k1, keeping yarn at back (right side), sl 1 purlwise, rep from * to end.

**Row 3** Using yarn M, *sl 1 purlwise, k1, rep from * to end.

**Rows 4 and 5** Using yarn M, *p1, k1, rep from * to end.
Repeat Rows 2 to 5 (3, 4, 5, 6, 7, 8) times, then work Rows 2 to 4 once. Break yarn B.
*Shape armholes:* Bind off 6 (6, 6, 8, 8, 8) sts, k to end. Bind off 5 (5, 5, 9, 9, 9) sts, p to end. K2 tog beginning next 4 rows incorporating sts yarn B as on skirt – 65 (65, 65, 73, 73, 73) sts. Continue in pattern without shaping for a further 2 (2¼, 2¾, 3¼, 3¼, 3½)in, ending with a purl row.
*Shape neck:* Knit 25, bind off 15 (15, 15, 23, 23, 23), k25. Continue to work on these last 25 sts: K2tog beginning next 3 knit rows (neck edge) – 22 sts. Work without shaping until armhole measures 3½ (4, 4¼, 4¾, 4¾, 5)in from beginning of shaping. Bind off. Work other side to match, reversing shaping.

## Back

Work skirt as front to **
*Right back:*

**Row 1** *Knit 1, p1, k2tog, rep from * 19 (19, 19, 22, 22, 22) times, k0 (0, 0, 1, 1, 1), turn – 40 (40, 40, 47, 47, 47) sts.

**Row 2** Cast on 3 sts, then k1, p1, k1 across cast-on sts, p to end.
Continue in skirt pattern but work last 4 sts (right-side rows) and first 4 sts (wrong-side rows) in moss st (button-bands). Make button-holes next and every 4th (6th, 8th, 10th, 12th, 14th) row as follows:
Knit to last 2 sts, yo, k2tog.
When work measures same as front to armholes, ending with a purl row, continue as follows:
*Shape armhole:* Bind off 6 (6, 6, 8, 8, 8) sts, k to end. K2tog beginning next two k rows (armhole edge), work without shaping until back measures as front to neck shaping, ending with a k row.
*Shape neck:* Bind off 9 (9, 9, 11, 11, 11) sts, p

to end. K2tog beginning next three p rows (neck edge). Continue without shaping until work measures same as front to shoulder and bind off.
*Left back:* Right side facing, rejoin yarn to remaining sts.

**Row 1** Cast on 2 sts, k, p1 across cast-on sts; k1 (1, 1, 2, 2, 2); *k1, k2tog, rep from * 19 (19, 19, 22, 22, 22) times – 43 (43, 43, 50, 50, 50) sts.
Continue as right back, reversing shaping and omitting buttonholes.

## Sleeves

Cast on 85 (85, 85, 97, 97, 97) sts using yarn A. Break yarn. Change to yarn M:

**Row 1** *Sl 1, k5, turn, p5, turn, k5, rep from * to last st; sl 1.

**Row 2** Purl.

**Row 3** Knit 1, k2tog to end – 43 (43, 43, 49, 49, 49) sts.

**Row 4** Using yarn A, *k1, keeping yarn at back (right side), sl 1 purlwise, rep from * to last st, k1.

**Row 5** Using yarn M *sl 1 purlwise, k1, rep from * to last st, sl 1.

**Row 6** Purl.

**Row 7** Double sts by knitting into front and back of each st – 86 (86, 86, 98, 98, 98) sts.
Continue in st st incorporating sts yarn B as skirt until sleeve measures 1¼ (1½, 2, 2¼, 2¾, 3¾)in (or more or less as required) ending with a wrong-side row.
Bind off 6 (6, 6, 8, 8, 8) sts beginning of next two rows. Then k2tog beginning every row until 50 sts remain. K2tog across all sts and bind off.

## Neck

Sew shoulder and side seams. Right side facing, working from left edge of left button-band, and using yarn B, *pick up 1 st ¼in down from neck edge, then k up 3 sts along edge, rep from * around neck ending with a long st at right of second button-band. Bind off.

## Finishing

Sew sleeve seams and set sleeves into armholes easing in fullness. Attach length of ribbon to either side of waist over seam. Sew base of button-bands together and to body of work. Attach buttons to correspond with holes.

## DRESS

### Yarn
Main yarn M 3½ (5¼, 5¼, 7, 8¾, 10½)oz 4-ply silk (black)
Yarn A 1¾oz 4-ply silk (ivory)
Yarn B 1¾oz 4-ply silk (pink)

### Needles
1 pair no 3 (4, 5, 3, 4, 5)

### Notions
2yd satin ribbon (black)
5 mother-of-pearl buttons

### Stitch gauge
30 sts and 34 rows to 4in on no 3 needles;
28 sts and 32 rows to 4in on no 4 needles;
26 sts and 30 rows to 4in on no 5 needles
(or size needed to obtain given tension).

**Graph A** Shoulder straps

4

**Graph B** Cross strap

5

**Measurements**

**Blouse**
*To fit sizes 1, 2, 3, 4, 5, 6*
All sizes very full across chest
Neck to waist 5 (6, 7, 7¾, 9, 10¼)in
Sleeve seam 6 (7½, 9, 9¾, 11, 11¾)in
**Skirt**
*To fit sizes 1–2, 3–4, 5–6*
Length 9 (10¼, 11¾)in
Waist 19¾in (stretching to about 21¾in)
**Suspenders**
*One size only*
Waist–shoulder–waist 19in (adjustable)

# Heidi and Peter

Based on the traditional German Lederhosen, this skirt and shorts (see overleaf) are made in bulky Shetland yarn with leather strips worked into the waist and hem. The shorts should be worn with a checked shirt; make this pretty "peasant" blouse to wear with the skirt.

## BLOUSE

### Yarn

Main yarn M 3½oz fine acrylic yarn or 3½ (3½, 4½, 4½, 5¼, 5¼)oz fine cotton (white)
Yarns A Scraps medium-weight cotton (green)
Yarn B Scraps medium-weight cotton (pink)
Yarn C Scraps medium-weight cotton (blue)
Scraps yarn for working flowers on yoke

### Needles

1 pair no 2 (3, 4, 2, 3, 4)
Similar size set of 4 double-pointed (or short circular) for yoke

### Notions

Stitch holder

### Stitch gauge

32 sts and 36 rows to 4in over st st on no 2 needles; 28 sts and 36 rows to 4in over st st on no 3 needles; 26 sts and 36 rows to 4in over st st on no 4 needles (or size needed to obtain given tension).

## Front

With yarn A, cast on 80 (80, 80, 100, 100, 100) sts using 2-needle method. Change to yarn M. Work 8 rows garter st. Change to yarn A, k2tog across all sts and k 1 row. Then, k 2 rows yarn C and 2 rows yarn B.
Change to yarn M. Double sts on row: k into front and back each st. Working in st st, continue without shaping until work measures 5 (6, 7, 7¾, 9, 10¼)in from waist (or more or less as required).
*Shape armhole:* Bind off 5 sts beginning next 2 rows. K2tog beginning next 4 rows – 66 (66, 66, 86, 86, 86) sts. Work 6 rows without shaping.
*Larger 3 sizes:* Knit 30 sts, turn. Purl 1 row.
*All sizes:* Knit 26 sts, turn.
**Row 1** *and every alternate row:* Purl.
**Row 2** Knit 22, turn.
**Row 4** Knit 18, turn.
**Row 6** Knit 14, turn.
**Row 8** Knit 10, turn.
**Row 10** Knit 6, turn.
Break yarn and slip all sts to end of needle. Work right armhole similarly, reading p for k and k for p.
Work back similarly. Slip all sts onto stitch holder.

## Sleeves

With yarn A, cast on 50 (50, 50, 60, 60, 60) sts using 2-needle method. Change to yarn M and work 4 rows garter st. With yarn A k2tog across all sts then k 1 row, k 2 rows yarn C and 2 rows yarn B. Change to yarn M and double sts on row: k into front and back each st.
Continue in st st without shaping until work measures 6 (7½, 9, 9¾, 11, 11¾)in (or more or less as required).
*Shape top:* Bind off 5 sts beginning next 2 rows, then bind off 1 st beginning next 4 rows – 36 (36, 36, 46, 46, 46) sts. Work 10 (10, 10, 12, 12, 12) rows without shaping.
*Smaller 3 sizes:* Knit 26, turn. Sl 2, p16, turn. Sl 2, k11, turn. Sl 2, p6.
*Larger 3 sizes:* Knit 36, turn. Sl 2, p26, turn. Sl 2, k21, turn. Sl 2, p16, turn. Sl 2, k11, turn. Sl 2, p6.
Work another sleeve similarly.
*Work yoke:* Slip all sts onto double-pointed needles or circular needle – 204 (204, 204, 264, 264, 264) sts. Move sts around so that knitting commences center front. Using yarn M, k2tog across all sts.
Working back and forth on needles, work 5 rows st st. Then change to yarn A and k 2 rows.
**Next row** Change to yarn M, *k2tog, k3, rep from * to end.
Work 3 rows st st. Then, keeping first and last 5 sts in st st yarn M, k 2 rows yarn C.
**Next row** Change to yarn M, *k2tog, k2, rep from * to end.
Work 3 rows st st. Keeping first and last 5 sts in st st yarn M, k 2 rows yarn B. Change to yarn M, work 5 rows st st. Right side facing and using yarn A, bind off.

## Finishing

Sew up underarm, side and sleeve seams.
Right side work facing, using yarn A, k up sts down both sides front neck opening. Turn and bind off.
Make 2 loops yarn A and crochet a cord yarn A to thread through loop and tie in bow.
Embroider small colored flowers with 4 petals and a yellow center up both sides front opening, if desired.

## SKIRT

### Yarn

6 (8, 8)oz 3-ply chunky Shetland (green)

### Needles

1 pair no 7

### Notions

2 traditional buttons for skirt fastening
4 traditional buttons for suspenders

### Stitch gauge

16 sts and 23 rows to 4in over st st on no 7 needles (or size needed to obtain given tension).
and a yellow center up both sides front opening, if desired.

## Front

**NB** *A thin band of leather or suede can be knitted in with the yarn on garter st rows at hem and waist. Simply take a piece of suede or leather in olive green (or similar color to yarn used) and cut into ⅛in-wide strips.*
*Starting at waist:*
Cast on 34 sts using no 7 needles and yarn and leather strips together if applicable. Work 4 rows garter st, but make buttonholes beginning rows 2 and 3 by k1, yfwd, k2tog, k15 to last 3 sts, k2tog, yo, k1. Break off leather strip.
**Row 5** Knit.
**Row 6** Knit 2, p13, k4, p13, k2.
**Row 7** Knit 2, inc 1, k13, inc 1, k4, inc 1, k13, inc 1, k2.
Continue in this way increasing 4 sts every 4th row until work measures 8¾ (9¾, 11½)in (or more or less as required).
Join in leather strips again if applicable. Work 3 rows garter st and bind off with wrong side work facing.

## Back

Work as front but without buttonholes.

## Finishing

Sew side seams leaving 3½in opening at the top of each seam. Attach buttons to correspond with buttonholes. Attach buttons for suspenders as specified in suspenders pattern.

# SUSPENDERS

### Yarn

Main yarn M 2oz 3-ply Shetland (green)
Yarn A Scraps 3-ply Shetland (red) for hearts.
Yarn B Scraps 3-ply Shetland (yellow, white) for edelweis pattern
### Needles
1 pair no 7

## Method

*Commence at front:* Cast on 9 sts. Work 2 rows garter st.
**Row 3** Knit 4, yo, k2tog, k3.
**Row 4** Knit 2, p5, k2.
**Row 5** Knit, commencing pattern from Graph A.
Repeat rows 4 and 5 working in pattern until work measures 2¾ (4)in from beginning, ending with a wrong-side row. Break yarn.
Work another strap to match but do not break yarn.
*Work bodice:* Knit across sts of latter strap, cast on 21 sts yarn M then k across sts of first strap – 39 sts.
**Row 1** Knit 2 yarn M, p5 (in patt), k25 yarn M, p5 (in patt), k2 yarn M.
**Row 2** Knit yarn M.
**Row 3** As row 1.
**Row 4** As row 2.
**Row 5** Knit 2 yarn M, p5 (in patt), k2 yarn M, p21 following Graph B, k2 yarn M, p5 (in patt), k2 yarn M.
Work 6 further rows working central 5 sts on straps and 21 sts on bodice panel in st st.
**Row 13** As row 1.
**Row 14** As row 2.
**Row 15** Knit 2, p5, k2, bind off 21, k2, p5, k2.
Continue working last 9 sts in pattern until work measures 9¾in, then work in plain st st

with first and last 2 sts garter st until strap measures 18in overall (or more or less as required). Make buttonholes on next right side row as row 4 of suspender straps. Knit 2 rows and bind off.
Complete second strap to match.

## Finishing

Press all pieces well and sew buttons onto front and back of shorts or skirt to correspond with buttonholes on suspenders.

# SHORTS

### Yarn
4 (4, 4)oz 3-ply bulky Shetland (green)
### Needles
1 pair no 7
### Notions
2 buttons
### Stitch gauge
16 sts and 23 rows to 4in over st st on no 7 needles (or size needed to obtain given tension).

## Left leg

**NB** *A thin band of leather or suede can be knitted in with the yarn on garter st rows at hem and waist (see photograph of skirt, pp. 88–9). Simply take a piece of suede or leather in olive green, or color to match yarn used, and cut into ⅛in-wide strips.*
Cast on 27 sts. Work 3 rows garter st. Break yarn.
Cast on 27 sts onto same needle as first 27 sts and work 3 rows garter st on these sts. * *With all sts right side facing on one needle, bind off 5, k to end across all sts on needle.
**Next row** Bind off 5, p to end.
Continue k2tog beginning next 4 rows – 40 sts.
Work without shaping until work measures 5½in from beginning ending with a purl row. * *
*Work back:* Divide sts for side slit.
**Row 1** Knit 24, turn.
**Row 2** Knit 2, p22.
Repeat these 2 rows 3 (5, 6) times.
Work 3 rows garter st and bind off with wrong side facing.
*Work front:* Right side facing,
**Row 1** Knit across the 17 sts on needle.
**Row 2** Purl 15, k2.
Repeat these 2 rows 3 (5, 6) times. Work 2 rows garter st.
**Next row** Make buttonhole: k1, yfwd, k2tog; k to end.
Bind off.

## Right leg

Work as left leg to * *
*Work front:*
**Row 1** Knit 17, turn.
**Row 2** Knit 2, p15, turn.
Repeat these 2 rows 3 (5, 6) times. Work 2 rows garter st.
**Next row** Make buttonhole: K to last 3 sts, k2tog, yfwd, k1.
Bind off.
*Work back:*
**Row 1** Knit across the 24 sts on needle.
**Row 2** Purl 22, k2.
Repeat these 2 rows 3 (5, 6) times. Knit 3 rows.
Bind off.

## Finishing

Sew center seams. Attach buttons to side openings to correspond with buttonholes. If making suspenders, attach buttons to shorts as specified in suspenders pattern.

## Measurements

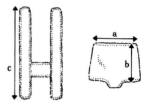

### Shorts
*To fit sizes 1–2, 3–4, 5–6*
**a** Waist 19¾in (stretching to about 21¾in)
**b** Length at side seam 7½ (7¾, 8¼)in
### Suspenders
*One size only*
**c** Waist-shoulder-waist 19in (adjustable)

**Graph B** Cross strap

**Graph A** Shoulder straps

Repeat these sts 3 times for lower section

A warm, pretty dress and matching frilly cape ideal for play-going
or parties of all sorts.

## DRESS

### Yarn

Main yarn M 4 (4, 5, 5, 6, 7)oz 2-ply Shetland (camel)

Yarn A ½oz 2-ply Shetland (natural or white)

### Needles

1 pair no 2 (3, 4, 2, 3, 4)

Cable needle

Small crochet hook

### Notions

3 (4, 4, 5, 5, 6) mother-of-pearl buttons

### Stitch gauge

28 sts and 36 rows to 4in over st st on no 2 needles; 26 sts and 34 rows to 4in over st st or no 3 needles; 24 sts and 32 rows over 4in over st st on no 4 needles (or size needed to obtain given tension).

### Measurements

*To fit sizes 1, 2, 3, 4, 5, 6*

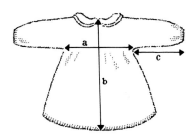

**a** Chest 18½ (20½, 21¼, 22½, 24½, 25¾)in
**b** Neck to hem 11¾ (14½, 16½, 19¼, 22, 23¾)in
**c** Sleeve seam 5½ (6¼, 7¾, 8¾, 9½, 10¼)in

### Front

With yarn M cast on 100 (100, 100, 130, 130, 130) sts. Work 5 rows moss st then change to st st and work until front measures 7¾ (9, 9¾, 11, 12¼, 13)in from beginning, ending on a purl row.

*Shape bodice:* Knit 1, *yo, k3tog, rep from * to end – 67 (67, 67, 87, 87, 87) sts. Bind off 5 (5, 5, 10, 10, 10), purl to last 4 (4, 4, 10, 10, 10) sts, bind off 4 (4, 4, 10, 10, 10) sts. Break yarn. Rejoin yarn to remaining 58 (58, 58, 67, 67, 67) sts and work as follows * *:

**Row 1** *C4b (cable 4 back – and hold at back, sl 2 onto cable needle, k2, k2 sts from cable needle), p1, ladder 3 (k into front and back of next st, yo, k2tog into front and back of next 2 sts), p1, rep from * to last 4 sts, c4b.

**Row 2** Purl 4; *k1, p2tog, p1, p2tog, k1, p4, rep from * to end.

**Row 3** Knit 4; *p1, ladder 3, p1, k4, rep from * to end.

**Row 4** As row 2.

Repeat these 4 rows until work measures 3¼ (4¾, 6, 7½, 9, 9¾)in (or more or less as required) from waist, ending on a right-side row.

*Shape neck:* Work 19 (19, 19, 21, 21, 21) sts, bind off 20 (20, 20, 25, 25, 25), work 19 (19, 19 21, 21, 21).

*Shape shoulder:* Bind off one st at neck edge at the beginning of the next 2 alternate rows; work further 2 rows without shaping. Bind off. Finish other shoulder similarly – reversing shaping.

The bodice combines traditional aran cable with ladder stitch and moss stitch.

## Back

Work as front to **.
*Smaller 3 sizes:* *C4b, p1, ladder 3, p1, rep from
* 3 times, k2, turn.
*Larger 3 sizes:* *C4b, p1, ladder 3, p1, rep from
* 3 times; c4b; work 3 sts moss st, turn.
*All sizes:* Continue on these stitches, begin
buttonhole bands, cast on 2 sts, work 4 (4, 4, 5,
5, 5) moss st, cont in pattern to end. Continue
in pattern, working last 4 (4, 4, 5, 5, 5) sts on
right-side rows in moss st, and first 4 (4, 4, 5, 5,
5) sts on wrong-side rows in moss st.
*Buttonholes:* Make buttonholes on 3rd (3rd,
3rd, 4th, 4th, 4th) st (yo, k2tog) of row 4 and
every following 8th row. Continue until work
measures $3\frac{1}{2}$ (5, $6\frac{1}{4}$, $7\frac{3}{4}$, $9\frac{1}{2}$, $10\frac{1}{4}$)in from waist,
ending with a right-side row.
*Shape neck:* Bind off 12 (12, 12, 15, 15, 15) sts;
work in pattern to end. Bind off one st at the
beginning of the next 2 alternate rows. Work
one row in pattern without shaping. Bind off.
Work left back similarly, reversing shaping,
omitting buttonholes and casting on 3 sts
instead of 2 for button-bands.

## Sleeves

Sew shoulder seams together. With right side of
work facing, pick up sts evenly from waist over
shoulder back to other side waist – about 56
(72, 80, 110, 130, 130) sts. Work 8 (8, 8, 18, 18,
18) rows without shaping in st st, then bind off
3 (5, 7, 10, 12, 12) sts at the beginning of the
next 2 rows. Bind off one st at the beginning of
the next 4 (10, 10, 16, 20, 20) rows. Continue
without shaping until work measures $5\frac{1}{2}$ ($6\frac{3}{4}$,
$7\frac{3}{4}$, $8\frac{3}{4}$, $9\frac{1}{2}$, $10\frac{1}{4}$)in from shaping (or more or less
as required), ending with a wrong-side row.
K2tog across all sts. Work 5 rows in moss st.
Bind off in moss st.
Work another sleeve similarly.

## Collar

Using yarn A and 2-needle method, cast on 25
(25, 25, 35, 35, 35) sts.
**Row 1** Yo, k to end.
**Row 2** Repeat this row.
**Row 3** *Yo, k2tog, rep from * 3 times, k to end.
**Row 4** *Yo, k2tog, rep from * 3 times, k15,
turn.
**Row 5** Yo, k15, turn.
**Row 6** Yo, k13, turn.
**Row 7** Yo, k11, turn.
Continue in this way knitting 2 less sts per row
until knitting 3 sts. Turn and k to end. Work a
row of eyelets – yo, k2tog – to end. Knit one
row.
**Next row** *Yo, k1, rep from * to end.
Bind off.
Work another collar similarly. If desired, work a
further pair of collars to make a double collar.

## Finishing

Sew straight edge at base of sleeve (underarm)
to bound-off edge of all 4 skirt sections then
sew side and sleeve seams. Using yarn A, make
a long chain to thread through eyelets at waist.
Attach buttons to correspond with holes.
Overlap buttonhole band over button-band and
sew at base. Attach collars to neck starting
either side of back bands. Press gently on
wrong side.

## CAPE

### Yarn
*8oz* 2-ply Shetland
### Needles
1 pair no 5 – $13\frac{3}{4}$in long
1 no 6 circular
### Stitch gauge
21 sts and 40 rows to 4in over garter st on
no 5 needles (or size needed to obtain given
tension).

### Measurements

*One size only*

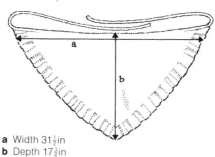

**a** Width $31\frac{1}{2}$in
**b** Depth $17\frac{3}{4}$in

### Body

Using no 5 needles, cast on 206 sts. Work in
garter st throughout.
**Row 1** *and every alternate row:* Knit.
**Row 2** Knit 1, sl 1, k1, psso, k97, sl 1, k1, psso,
k2, k2tog, k97, k2tog, k1.
**Row 4** Knit 1, sl 1, k1, psso, k95, sl 1, k1, psso,
k2, k2tog, k95, k2tog, k1.

**Row 6** Knit 1, sl 1, k1, psso, k93, sl 1, k1, psso,
k2, k2tog, k93, k2tog, k1.
Continue decreasing in this way until 10 sts
remain. Knit one row.
**Next row** Knit 1, sl 1, k2tog, psso, k2, k3tog,
k1 – 6 sts.
Bind off.

### Frill

Using circular needle, knit up 412 sts along
cast-on edge of shawl by knitting and purling
into each st. Work back and forth in rows.
Purl one row.
**Next row** Knit 2, *pick up strand between sts
and knit, k2, rep from * to end – 617 sts.
Beginning with purl row, work 11 rows st st.
Work 6 rows garter st. Bind off.

### Band

Using circular needle, cast on 100 sts, with
right side of work facing, pick up 105 sts across
top of shawl, and cast on a further 100 sts –
305 sts. Work 5 rows st st starting with purl row.
**Row 6** Purl.
Work 5 further rows st st starting with a purl
row. Bind off.

### Finishing

Fold tie band in half, and sew along ends and
length, catching neatly on wrong side work at
top of shawl. Press frill carefully.
Cross tie bands over the child's chest and tie
center back.

# Toy Blanket

Mother's helper – lay it out flat for a baby to play on, pull up the ribbons and it makes an ideal bag for carrying around any toys and playthings.

## BLANKET

### Yarn
*12oz* different colored and textured yarn, preferably machine washable

### Needles
1 pair no 5 (long) or similar size circular

### Notions
10yd × ½in-wide bright ribbon or tape

## Measurements

43¼in diameter

## Method

Cast on one st and work in st st. Increase one st beginning of next 6 rows: K into the front and back of first st. Then work 2 rows without shaping. Repeat these 8 rows until work measures 19¾in from beginning. Work a row of eyelet holes (yo, k2tog). Work 5 rows garter st and bind off.

Work a further 5 sections similarly.

## Finishing

Sew sections together. Halve ribbon and, commencing in the middle of one section, thread one ribbon through every 3rd hole until it is back at starting point. Sew these two ends together. Commencing in the middle of the opposite section, thread other half of ribbon through remaining eyelet holes until it comes back to starting point. Sew these two ends together. Press work carefully and pull up ribbons to form bag.

# Spanish Frills

Generous, circular shawl which will keep any baby really warm and cosy. Its frilled edges give it a lovely shape as it drapes abundantly over your arms.

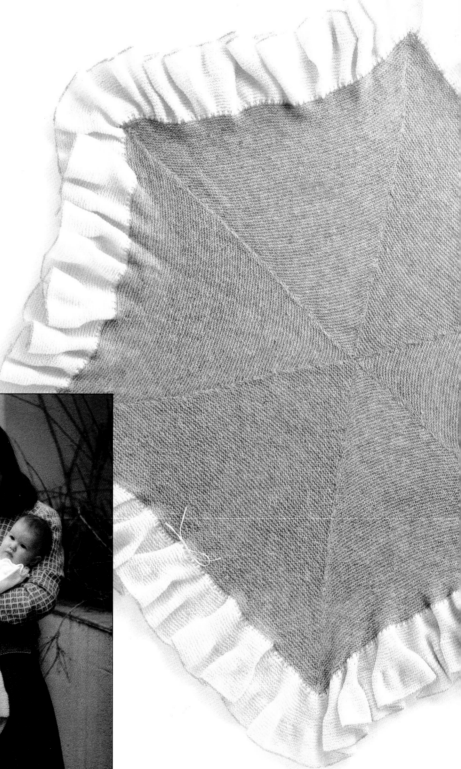

## SHAWL

**Yarn**
Yarn A *12oz* 2-ply Shetland (pink)
Yarn B *19oz* 2-ply Shetland (white)
**Needles**
1 pair no 5 (long) or similar size circular
1 no 7 for binding off
**Notions**
10yd very fine ribbon to match yarn A

## Measurements

Diameter 55in

## Method

With yarn A, cast on 1 st. Work in garter st. Increase 1 st beginning of next 6 rows: K into front and back of st and k to end. Then work 2 rows without shaping. Repeat these 8 rows until there are 132 sts on needle.
Change to yarn B. Double sts: K into front and back every stitch. Then work a row of eyelets (yo, k2tog). Continue in garter st and work 2¾in then double sts: K into front and back of every stitch – 528 sts.
Work a further 2¾in on these sts, then right side facing, bind off in yarn A using no 7 needle. Work 5 further sections similarly.

## Finishing

Assemble all sections and press gently. Thread ribbon through eyelet holes tying in center of one section on right side of work.

A soft, absorbent blanket; ideal for the new baby. Quick and easy to knit up and care for.

## BLANKET

**Yarn**
8¾oz medium-weight cotton (white)
**Needles**
1 pair no 3 – 13¾in long
**Notions**
4yd of 2in satin ribbon
**Stitch gauge**
18 sts and 30 rows to 4in

## Measurements

45¼in × 24½in

## Method

Cast on 200 sts.
**Row 1** **Knit.
**Row 2** Knit 1, *yfwd, k2tog, rep from * to last st, k1.
**Row 3** Knit.
**Row 4** Knit 2, *yfwd, k2tog, rep from * to end.
Repeat these 4 rows 5 times then k 1 row. **
Repeat from ** to ** 6 times, or until work measures approx 23in. Bind off.

## Finishing

Press gently and sew ribbon folded around edge.

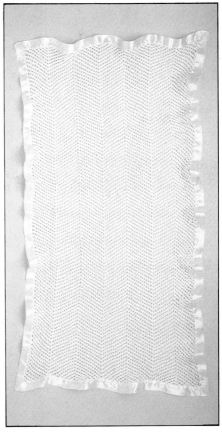

# Butterfly Quilt

A personalized carriage or crib quilt makes a very special present for a new baby. Save the last two squares until the baby is born so that you can include his or her initials and birthdate. Work the back panels in any colors you wish, or even leave them plain.

## QUILT

### Yarn

*Front*

Main yarn M 7 (12)oz 2-ply Shetland (white)
Yarn A 2 (4)oz 2-ply Shetland (green)
Yarn B 2 (4)oz 2-ply Shetland (black)
Yarn C 3 (6)oz 2-ply Shetland (blue)
Scraps different shades for butterfly wings

*Back*

$6\frac{1}{4}$ ($12\frac{1}{4}$)oz of 5 or 6 favorite shades and use
them as you choose.

### Needles

1 pair no 4

### Notions

3yd narrow ribbon

### Stitch gauge

24 sts and 34 rows to 4in over plain st st.

## Measurements

Carriage quilt $23\frac{3}{4}$in $\times$ $31\frac{1}{2}$in (photographed)
Crib quilt $39\frac{1}{2}$ $\times$ $31\frac{1}{2}$in

## Front

Work 10 (18) butterfly squares by casting on 51
sts and work as Graph A. Work 2 white
squares with baby's initials, birthdate and
ribbons working from chart.

## Back

Work three $7\frac{3}{4} \times 31\frac{1}{2}$in strips for carriage quilt
and four $7\frac{3}{4} \times 39\frac{1}{2}$in strips st st for crib quilt.
Experiment with pictorial and annual designs
which might appeal to a young child such as
flowers, trees, cats and birds. Tiny ladybugs
and butterflies would look charming.

## Finishing

Press all pieces well and assemble carefully.
Make sure the squares are lined up and that
all the knitting lies in the same direction.
Make up the front and back sections and sew
them together around the edge. Quilt or thread
a narrow ribbon through the center of each
square and tie it carefully at the back in a
big bow.

**Graph A**

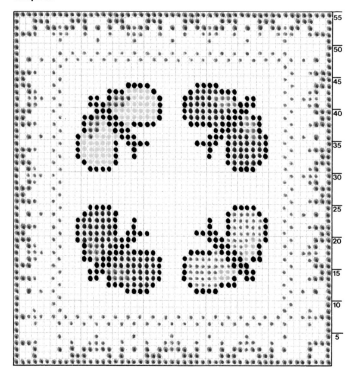

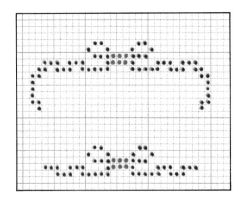

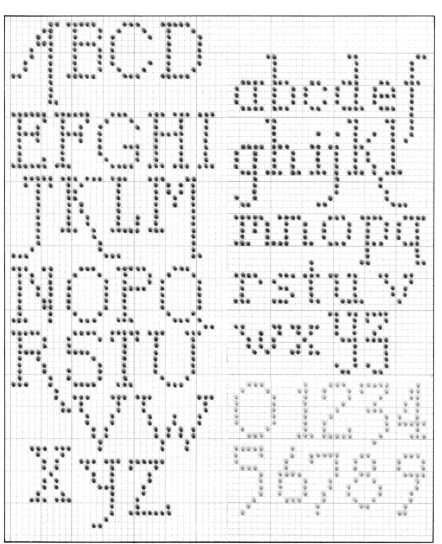

# STYLISH SOCKS

Three simple patterns which can be adapted to make socks to match
any garment in the book. The slipper socks have strips of non-
slippable suede worked into the sole, alternatively you can sew suede
patches onto the bottom of the other two socks to make soles.

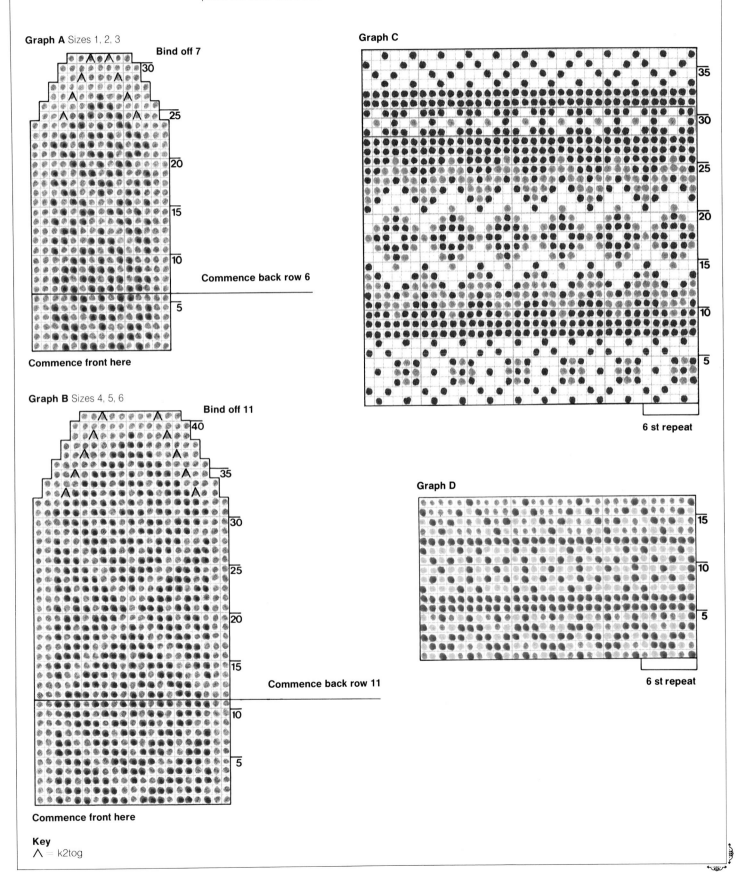

**Graph A** Sizes 1, 2, 3

Bind off 7

30

25

20

15

Commence back row 6

10

5

Commence front here

**Graph B** Sizes 4, 5, 6

Bind off 11

40

35

30

25

20

Commence back row 11

15

10

5

Commence front here

**Graph C**

35

30

25

20

15

10

5

6 st repeat

**Graph D**

15

10

5

6 st repeat

**Key**

∧ = k2tog

101

## SLIPPER SOCKS

**Yarn**
Yarn A 1 (1, 1, 2, 2, 2)oz bulky Shetland (blue)
Yarn B ½ (½, ½, 1, 1, 1)oz bulky Shetland (red)
**Needles**
1 pair no 5 (6, 7, 5, 6, 7)
**Notions**
About 1 sq foot navy clothing-weight suede cut into one long strand about ¼in wide.
**Stitch gauge**
23 sts and 28 rows to 4in over st st on no 5 needles; 21 sts and 26 rows to 4in over st st on no 6 needles; 19 sts and 24 rows to 4in over st st on no 7 needles (or size needed to obtain given tension.

### Sole

Using suede cord and yarn A together, cast on 5 sts. Work in st st throughout.
Increase 1 st at beginning of next 4 (4, 4, 8, 8, 8) rows – 9 (9, 9, 13, 13, 13) sts.
Continue until sole measures 3¼ (3½, 4, 4¼, 4¾, 5)in from beginning (or more or less as required). K2tog at beginning of next 4 (4, 4, 8, 8, 8) rows. Bind off.

### Front

Using yarn A cast on 15 (15, 15, 21, 21, 21) sts. K 1 row, then refer to Graph A or B (see p. 101) for pattern and shaping.

### Back

Work as front, starting 6 (6, 6, 11, 11, 11) rows further up the Graph as marked.

### Finishing

Sew side seams until back shaping is reached, then sew tops to sole with smooth st st surface inside for comfort.

## PINK SOCKS

**Yarn**
Main yarn M 1 (1, 1, 1¾, 1¾, 1¾)oz 2-ply Shetland (oatmeal)
Yarn A scraps 2-ply Shetland (red)
Yarn B scraps 2-ply Shetland (pink)
Yarn C scraps 2-ply Shetland (brown)
**Needles**
Set 4 double-pointed no 2 (3, 4, 2, 3, 4)
**Stitch gauge**
28 sts and 36 rows to 4in over st st on no 2 needles; 26 sts and 34 rows to 4in over st st on no 4 needles; 24 sts and 32 rows to 4in over st st on no 4 needles (or size needed to obtain given tension).

### Method

With yarn A cast on 30 (30, 30, 42, 42, 42) sts evenly over 3 needles. Work 6 rounds alternate k and p rounds. Change to st st and work 17 rounds pattern following Graph C, see p.101 (or make up your own to match a garment). Change to yarn M and continue until 30 (35, 40, 45, 50, 55) rounds have been worked from beginning (or more or less as required).
*Shape heel:* Knit 16 (16, 16, 20, 20, 20) sts, turn. Purl 15 (15, 15, 19, 19, 19), turn. Continue in this way knitting or purling one less st per row until purling 7 sts, then turn and k8. Turn, p9.

Continue in this way knitting or purling one more st per row until purling 15 (15, 15, 19, 19, 19) sts.
**Next round** Knit 16 (16, 16, 20, 20, 20); *k2tog, k1, rep from * 4 (4, 4, 7, 7, 7) times; k2 (2, 2, 1, 1, 1) – 26 (26, 26, 35, 35, 35) sts.
Work a further 14 (16, 18, 20, 22, 24) rounds (or more or less as required).
*Shape toe:*
**Round 1** K2tog, k9 (9, 9, 14, 14, 14), k2tog, k2tog, k9 (9, 9, 13, 13, 13), k2tog.
**Round 2** *and every alternate round:* Knit without shaping.
**Round 3** K2tog, k7 (7, 7, 12, 12, 12), k2tog, k2tog, k7 (7, 7, 11, 11, 11), k2tog.
**Round 5** K2tog, k5 (5, 5, 10, 10, 10), k2tog, k2tog, k5 (5, 5, 9, 9, 9), k2tog.
*Larger 3 sizes only:*
**Round 7** K2tog, k8, k2tog, k2tog, k7, k2tog.
**Round 9** K2tog, k6, k2tog, k2tog, k5, k2tog.
*All sizes:* K 1 round, bind off.

### Finishing

Sew up toe seam. Press work carefully.

## BLUE SOCKS

**Yarn**
Main yarn M 1 (1, 1, 2, 2, 2)oz 2-ply Shetland (blue)
Yarn A ½oz 2-ply Shetland (white)
Yarn B ½oz 2-ply Shetland (green)
**Needles**
1 pair no 2 (3, 4, 2, 3, 4)
**Notions**
Square of soft suede for soles
**Stitch gauge**
30 sts and 38 rows to 4in over st st on no 2 needles; 28 sts and 36 rows to 4in over st st on no 3 needles; 26 sts and 34 rows to 4in over st st on no 4 needles (or size needed to obtain given tension).

### Left sock

**Using yarn M, cast on 50 (50, 50, 70, 70, 70) sts. Work 20 rows k1, p1 rib.
**Next row** Knit 4, *k into front and back next st, k1, rep from * to last 4 sts; k4 – 71 (71, 71, 101, 101, 101) sts.
With st st, work 5 (6, 7, 7¾, 9, 9¾)in (or more or less as required) in pattern following Graph D, page 101.
**Next row** With yarn M and right side facing: K2tog across all sts – 36 (36, 36, 51, 51, 51) sts.
Work 10 rows k1, p1 rib.**
*Shape foot as follows:*
**Row 1** Knit 15 (15, 15, 20, 20, 20), turn.
**Row 2** Purl 8 (8, 8, 12, 12, 12), turn.
Work 8 (8, 8, 12, 12, 12) further rows st st on these sts. Break yarn.
With yarn M, knit up 5 (5, 5, 8, 8, 8) sts from right side of heel. Knit across 8 (8, 8, 12, 12, 12) sts on needle and knit up further 5 (5, 5, 8, 8, 8) sts from other side of heel.
**Next row** Knit 7 (7, 7, 8, 8, 8); *k2tog, k1, rep from * 4 (4, 4, 7, 7, 7) times; k to end – 42 (42, 42, 60, 60, 60) sts.
Then continue as follows:
**Row 1** *and every alternate row:* Purl.
**Row 2** Knit 6 (6, 6, 7, 7, 7), k2tog, k17 (17, 17, 27, 27, 27), k2tog, k6 (6, 6, 7, 7, 7), turn.
**Row 4** Knit 5 (5, 5, 6, 6, 6), k2tog, k17 (17, 17, 27, 27, 27), k2tog, k5 (5, 5, 6, 6, 6), turn.
**Row 6** Knit 4 (4, 4, 5, 5, 5), k2tog, k17 (17, 17,

27, 27, 27), k2tog, k to end – 36 (36, 36, 54, 54, 54) sts.
Continue in this way decreasing 2 sts per k row until 28 (28, 28, 44, 44, 44) sts remain on needle. Work without shaping until sole measures 2¾ (3½, 4¼, 4¾, 5, 6)in from heel, turn.
*Shape toe:* K2tog; k10 (10, 10, 18, 18, 18); (k2tog) twice; k10 (10, 10, 18, 18, 18); k2tog.
Purl the next and alternate rows. K2tog, k8 (8, 8, 16, 16, 16), (k2tog) twice; k8 (8, 8, 16, 16, 16), k2tog. Continue in this way decreasing 4 sts per k row until 16 (16, 16, 24, 24, 24) sts remain on needle, bind off.

### Right sock

Work as for left sock from ** to ** – 36 (36, 36, 51, 51, 51) sts on needle.
*Shape foot:*
**Row 1** With wrong side facing, p15 (15, 15, 20, 20, 20), turn.
**Row 2** Knit 8 (8, 8, 12, 12, 12), turn.
Work 9 (9, 9, 13, 13, 13) further rows in st st on these sts. Break yarn.
Starting from the beginning of the row: knit 2; *k2tog, k1, rep from * 4 (4, 4, 7, 7, 7) times; k7 (7, 7, 8, 8, 8). Knit up 5 (5, 5, 8, 8, 8) sts from the

right side of the heel, knit across 8 (8, 8, 12, 12, 12) sts on needle and knit up further 5 (5, 5, 8, 8, 8) sts from other side of the heel, k7 (7, 7, 8, 8, 8) – 42 (42, 42, 60, 60, 60) sts. Work as follows:

**Row 1** Purl 33 (33, 33, 45, 45, 45), turn.
**Row 2** Knit 6 (6, 6, 7, 7, 7), k2tog, k17 (17, 17, 27, 27, 27), k2tog, k6 (6, 6, 7, 7, 7), turn.
**Row 3** Purl 31 (31, 31, 43, 43, 43), turn.
**Row 4** Knit 5 (5, 5, 6, 6, 6), k2tog, k17 (17, 17, 27, 27, 27), k2tog, k to end.
**Row 5** Purl to end.
Continue in this way decreasing 2 sts per knit row until 28 (28, 28, 44, 44, 44) sts remain on needle. Complete as left sock.

## Finishing

Press well and assemble, sewing up inside leg and foot seams.
*Make soles:* Place socks on child and stand child on square of suede. Using ballpoint pen, outline the foot and cut. Sew sole onto sock.

## Measurements

*To fit sizes 1, 2, 3, 4, 5, 6*

**Slipper socks**
**a** Sole 4 (4¼, 4¾, 5½, 6, 6¾)in
**b** Ankle to top 2¾ (3, 3¼, 3¼, 3¼, 3½)in
**Pink socks**
**c** Heel to toe 3½ (4¼, 4¾, 5¼, 6, 6¼)in
**Blue socks**
**d** Length: top to ankle 7¾ (9, 10¾, 11½, 13, 14¼)in
**e** Heel to toe 3½ (4¼, 4¾, 5½, 6, 6¾)in

# CARRIER AND REINS

Make a pretty, practical carrier for a newborn baby or a pair of walking reins to help keep hold of a wandering toddler. Work any graph you wish into the panel of the carrier. We have used the pattern from the butterfly quilt (see pp. 98–100).

## CARRIER

### Yarn

Main yarn. M 5¼oz medium-weight cotton (blue)
Yarn A 1¾oz medium-weight cotton (white)
Scraps of green, light blue and 5 other colors

### Needles

1 pair no 5 (long)

### Notions

11 × 11in piece strong washable cloth

## Measurements

*For use with baby up to about 6 months*
11in square with straps 53¼in overall length

## Body

Using yarn M cast on 51 sts. Work 1½in yarn M then work 55 rows in plain or pattern.
Continue in yarn M and work 12½in. Bind off.

## Straps

Using yarn M cast on 300 sts. Work 9 rows st st, then knit 1 row to make fold line. Work further 9 rows st st and bind off.
Make another strap similarly.

## Finishing

Lie work pattern face up on cloth with short blue section at top. Lay open strap right side down on right edge and sew through all 3 thicknesses with a sewing machine or by hand. Repeat with other strap on left edge. Turn work over and fold up plain section. Sew top edges together. Fold strap over and sew ends and along whole length.

## REINS

### Yarn

Yarn A 1¾oz medium-weight cotton (yellow)
Yarn B 1¾oz medium-weight cotton (orange)

### Needles

1 no 3 circular (or similar size double-pointed)

### Notions

2 large buttons

### Stitch gauge

28 sts and 36 rows to 4in over st st on no 3 needles (or size needed to obtain given tension).

## Measurements

Chest 19in stretches to fit up to 23in

## Front

Using yarn A cast on 111 sts and, working back and forth on needles:
**Row 1** Knit.
**Row 2** Purl.
**Row 3** *Yfwd, k2tog, rep from * to end.
**Row 4** Purl.
**Row 5** Change to yarn B. Knit.
**Row 6** Purl.
**Row 7** Change to yarn A, knit up hem.
**Row 8** Starting at same end, change to yarn B, knit.
**Row 9** Purl 45, work central 27 sts in pattern as Graph, p37.
**Row 10** Knit 37, pattern 27, k45.
Continue in this way in st st to Row 19, then: Purl 81, turn.
**Row 20** Sl 2, k41, turn.
**Row 21** Sl 2, p37, turn.
**Row 22** Sl 2, k33, turn.
**Row 23** Sl 2, p29, turn.
**Row 24** Sl 1, k27, turn.
**Row 25** Sl 1, p25, turn.
**Row 26** Sl 1, k to end row.
*Work fold line for bodice:*

**Row 27** Change to yarn B: Purl.
**Row 28** Change to yarn A: Knit.
**Row 29** Change to yarn B: Purl.
**Row 30** Knit.
**Row 31** Change to yarn A: Purl.
**Row 32** *Yfwd, k2tog, rep from * to end.
*Commence working on back:* Continue yarn A work 4 rows st st then work as follows:
**Row 5** Purl 73, turn.
**Row 6** Sl 1, k27, turn.
**Row 7** Sl 1, p29, turn.
**Row 8** Sl 2, k33, turn.
**Row 9** Sl 2, p37, turn.
**Row 10** Sl 2, k to end.
Work 10 rows st st and bind off.
Sew bound-off edge to cast-on edge and up both sides, making 2 loop buttonholes on shorter back bodice that are *just* large enough to allow button through – attach buttons firmly and securely.

## Shoulder straps

Using yarn A, cast on 50 sts, work 2 rows st st then:
**Row 3** *Yfwd, k2tog, rep from * to end.
**Row 4** Purl.
**Row 5** Change to yarn B: Knit.
Work 4 rows st st but knit up hem into row 7.
**Row 10** Change to yarn A: Purl.
**Row 11** *Yfwd, k2tog, rep from * to end.
Work 3 rows st st. Bind off. Sew cast-on and bound-off edges together at center back of strap. Work another strap similarly.

## Restraining strap

Using yarn B cast on 180 sts. Work 5 rows garter st and bind off.

## Finishing

Attach shoulder straps to front of bodice very securely on either side of sun motif. Attach shoulder straps to back of bodice about 3½in away from front attachment (or as required). Attach restraining strap to either side of bodice directly below back shoulder straps in center of work by sewing through both thicknesses of bodice. Press work carefully.

**Graph for reins**

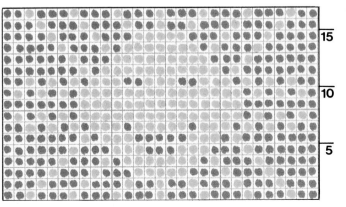

# CHANGING BAG

Pretty changing bag with a waterproof lining and long zippers so that it will open out flat. It is ideal for travelling, you can change the baby's diaper on the waterproof side, then zip it up and store things inside. It has a special pocket for keeping essential items to hand.

## CHANGING BAG

### Yarn

Yarn A 5¼oz medium-weight cotton (white)
Yarn B 5¼oz medium-weight cotton (green)

### Needles

1 no 3 circular

### Notions

2 × 23¾in open ended white nylon zipper
23¾ by 35½in sheet of vinyl or similar washable waterproof material
23¾ by 35½in piece of washable wadding

### Measurements

Width 20in
Depth 15¾in (folded)

### Bag

Using yarn A cast on 115 sts. Change to yarn B and p 1 row. Knit 1 row yarn A, and, starting at same end, k 1 row yarn B. Purl 1 row yarn A, p 1 row yarn B.
Continue working back and forth in this manner, increasing one st at the beginning of every row until 125 sts on needle.
Continue without shaping alternating yarns A and B until work measures 29½in from beginning.
*Shape ends:* Decrease one st at the beginning of every row until 115 sts remain on needle.
Bind off.

### Edges

Fold body of work in half with right side facing. Using yarn B, starting at fold, knit up sts around three edges ending same point opposite side. Knit 4 rows garter st, increasing 1 st every row at corners. Bind off.
Repeat on other half of work.

### Pocket

Using yarn B, cast on 40 sts. Working in alternate stripes as bag, work in st st without shaping until work measures 8¾in from beginning. Using yarn B, work 5 rows garter st. Bind off.

### Straps

With yarn B, cast on 300 sts. Work in st st.
**Row 1** Knit.
**Row 2** *Purl 3 yarn B, p1 yarn A, rep from * to end.
**Row 3** *Knit 1 yarn B, k1 yarn A, rep from * to end.
**Row 4** Purl 1 yarn B, *p1 yarn A, p3 yarn B, rep from * to end.
**Rows 5, 6 and 7** Knit yarn B.
**Rows 8 and 10** Purl yarn A.
**Row 9** Knit yarn A.
Bind off in yarn B.
Work another strap similarly.

### Finishing

Fold main body of work in half, base pocket on fold line and sew in place.
Fold straps and sew up sides. Sew ends of straps together, making one long strap. Center these joins on fold line and pattern side out, sew straps up either side of pocket to top of work. Sew up other side similarly. Lay work flat on table or floor and cut out waterproof lining and wadding to same size and shape. Fold lining right sides together and attach zippers, starting with end ¾in above fold line and work around corner so that they will join between straps.
Lay wadding and opened out lining on inside of bag and join zipper to main body of work.

The changing bag can also be made in several different colors. To make a bag in the colors below work one row stripes as follows: white, blue, white, green, white, yellow, white, pink, then repeat these eight rows.

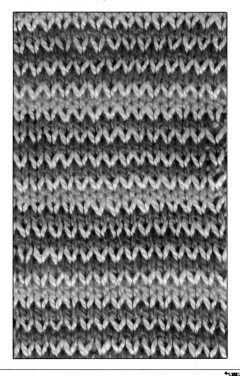

# NURSERY FRIENDS

What young child can resist a cuddly doll, especially if it's dressed to match. All their clothes can be removed for maximum play value, and included here are patterns for several different outfits.

## DOLLS

### Yarn
Main yarn M *1oz* 2-ply Shetland – or equivalent 4-ply – (pink, beige or brown) for body
Yarn A Scraps of any yarn for hair, eyelashes and brows
Yarn B Colored yarn for lips
Yarn C Colored yarn for eyes

### Needles
1 pair no 4

### Notions
Small quantity of stuffing

## Measurements
13½in tall

## Body

*Start at toes:* Using yarn M cast on 16 sts. Work 10 rows st st.
*Shape heel:* Knit 8 sts, turn, sl 1, p6, turn. Sl 1, k5, turn. Continue until purling 2, then turn. Sl 1, k3, turn and so on until knitting 8. Turn and sl 1, p to end. Work 40 rows st st without shaping. Break yarn.
Work another leg similarly, working heel on *last* 8 sts on needle instead of first 8 sts.
*Shape body:* Wrong side facing, cast on 2, p across sts of right leg, cast on 4, p across sts of left leg, cast on 2. Work 30 rows st st without shaping, ending with a wrong-side row.
*Shape armholes:* Knit 9 sts, bind off 2, k18, bind off 2, k9. Work on these last 9 sts in st st. Purl 1 row.
**Next row** K2tog, k7.
Work 5 rows without shaping.
**Next row** Bind off 4 sts, k4. Break yarn.
Working on front, purl 1 row, then k2tog beginning of next 2 rows, work further 5 rows st st without shaping.
**Next row** Bind off 4 sts, k8, bind off 4. Break yarn.
Working on left back p2tog beginning next p row and work 6 rows st st without shaping.
**Next row** Knit 4, bind off 4. Break yarn.
Right side facing, k across neck sts – 16 sts. Work 3 rows st st.
*Shape head:* Knit into front and back every st – 32 sts. Cast on 1 st at beginning next 4 rows – 36 sts. Work 3 rows st st without shaping.
*Work nose as follows:* Knit 18 sts, k 3 times into next st, turn, p3, turn, k3, turn, p3tog, turn. Sl 1 and k to end.
Then p17, sl 1, p18. Work further 12 rows st st.
*Shape top head:*
**Row 1** *K2tog, k7, rep from * to end – 32 sts.
**Row 2** *and every alternate row:* Purl.
**Row 3** *K2tog, k6, rep from * to end – 28 sts.
Continue decreasing 4 sts per k row until 16 sts remain. Break yarn and thread through remaining sts.

## Arms

Using yarn M cast on 10 sts and work 6 rows st st. Break yarn.
*Shape thumb:* Cast on 3 sts, work 4 rows st st.
**Row 1** Knit 3 thumb sts, k 10 hand sts.
Work further 3 rows st st.
**Row 5** K2tog, k11.
Work 29 rows on these 12 sts.
K2tog beginning of next 4 rows. Work 4 rows st st. K2tog beginning of next 4 rows. Bind off. Work another arm similarly.

## Finishing

Sew up inside legs and crotch. Stuff legs. Sew up and stuff arms, sew up back and set arms into armholes. Stuff body. Stuff head firmly, then embroider on face using yarns A, B and C. Embroider hair, knotting each strand of hair firmly to another strand.

## CLOTHES

**Yarn**
Main yarn M *1oz* medium-weight cotton (blue)
Yarn A *1oz* medium-weight cotton (white)
Yarn B Scraps 2-ply Shetland (beige)
Yarn C Scraps 2-ply Shetland (brown)
**Needles**
1 pair no 5
**Notions**
½yd length ribbon
Thin elastic

### SHIRT AND DRESS

*Work front:* Cast on 24 sts. Starting from top, work 3 rows garter st then change to st st. Work 23 rows (for shirt) or 37 rows (for dress). Work another 2 rows garter st and bind off. Work another piece similarly for back.
*Shape sleeves:* Sew small shoulder seam along cast-on edge of work. With right side work facing pick up 24 sts (12 either side of seam) and knit 24 rows st st for sleeve. Right side work facing, change to contrast yarn, work 2 rows garter st. Change and work 1 row garter st in main yarn. Bind off. Work another sleeve similarly.
Join side and sleeve seams.

### Collar

Using contrast color, cast on 16sts. Knit 1 row. Change to main yarn. K2tog each end of next 2 rows in garter st – 12 sts. Change back to contrast yarn and work 12 rows st st. Right side work facing, k 3 sts, bind off 6, k3. Work 16 rows on these 3 sts, then p2tog, p1, turn. Knit 2, turn. P2tog, break yarn and thread through remaining st. Work other point of collar similarly.
*Work collar trim:* Right side facing and using yarn M, pick up 24 sts along outside of collar from point to back edge. Turn. Knit into front and back next st and k to end. Change to contrast color, k into front and back of next st and knit to end. Repeat this row. Bind off. Finish other side of collar similarly.

### Finishing

Sew small seam at back corners. Attach to back inside neck of shirt or dress. Tie length of ribbon around collar points.

### SHORTS AND UNDERPANTS

Cast on 4 sts using chosen yarn. Work 4 rows st st. Break yarn. Cast on 36 sts and work all 40 sts in st st for 14 rows.
Work a row of eyelets: Knit 2, *yfwd, k2tog, rep from * to end. Bind off.
Sew up back seam and attach crotch sts to back of garment. Thread thin elastic through waist eyelets if required.

### SOCKS

Work as doll's foot and bind off at required length. Work 2-row stripe contrast color at top if desired.

### GIRL'S SHOES

Cast on 8 sts. Work in garter st increasing 1 st beginning every row until 12 sts on needle. K2tog beginning every row until 8 sts remain. Cast on 4 sts, k to end. Increase 1 st beginning

next and every alternate row until 14 sts on needle.
**Next row** Bind off 8 sts, k to end.
Work 7 rows. Cast on 8 sts. Bind off 1 st beginning next and every alternate row at toe edge – 12 sts. Bind off. Butt heel edges together and pick up 3 sts from each. Turn. *Shape ties:* Cast on 30 sts beginning next row. Bind off 30 sts. Knit across 6 heel sts and cast on 30. Bind off all sts. Sew heel and side seams. Work another shoe similarly.
Tie onto foot with a bow.

### BOY'S SHOES

Cast on 12 sts yarn C, work 12 rows garter st and bind off. Fold work in half and sew up both ends.
Work another shoe similarly.

### DRESS

**Yarn**
Scraps knitting worsted
**Needles**
1 pair no 5
**Notions**
3 mother-of-pearl buttons

### Method

Cast on 80 sts. Work 3 rows garter st.
Continue on st st until skirt measures 3¼in from beginning, then k2tog across all sts.
*Shape waist:* Knit 1 row. Work 5 rows st st making buttonhole in rows 1, 7 and 13 (k1, yo, k2tog). Purl 9, bind off 2, p18, bind off 2, p9.
*Shape left back:* Knit to last 2 sts, k2tog. Continue on these 8 sts, work 7 rows st st without shaping then bind off 5, k3. Purl 1 row and bind off.
*Shape front:* K2tog, k to last 2 sts, k2tog. Work 7 rows st st, then k4, bind off 8, k4. Purl 1 row and bind off. Repeat with other shoulder.
*Shape right back:* Work as left, reversing shaping.

### Sleeves

Cast on 10 sts. Double sts on needle knitting into front and back every st. Work 6 rows st st. Bind off.

### Finishing

Sew up side and sleeve seams. Set sleeves into armholes. Press work well.

### APRON

**Yarn**
Small quantity white 2-ply Shetland yarn (or equivalent 4-ply)
**Needles**
1 pair no 4

### Method

Cast on 100 sts. Bind off 40, k to end. Bind off 40, k to end. Increase 1 st beginning each row. Work central 16 sts st st and extra sts at beginning and end each row in garter st. Work 18 rows.
*Make frill:* Knit into front and back each st. Knit 2 rows garter st and bind off.

## BABY DOLL

**Yarn**
Main yarn M *1oz* 4-ply yarn for body (pink, beige or brown)
Yarn A dark yarn for hair, eyelashes and brows
Yarn B colored yarn for lips
Yarn C colored yarn for eyes
*Diaper*
Yarn D scraps bulky yarn (white)
**Needles**
1 pair no 4
1 pair no 5
**Notions**
Small quantity washable stuffing
4 pipe cleaners

### Measurements

Approx 6in tall

### Body

Using no 4 needles work as larger doll *but* work 24 rows st st for leg; 20 rows st st for body; 1 row at neck; 19 rows for arms; and omit upper arm shaping.

### Diaper

Using yarn D and no 5 knitting needles, cast on 30 sts. Work in garter st, k2tog beginning every row until 6 sts remain. Work 2 rows without shaping and bind off.

### Finishing

As for larger doll, then place pipe cleaners, with ends folded over to avoid sharp spikes, down legs and arms in order to bend limbs into baby-like positions. Attach thumb to mouth with several stitches of yarn if you wish.

# THE BEARS

Three old favorites: Daddy, Mommy and Baby bear. Make a
Goldilocks doll to complete the story using patterns on pp. 108–9.

## BEARS

### Yarn
3½oz knitting worsted (yellow, gold or brown) to
make all three bears

### Needles
1 pair no 5

### Notions
Small quantity of washable stuffing

## Measurements

Height 7¾ (10¼, 12½)in

## Body

Starting at legs, cast on 15 (20, 25) sts. Work 20
(25, 30) rows st st. Increase 2 (3, 4) sts
beginning next 2 rows, then k2tog beginning
next 3 (5, 7) rows. Work 12 (16, 20) rows
without shaping.
*Shape arms:* Knit 7 (9, 11), bind off 2, sl last st
back onto other needle. Cast on 20 (25, 30) sts
and k to end. Work 5 (7, 9) rows st st. Knit 4 (5,
6), bind off 26 (34, 42), k4 (5, 6). Break yarn, sl
sts onto end of needle.
Work another half body similarly but do not
break yarn.

### Head
Right side facing, k across all 16 (20, 24) sts.
Purl 1 row. Double sts by knitting into front and
back of each st – 32 (40, 48) sts. Purl 20 (24,
28), turn. Knit 8 (10, 12), turn. Purl 7 (9, 11),

turn. Continue until knitting 4 (6, 6), turn. Then
p5 (7, 7), turn. Knit 6 (8, 8), turn. Purl 7 (9,
9), turn.
*Largest size only:* Knit 10, turn. Purl 11, turn.
*All sizes:* K2tog 4 (5, 6) times, k to end. Work 3
(5, 7) rows st st.
**Row 1** *Knit 5, k2tog, rep from * to end.
**Row 2** *and every alternate row:* Purl without
shaping.
**Row 3** *Knit 4, k2tog, rep from * to end.
Continue this way until 16 (20, 24) sts remain.
K2tog across all sts, break yarn and thread
through loops.

## Finishing

Sew seams leaving a small hole at the back for
stuffing. Stuff the bear, then sew up hole.
Embroider on nose, eyes, fingers and toes.
*Shape ears:* Pick up 3 (5, 7) sts from side of
head. Double them and work 2 (3, 4) rows.
Bind off. Sew edges down to head.

# KNITTING KNOW-HOW

# KNITTING AIDS

Straight needles and yarn are all that is necessary for plain knitting but additional accessories come in useful from time to time. For example when knitting in the round you will need a circular needle or a set of four double-pointed needles and you will need a special cable needle for cable work. Stitch holders and yarn bobbins keep unworked stitches and yarns separate;

needle guards prevent dropped stitches; a counter keeps track of rows; small rings keep track of rounds. A crochet hook, scissors, a blunt-ended needle and pins can be used for finishing off and putting together, a tape measure is necessary for keeping track of vital measurements during both the construction and blocking of a garment.

2mm

No 0

No 1

No 2

No 3

No 4

No 5

No 6

No 7

No 8

No 9

No 10

No 10½

No 11

No 13

No 15

10mm

**Key**
1 Cable needles
2 Stitch holder
3 Yarn bobbins
4 Circular needle
5 Tape measure
6 Needle guards
7 Pins
8 Double-pointed needles
9 Crochet hook
10 Marker rings
11 Scissors
12 Wool needle
13 Stitch and row counter

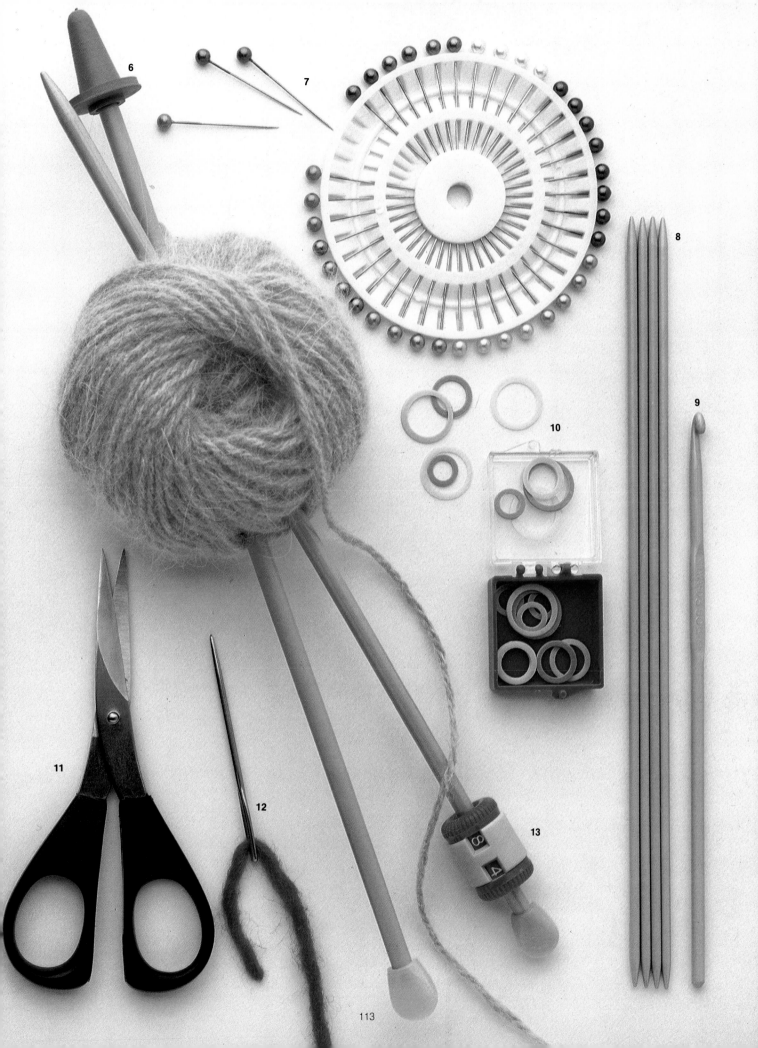

# BASIC KNITTING

To start knitting all you need are two needles and some yarn. The information on the following pages will tell you all you need to know to make the patterns in the book as well as helping you to design your own knitting. An illustrated glossary of yarns (see pp. 138–41) will enable you to be more inventive in choosing colors and textures for the patterns.

The instructions in this section are all written and illustrated for right-handed knitters. If you are left-handed, reverse any instructions for left and right, or prop the book up in front of a mirror and follow the diagrams in reverse.

## STITCH GAUGE

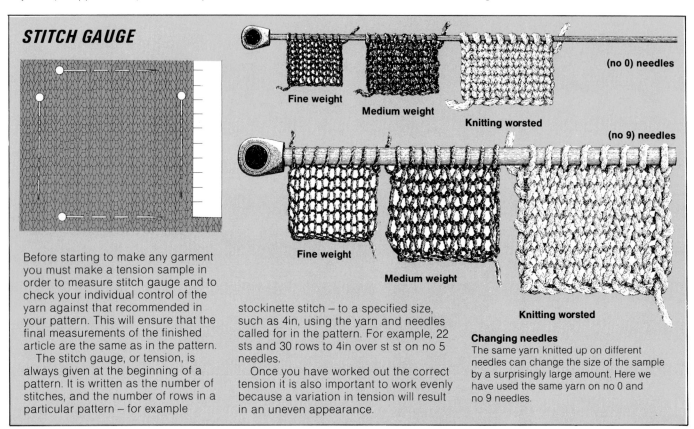

**Fine weight**

**Medium weight**

**Knitting worsted**

**(no 0) needles**

**(no 9) needles**

**Fine weight**

**Medium weight**

**Knitting worsted**

**Changing needles**
The same yarn knitted up on different needles can change the size of the sample by a surprisingly large amount. Here we have used the same yarn on no 0 and no 9 needles.

Before starting to make any garment you must make a tension sample in order to measure stitch gauge and to check your individual control of the yarn against that recommended in your pattern. This will ensure that the final measurements of the finished article are the same as in the pattern.

The stitch gauge, or tension, is always given at the beginning of a pattern. It is written as the number of stitches, and the number of rows in a particular pattern – for example stockinette stitch – to a specified size, such as 4in, using the yarn and needles called for in the pattern. For example, 22 sts and 30 rows to 4in over st st on no 5 needles.

Once you have worked out the correct tension it is also important to work evenly because a variation in tension will result in an uneven appearance.

## Making a tension sample

Using the same yarn, needles and stitch pattern called for in the pattern, knit a sample slightly larger than 4in square. Smooth out the finished sample on a flat surface being careful not to stretch it. Using long pins, mark out the tension measurement given in the chosen pattern (e.g., 4in sq).

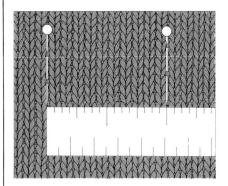

**Measuring the number of stitches**
To determine the width of the knitting, place a steel ruler or tape measure across the sample and count the number of stitches between the pins. Remember to include any half stitches over the width of a garment; a half stitch which is left uncalculated may amount to several inches in the final width.

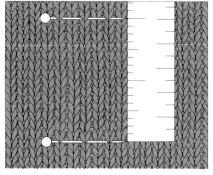

**Measuring the number of rows**
To determine the length of the knitting, place a steel ruler or tape measure vertically along the fabric and count the number of rows to the inch.

## Adjusting the stitch gauge

If the number of stitches given in the pattern knit up too wide a measure your knitting is too loose and you should change your knitting needles to a smaller size. If they knit up too small a measure, then your knitting is too tight and you should change your knitting needles to a larger size.

Changing to needles one size larger or one size smaller makes a difference of one stitch usually every two inches. Changing your needle size will normally be sufficient to adjust the dimensions. Sometimes, however, the width will match but not the length. If there are too many vertical rows to that called for in the pattern, you must calculate the length of the garment from your tension sample and adjust the increasing and decreasing rows accordingly. However, in certain patterns, such as raglan or set-in sleeves, the shaping is dependent on a specific number of vertical rows. If your vertical tension matches but not your horizontal then in this case it is better to lose some stitches across the width.

# CASTING ON

When you begin to work on a pattern placing the first row of stitches on the needle is known as "casting on". All further rows are worked into these initial loops. This can be done on one or two needles and the method may be specified in the pattern. Single cast on is often used for fine knitting and baby clothes because it produces a loose, soft edge.

## Making a slip loop

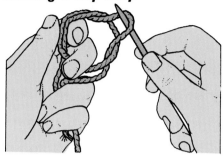

**1** Wrap your yarn around two fingers twice and pull a loop through the twisted yarn with a knitting needle.

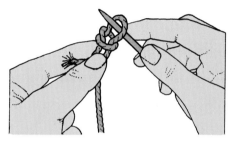

**2** Pull both ends of the yarn to tighten the slip loop.

## Single cast on

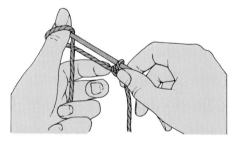

**1** With the slip over loop on your right-hand needle wrap the working end of the yarn around your left thumb and hold it in the palm of your hand. Put the needle through the yarn behind the thumb.

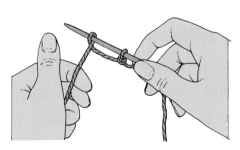

**2** Lift the yarn and slide the new "stitch" towards the slip loop. Tighten the working end to secure the stitch until you have the required number.

## Two-needle method

**1** With the slip loop on your left-hand needle, insert your right-hand needle through the loop from front to back.

**2** Bring the yarn under and over your right-hand needle.

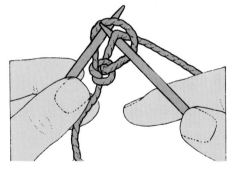

**3** Draw up the yarn through the slip loop to make a stitch.

**4** Place the stitch on your left-hand needle. Continue to make stitches drawing the yarn through the last stitch on your left-hand needle.

## Binding off

When you end a piece of knitting you must secure all the stitches you have finished by "binding off". This should be done on a knit row but you can employ the same technique on a purl row: the stitches, whether knit or purl, should be made loosely. When binding off rib, you must use both knit and purl.

**IN A KNIT ROW**

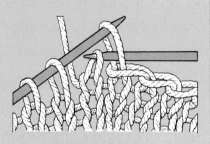

**1** Knit the first two stitches and insert the tip of your left-hand needle through the first stitch.

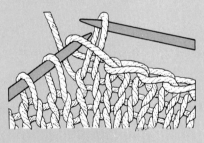

**2** Lift the first stitch over the second stitch and discard it. Knit the next stitch and continue to lift the first stitch over the second stitch to the end of the row. Be careful not to knit too tightly. For the last stitch, cut your yarn, slip the end through the stitch and pull the yarn tight to fasten off securely.

**IN A PURL ROW**

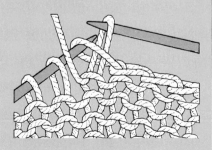

Purl the first two (and all subsequent) stitches and continue as for knit stitch above.

## Holding the needle and yarn

The way in which you hold your knitting will affect the tension and evenness of the fabric. Threading the working end of the yarn through the fingers not only makes knitting faster but it helps produce a firm, even result.

**HOLDING THE YARN IN THE RIGHT HAND**

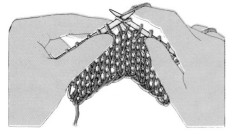

With the working yarn in your right hand, use the right forefinger to wrap the yarn over the needles.

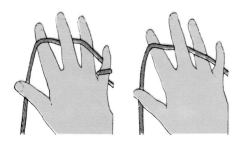

**Threading the yarn**
Place the working end of yarn through the fingers of your left hand using one of these two methods.

**HOLDING THE YARN IN THE LEFT HAND**

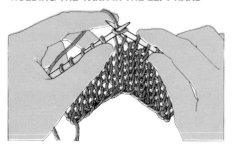

With the working yarn in your left hand, use the left forefinger to position the yarn while you move the right needle to encircle the yarn to form a new loop.

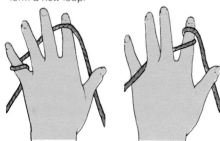

**Threading the yarn**
Place the working yarn through the fingers of your right hand either way.

# BASIC STITCHES

Knit stitch and purl stitch are the two basic knitting stitches. Either one worked continuously in rows forms Garter stitch pattern and worked alternately forms Stockinette stitch pattern.

## Knit stitch (K)

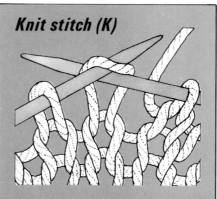

**1** With the yarn at the back, insert your right-hand needle from front to back into the first stitch on your left-hand needle.

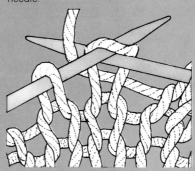

**2** Bring your working yarn under and over the point of your right-hand needle.

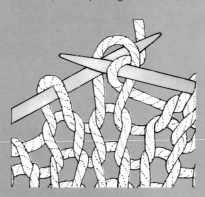

**3** Draw a loop through and slide the first stitch off your left-hand needle while the new stitch is retained on your right-hand needle. Continue in this way to the end of the row.

**4** To knit the next row, turn the work around so that the back is facing you and the worked stitches are held on the needle in your left hand. Proceed to make stitches as above, with the initially empty needle held in your right hand.

## Purl stitch (P)

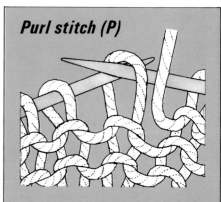

**1** With the yarn at the front, insert your right-hand needle from back to front into the first stitch on your left-hand needle.

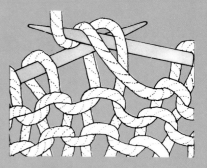

**2** Bring your working yarn over and around the point of your right-hand needle.

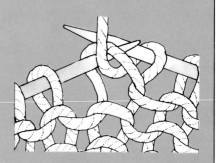

**3** Draw a loop through and slide the first stitch off your left-hand needle while the new stitch is retained on your right-hand needle. Continue in this way to the end of the row.

**4** To purl the next row, turn the work around so that the back is facing you and the worked stitches are held on the needle in your left hand. Proceed to make stitches as above, with the initially empty needle held in your right hand.

## Garter stitch

Knitting or purling every row back and forth on two needles produces Garter stitch.

## Stockinette stitch (st st)

Knitting the first and every odd row and purling the second and every even row produces Stockinette stitch when made on two needles. When working in the round (see p. 123) the work does not have to be turned around because the knit stitch will always be on the outside and the ridged purl will be on the inside.

## Ribbing

A combination of knit and purl stitches, usually one or two knit stitches and then one or two purl stitches, in the same row is known as ribbing. Ribbing is used on sleeve and body edges to form a neat, stretchable finish. It is usually worked on smaller needles than the main body of the garment.

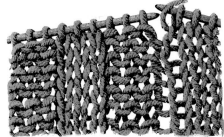

**Changing from a knit stitch to a purl stitch (on a k3, p3 rib)** Knit three in the usual way and bring the yarn to the front. Purl three in the usual way.

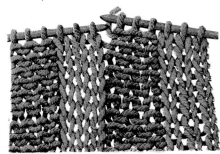

**Changing from a purl stitch to a knit stitch (on a p3, k3 rib)** Having purled three in the usual way, bring the yarn to the back and knit three in the usual way.

## Dropped stitches

Occasionally, a stitch may fall off your needle, in which case correct it by following one of the techniques described below. Dropped stitches are often the result of leaving work in the middle of a row.

## Ladders

If a dropped stitch is left, it can unravel down the work and form a "ladder". The easiest way to correct this is to use a crochet hook to pick up the stitches in pattern, although you can try to correct it with your needles.

If you make a mistake in your knitting, you may have to "unpick" a stitch, which can result in a ladder. Pick up one dropped stitch at a time, securing any others with a safety pin to prevent further unraveling.

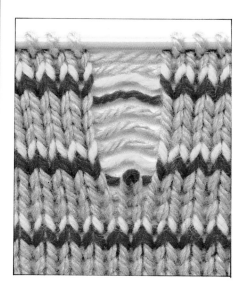

| PICKING UP A DROPPED KNIT STITCH | PICKING UP A DROPPED PURL STITCH |
|---|---|
| 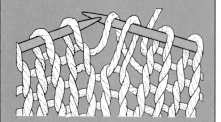 | 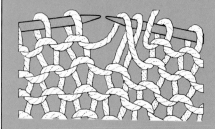 |
| **1** Pick up both the stitch and strand on your right-hand needle, inserting the needle from front to back. | **1** Pick up both the stitch and strand on your right-hand needle, inserting the needle from back to front. |
| 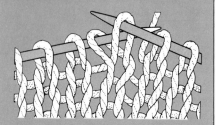 | 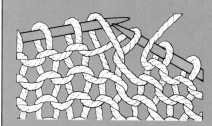 |
| **2** Insert your left-hand needle through the stitch only, from back to front. With your right-hand needle only, pull the strand through the stitch to make the extra stitch. (Drop the stitch from your left-hand needle.) | **2** Insert your left-hand needle through the stitch only, from front to back. With your right-hand needle only, pull the strand through the stitch to make the extra stitch. (Drop the stitch from your left-hand needle.) |
| 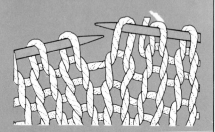 | 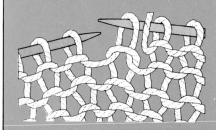 |
| **3** Transfer the re-formed stitch back to your left-hand needle, so that it untwists and faces the correct way. It is now ready for knitting again. | **3** Transfer the re-formed stitch back to your left-hand needle, so that it untwists and faces the correct way. It is now ready for purling again. |

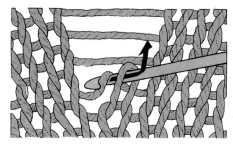

**Correcting a knit ladder**
Insert a crochet hook through the front of the dropped stitch. Hook up one strand and pull it through the stitch to form a new stitch one row up. Continue in this way to the top of the ladder then continue in pattern.

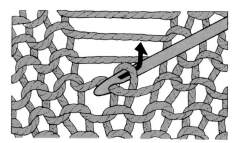

**Correcting a purl ladder**
Insert a crochet hook through the back of the dropped stitch. Hook up one strand and pull it through the stitch to form a new stitch one row up. Continue to re-insert hook to make stitches until you reach the top of the ladder, then continue in pattern.

## Unpicking mistakes

Holding the stitch on your right-hand needle insert your left-hand needle into the row below and undo the stitch. Transfer the stitch back to your right-hand needle and repeat undoing until the error has been reached. Correct stitch as if it had been a ladder, see right.

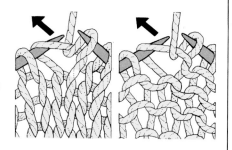

## INCREASING STITCHES

When shaping garments it is usually necessary to add additional stitches. If they are made "invisibly", there will be no hole or gap left in the fabric. The three "invisible" methods shown below all use part of an existing stitch to create a new one. Make two stitches from one, *Increase 1* "Inc 1", for shaping your side edges and use the *Raised increase* "M1" and *Lifted increase* "Up 1" for shaping within the body of the garment. The visible increase (see overleaf), variously written as yarn round needle "yrn", yarn forward "yfwd" and yarn over needle "yo", is used for decorative stitch patterns.

### Increase 1 (Inc 1)

**IN A KNIT ROW**

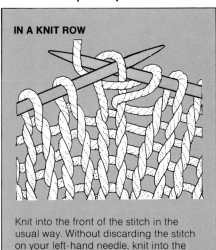

Knit into the front of the stitch in the usual way. Without discarding the stitch on your left-hand needle, knit into the back of it, making two stitches.

**IN A PURL ROW**

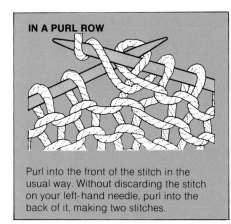

Purl into the front of the stitch in the usual way. Without discarding the stitch on your left-hand needle, purl into the back of it, making two stitches.

**Using invisible increase**
This frilled cuff was made by picking up stitches from white stripes and doubling every stitch on the needle.

### Lifted increase (Up 1)

**IN A KNIT ROW**

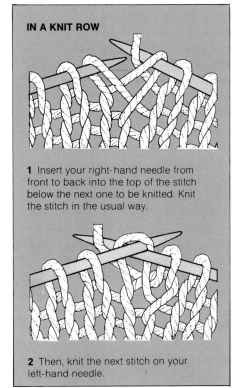

**1** Insert your right-hand needle from front to back into the top of the stitch below the next one to be knitted. Knit the stitch in the usual way.

**2** Then, knit the next stitch on your left-hand needle.

**IN A PURL ROW**

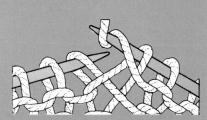

**1** Insert your right-hand needle from back to front into the top of the stitch below the next one to be purled. Purl the stitch in the usual way.

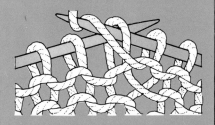

**2** Then purl the next stitch on your left-hand needle.

### Raised increase (M1)

**IN A KNIT ROW**

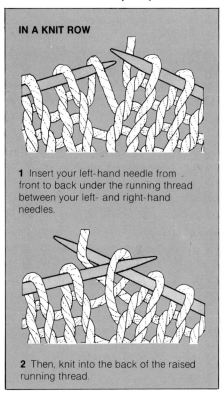

**1** Insert your left-hand needle from front to back under the running thread between your left- and right-hand needles.

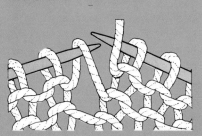

**2** Then, knit into the back of the raised running thread.

**IN A PURL ROW**

**1** Insert your left-hand needle from front to back under the running thread between your left- and right-hand needles.

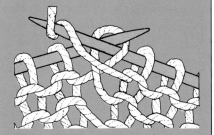

**2** Then, purl into the back of the raised running thread.

## Visible increase

This visible increase is usually used when making fancy patterns as in bobble stitches. Any number of stitches may be increased by the yarn-over method. Depending on the number of increases required in the pattern (and the position, see below), take your yarn forward, around or over your needle one, two, three, four or more times. On the subsequent row, knit the stitches in pattern order.

Patterns are usually written with: "yfwd" when the increase occurs between two knit stitches; as "yrn" when the increase occurs between two purl stitches or between a knit and a purl; as "yo" when the increase occurs between a purl and a knit; however, "yo" is also used to represent all three situations.

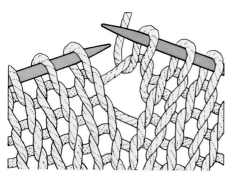

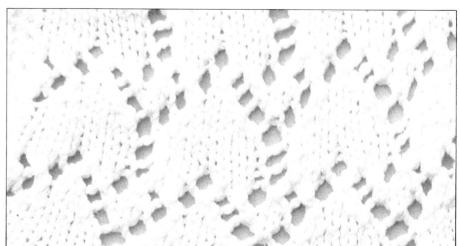

**Using a visible increase**
This technique can be seen clearly as a hole after the loop has been knitted into on the following row.

**IN A KNIT ROW**

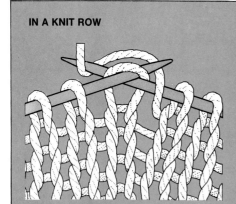

**1** Bring your yarn forward to the front and loop it over your right-hand needle.

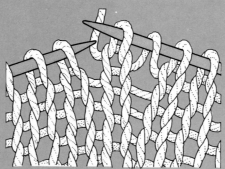

**2** Knit the next stitch.

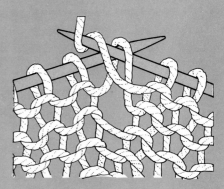

**3** On the subsequent row purl (or knit) the yarn-over loop in the usual way.

**IN A PURL ROW**

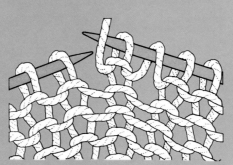

**1** Take your yarn back around your right-hand needle and then under to the front.

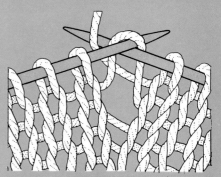

**2** Purl the next stitch.

**3** On the subsequent row, knit (or purl) the yarn-over loop in the usual way.

# DECREASING STITCHES

There are two ways to lose stitches for shaping or making decorative patterns and these are: to knit or purl two stitches together at the beginning, end or any given point in a row, or to use the slip stitch method.

The first method, knitting or purling two stitches together (k2tog, p2tog) is the simpler method and forms a slant to the right if the stitches are knitted together through the front and a slant to the left if the stitches are knitted together through the back of the work.

Slip-stitch decrease produces a more decorative effect on a garment. When on a knit row – abbreviated as Sl 1, k1, psso (slip one, knit one, pass slip stitch over) – the decrease forms a slant to the left on the front of the knitting; on a purl row – sl 1, p1, psso – a slant to the right is formed on the front.

## Knitting two stitches together

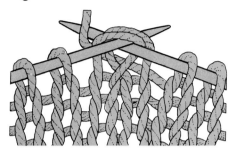

**In a knit row (K2tog)**
Insert your right-hand needle through the front of the first two stitches on your left-hand needle. Knit them together as a single stitch.

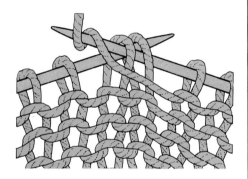

**In a purl row (P2tog)**
Insert your right-hand needle through the front of the first two stitches on your left-hand needle. Purl them together as a single stitch.

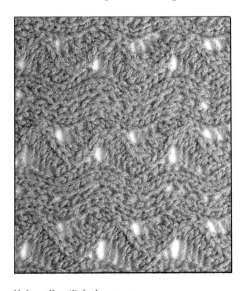

**Using slip stitch decrease**
Fancy openwork patterns such as Ric Rac depend on slip stitch decreases.

## Slip stitch decreases

**IN A KNIT ROW**

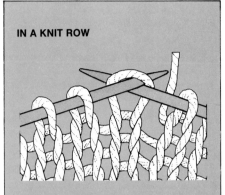

**1** Insert your right-hand needle "knitwise" and lift off the first stitch from your left-hand needle.

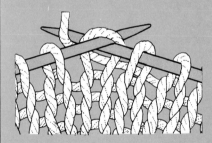

**2** Leave the stitch on the needle and knit the next stitch on your left-hand needle in the usual way.

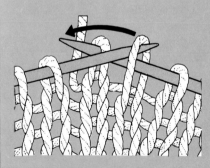

**3** Using the point of your left-hand needle bring the slipped stitch off your right-hand needle over the knitted stitch.

**IN A PURL ROW**

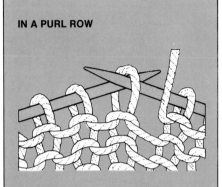

**1** Insert your right-hand needle "purlwise" and lift off the first stitch from your left-hand needle.

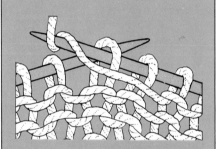

**2** Leave the stitch on the needle and purl into the next stitch on your left-hand needle in the usual way.

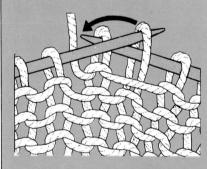

**3** Using the point of your left-hand needle, bring the slipped stitch off your right-hand needle, over the purled stitch.

## CABLES

Traditional cable-stitch patterns are created by moving stitches from one position on a row to another. For lightly embossed, lattice and ribbed patterns two stitches can be twisted on the needle. Special small double-pointed needles (cable needles) of varying shapes are used to produce individual rope or braided patterns. Such a needle is necessary to hold stitches at the front or back of work as required in the pattern.

Stitches held at the front of work will twist the cable right to left when knitted off; stitches held at the back will twist the cable from left to right when knitted off.

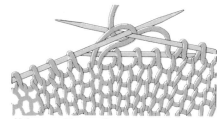

**Using a cable needle**
In the illustration of a six-stitch cable (below), the first three stitches are slipped onto a cable needle and held at the back of the work. The next three stitches are knitted from the left-hand needle followed by knitting the three stitches from the cable needle. This produces a cable twisting from left to right.

### Six stitch cable

A straightforward cable twist on a central panel of 10 sts is worked as follows:
**Rows 1 and 3** K2, p6, k2.
**Row 2** P2, k6, p2.
**Row 4** P2, sl next 3 sts to cn and hold at back (or front), k3, then k3 from cn, p2.
**Rows 5 and 7** As rows 1 and 3.
**Rows 6 and 8** As row 2.
Repeat rows 1–8.

### Double cable

A cable pattern with a central panel of 12 sts is worked as follows:
**Rows 1, 3, 5 and 7** K2, p8, k2.
**Row 2** P2, sl next 2 sts to cn and hold at front, k2, then k2 from cn, sl next 2 sts to cn and hold at back, k2, then k2 from cn, p2.
**Rows 4, 6 and 8** P2, k8, p2.
Repeat rows 1 to 8.

## BOBBLES

These patterns involve repeatedly increasing into a single stitch to form a cluster. Different patterns produce different effects ranging from fat bobbles to a slightly raised embossed look. After the increasing has been worked, the cluster is decreased and all but one stitch discarded.

You can make a simple bobble over five rows by following the instructions given right.

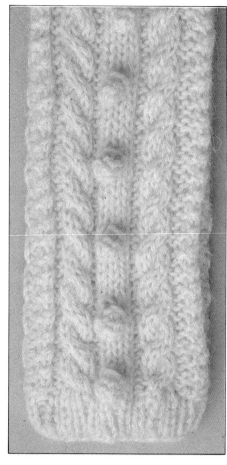

**Using bobbles**
Interesting texture can be created by combining bobbles and cable patterns.

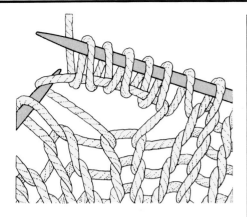

**Row 1** Knit two, take the yarn forward to the front of the work and over the needle. Knit one but do not discard the stitch. Instead, continue working into the stitch twice more.
*In a knitting pattern this would read:*
*\*K2, yfwd, k1, rep from \* twice more.*

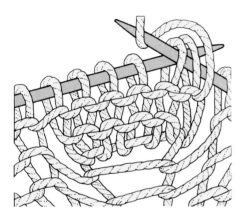

**Row 2** Turn the work. Slip the first stitch purlwise onto your right-hand needle and purl five stitches.
*Turn. Sl 1 pwise, p5.*

**Row 3** Turn the work. Slip the first stitch knitwise onto your right-hand needle and knit five stitches.
*Turn. Sl 1 kwise, k5.*

**Row 4** Turn. Purl two stitches together three times.
*Turn. P2tog 3 times.*

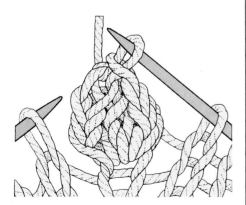

**Row 5** Turn. Slip one stitch knitwise, knit two stitches together, pass the slipped stitch over. One stitch remains on the needle.
*Turn. Sl 1 kwise, k2tog, psso. 1 st rem.*

# KNITTING IN THE ROUND

It is sometimes easier to make garments in the round working with circular or three or more double-pointed needles. This will produce a seamless garment, and the front of the work always faces you making patterns somewhat easier to follow. Circular needles are used from the beginning when knitting a garment, but a set of double-pointed needles will be more useful when picking up stitches such as when knitting necklines or when working small areas such as fingers for gloves. Two circular needles can also be used for flat knitting on very large items.

The most important thing to remember when working in the round is that to achieve stockinette stitch, you must *knit* every row because the outside of the work always faces you when working stockinette stitch.

## Using a circular needle

A circular needle is a flexible nylon tube which has two pointed metal ends (needles) sized in the normal way. You cast on stitches in the usual way and then knit into the first stitch to make a continuous round. You should always mark the beginning of a new row.

## Using double-pointed needles

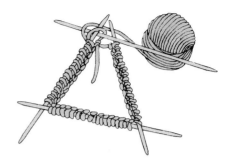

Sets of double-pointed needles are sold in the traditional sizes. Normally bought in fours, as many as six needles can be used if the area is large, the number of needles required will normally be specified in the pattern. When knitting with double-pointed needles, the stitches are divided among all but one of the needles. The remaining needle is used to knit off, so that each needle in turn holds stitches and then is used to knit off.

To knit, divide your stitches equally over the needles and knit a round. To close the circle, knit the first stitch with the working yarn from the last stitch. Keep your last and first needle as close together as possible. Make sure your first knitted stitch (you should mark this) is close to the last needle so that you do not end up with a gap in the knitting.

Continue to work rounds in this way, using your empty needles to knit off and keeping the stitches evenly divided. Hold the two working needles as usual, and drop the others to the back of the work when not in use.

# WORKING WITH MORE THAN ONE YARN OR COLOR

Work in a new ball of yarn or another color at the beginning of a row, if possible. With a new ball of yarn, the ends of both the old and the new yarn can then be darned neatly into the edge or the back of the work. When working with additional colors, the yarn can either be broken off and darned in, or carried up the side of the work until it is needed again.

When knitting with more than one color, you will find it necessary to adopt various techniques to keep the back of the work neat and to prevent holes appearing. There are three basic methods of working: stranding, weaving and crossing. Stranding and weaving yarns produces a thicker fabric.

To prevent the different yarns getting tangled when weaving or stranding, the strands must be caught up in the back of the work, but it must be done in such a way that they do not interfere with the pattern or produce undesired effects such as tightening tension.

## Adding yarn at the beginning of a row

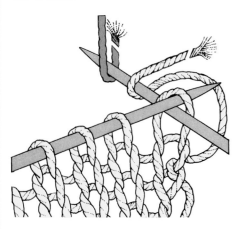

**1** Insert your right-hand needle through the first stitch on your left-hand needle and wrap the old yarn, and then the new yarn over it. Knit (or purl) the stitch using both yarns.

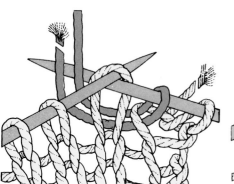

**2** Leaving the old yarn at the back, knit (or purl) the next two stitches using the double length of the new yarn.

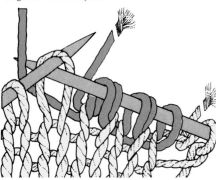

**3** Discard the short end of the new yarn and continue to knit as usual. On the following row, treat the three double stitches as single stitches.

## Adding yarn in the middle of a row

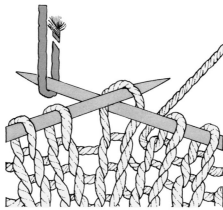

**1** Insert your right-hand needle through the first stitch on your left-hand needle. Wrap the new yarn over, and knit (or purl) the stitch with the new yarn. Leave the old yarn at the back of the work.

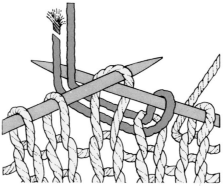

**2** Knit (or purl) the next two stitches using the double length of the new yarn.

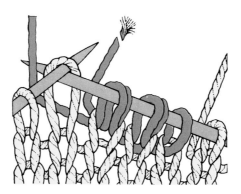

**3** Discard the short end of the new yarn and continue to knit as usual. On the following row, treat the two double stitches as single stitches.

## Stranding yarn

Use this method for working narrow stripes, small repeats of color such as Fair Isle, and other patterns requiring only two colors in a row. Strand yarn over a maximum of five stitches only.

**IN A KNIT ROW**

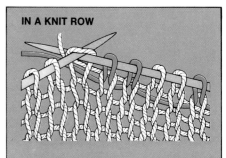

With both yarns at the back of the work, knit the required number of stitches with yarn A (in this case two), and then drop it to the back. Pick up yarn B and knit the required number of stitches and then drop it to the back. Both yarns should be stranded loosely along the back of the work.

**IN A PURL ROW**

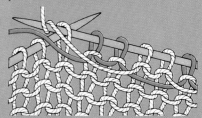

With both yarns at the front of the work, purl the required number of stitches with yarn A (in this case two), and then drop it. Pick up yarn B and purl the required number of stitches and then drop it. Both yarns should be stranded loosely along the front (side facing you).

## Winding bobbins

To help keep different yarns separate when working complicated color patterns, wind manageable lengths onto bobbins, yarn holders or spools. Replenish as necessary. Or, keep yarns in individual plastic bags secured at the "neck" with an elastic band.

## Weaving yarn

This method should be used when you are working large pattern repeats, for patterns requiring three or more colors, and when yarn has to be carried over more than five stitches.

### IN A KNIT ROW

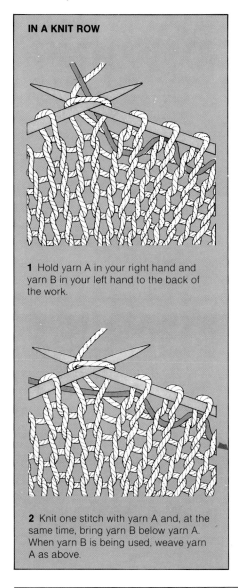

**1** Hold yarn A in your right hand and yarn B in your left hand to the back of the work.

**2** Knit one stitch with yarn A and, at the same time, bring yarn B below yarn A. When yarn B is being used, weave yarn A as above.

### IN A PURL ROW

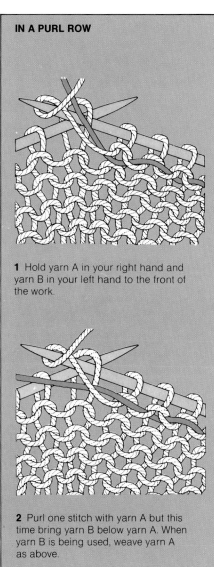

**1** Hold yarn A in your right hand and yarn B in your left hand to the front of the work.

**2** Purl one stitch with yarn A but this time bring yarn B below yarn A. When yarn B is being used, weave yarn A as above.

## Checking your technique

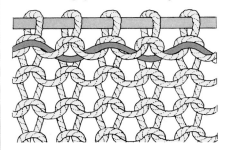

**Weaving**
If you have worked weaving correctly, the yarns will cross evenly and remain at the same depth. A "smocking" effect means that you have pulled the yarns too tightly. It is better for the yarns to be woven too loosely than too tightly.

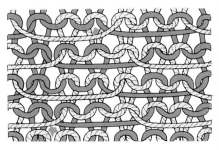

**Stranding**
If you have worked stranding correctly, the yarns will be running evenly across the back of the work at the same tension as the knitting. Puckering indicates that you have pulled the yarns too tightly.

## Crossing colors

Use this method for working large blocks of color (e.g., diagonal or wide vertical stripes or jacquard motifs). When crossing colors each color is kept as a separate ball or on a bobbin and is *not* taken across the work. Rather, the yarns are crossed at the join. Follow the instructions below for vertical color patterns as well, but cross the colors on every row.

### IN A KNIT ROW FOR A DIAGONAL STRIPE TO THE RIGHT

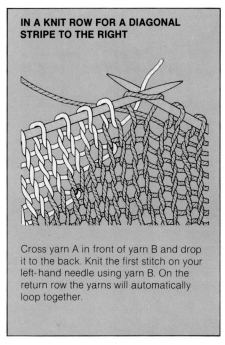

Cross yarn A in front of yarn B and drop it to the back. Knit the first stitch on your left-hand needle using yarn B. On the return row the yarns will automatically loop together.

### IN A PURL ROW FOR A DIAGONAL STRIPE TO THE LEFT

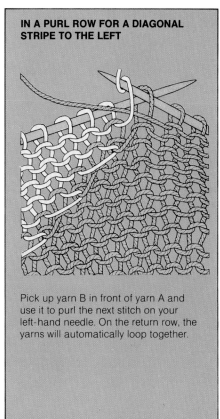

Pick up yarn B in front of yarn A and use it to purl the next stitch on your left-hand needle. On the return row, the yarns will automatically loop together.

# BUTTONHOLES

There are two main types of buttonhole used in knitting: horizontal and eyelet.

A horizontal buttonhole is the most useful for larger sweaters, cardigans and jackets. However, if you are using small buttons or making fastenings for baby's clothes, use an eyelet buttonhole: an *open eyelet buttonhole* is used for tiny buttons, while the *bold eyelet buttonhole* can take bigger buttons. A row of eyelets can also be used as slotting for ribbon.

Whatever type of buttonhole you are going to use, you should calculate the position of all the buttonholes before beginning to knit. Also it is a good idea to knit up a sample buttonhole before you start in order to check that your buttons will fit.

## Horizontal buttonhole

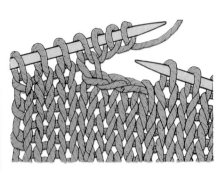

**1** To make the buttonhole, knit up to the marked position (about three to four stitches in from the main fabric or button-band), and bind off two or more stitches according to the size of the button. Continue in pattern to the end of the row.

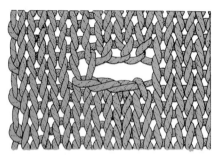

**2** On the following row work up to the bound-off stitches and replace them by casting on the same number of new stitches. Complete the row in pattern.

Bold eyelet buttonhole.

## Open-eyelet buttonhole

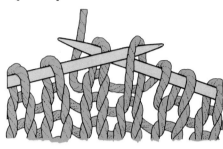

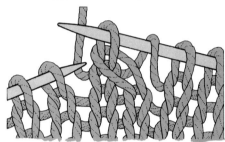

Knit 2, yfwd, sl the next kwise onto your right-hand needle, k1, psso. The yfwd increase replaces the stitch which was decreased by slipping.

## Bold-eyelet buttonhole

**Row 1** K3, k2tog, yfwd2, sl 1, k1, psso, k3.
**Row 2** P3, p2tog (one st is first yo), k2tog (one st is second yo), p3.
**Row 3** K4, yfwd2, k to end.
**Row 4** P3, p2tog (one st is first yo) and at the same time through the strand below, k1, p1 into second yo and, at the same time, knit and purl through the strand below. Purl to the end of the row.

## Button-stand

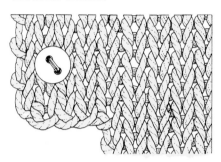

Sometimes when the knitting divides to form the opening of a garment, you will have to knit in an extra piece of fabric, a button-stand, in order to hold a button.

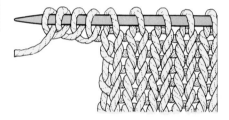

**Working button-stands**
To work in a button-stand, cast on an extra number of stitches at the end of a row (in this case four), and work these stitches until the fabric is large enough to support your button. Bind off the extra stitches.

## Button-bands

Patterns often call for button-bands which can either be knitted in two separate pieces or in one long piece which goes right up the front openings and around the neck. They can be knitted to match the garment's color or in contrasting shades and may be worked in either Garter or Moss stitch which give a flatter surface.

If you are knitting your button-bands in two parts (one to hold the buttons and one in which to place the buttonholes), knit them together using separate balls of yarn as this will ensure they are equal in length. In addition, when you work the buttonhole on one band you can mark the position for the button on the other.

You will have to sew the button-band onto the finished garment when putting together at the end.

## EDGES

The side of a piece of knitting are also known as the selvages. Special care must be taken while you are working to ensure that these are kept straight.

### Stockinette-stitch edge

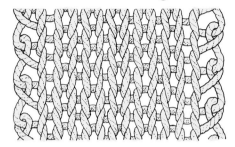

This is the most common edge and the first and last stitches must be firmly made. All knit row stitches are knitted and all purl row stitches are purled.

### Open edge

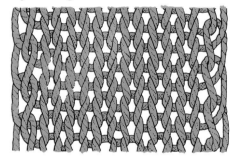

To produce this more decorative edge slip the first and last stitches of every knit row knitwise. Purl all the edge stitches in the purl row.

### Slip-stitch edge

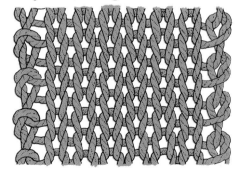

This is especially useful as a neat edge on cardigans. "Pips" are formed in a regular sequence which look neat and make row counting easier – each "pip" counts for two rows. Slip the first stitch of each row knitwise then knit the last stitch of each row.

## SEAMS

Your pattern will usually set out the order of seaming: normally the shoulder seams are joined first if you have to pick up stitches to make the neck band. There is a choice of two methods, the edge-to-edge seam and the backstitch seam.

An edge-to-edge seam is useful on lightweight knits because it is almost invisible and forms no ridge.

A backstitch seam is stronger and firmer and is suitable for all garments but it forms a ridge.

### Edge-to-edge seam

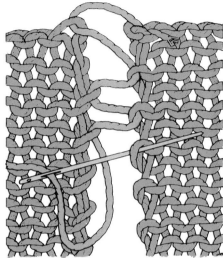

Place the pieces to be joined edge-to-edge with the "heads" of the knit stitches locking together. Match the pattern pieces carefully row for row and stitch for stitch. Using the main yarn, sew into the head of each stitch alternately.

### Backstitch seam

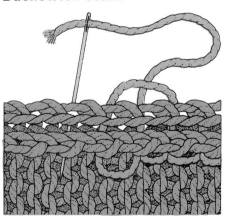

Place the pieces to be joined together with their right sides facing. Carefully match pattern to pattern, row to row and stitch to stitch. Sew along the seam using backstitch sewing into the center of each stitch to correspond with the stitch on the opposite piece. Sew $\frac{1}{4}$in in from the edge of the knitting.

## FINISHING TECHNIQUES

Before pattern pieces are joined up, they are usually blocked and pressed to ensure a good fit. It's always a good idea to check the yarn band for any special instructions. The pieces are blocked when dry and are pressed with a damp cloth.

### Blocking

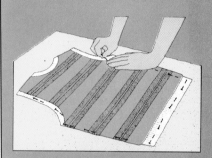

Garment pieces need blocking, or putting into shape before they can be joined up. Cover a table with a folded blanket and a sheet. Using rustless pins, "block" the pieces wrong-side out to the correct measurements. Be careful not to stretch or distort the fabric and make sure that all the rows run in straight lines.

### Pressing

After blocking, the garment pieces are usually pressed in position. Use a warm iron and a damp cloth on wool. Lay the iron on the fabric and lift it up, do not move it over the surface. Do not remove any of the pins until the work has cooled and dried completely.

Raised and embossed patterns should be pressed under a damp cloth, but remove the pins and adjust the fabric while it is still hot to avoid flattening the pattern.

Ribbing should be lightly stretched and pinned before ironing. Use a heavy cloth and remove the pins in order to adjust the fabric while it is still warm.

# BUTTONS AND TRIMMINGS

A strong decorative element can be added to handknits by the careful choice of buttons and trimmings. Metal, bone, wood and leather buttons look best on traditional garments such as Arans and Fair-Isles, while simple bright-colored buttons with motifs such as rabbits or cars look great on plain colored children's clothes.

Buttons can also be used to add to figurative or abstract motifs with or without embroidery. Threaded ribbon can be used to accentuate openwork patterns and wide satin ribbon can be used as ties. You can also buy ready-made motifs to sew onto any garment.

As well as using fancy stitch and color patterns, garments can be decorated by the addition of crochet, embroidery or smocking using contrasting or matching yarns.

Matching buttons, tassels and pom poms can brighten up any child's garment. Tassels and pom poms attached to crochet chains look particularly good on children's hats.

## YARN BUTTONS

Buttons made from the main yarn used in a garment can be a very neat finishing touch. Make solid buttons as shown in steps 1–6 right or open buttons by threading yarn around a plastic or metal curtain ring (see far right).

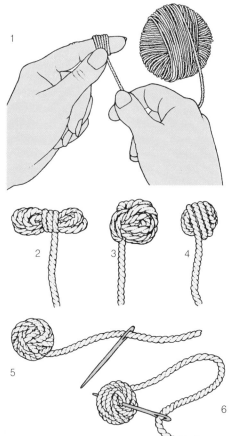

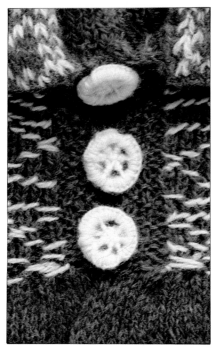

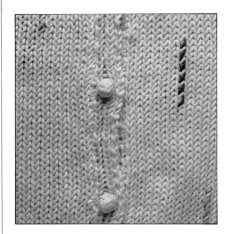

### Solid buttons

Wrap your main yarn around your forefinger approximately six times (1). Slip the loops off and hold them firmly. Wrap the yarn around the center three times making a bow shape (2). Fold in half and continue wrapping yarn around to make a small ball (3–4) – it should fit neatly in the buttonhole. Test for size. To hold the button together, snap off the end of the yarn, leaving about 15¾in.

Thread this into a darning needle and sew into the button securing the wrapped-around yarn (5–6). Sew the button onto the garment.

### Open buttons

To make these buttons embroider around a ½in chrome or plastic jewellery ring with buttonhole stitch. Then, make spokes by working long stitches from one side of the ring to the other.

## TASSELS

These are very simple to make and can be made to match any garment. Cut out a piece of card the length you want the tassel to be. Wind yarn (or yarns) around the card to the required thickness. Slip the yarn off the card and, holding the loop firmly, thread a needle with the main yarn and take it through the top of the loop twice and secure. Break yarn. Wind the same yarn around the tassel several times about ¼in from top and secure. Cut through bottom of loop to form tassel. Sew tassel onto garment or crochet chain.

## POM POMS

Cut two circular templates out of a piece of card. Cut large holes in the center and hold them against each other. Holding one end of the yarn wind the yarn around both pieces of card and through the center. Continue until the card is completely covered – the more yarn you wind around the templates, the thicker the finished pom pom. Holding the cards firmly, cut the yarn all around the outside edges. Thread a piece of yarn between the pieces of card around the yarn, pull it tight and secure. Remove the pieces of card.

# CROCHET

Occasionally, the finishing of some garments calls for the use of crochet stitches, as in collars, for instance. The stitches illustrated here are the most useful.

## Chains (Ch)

**1** Make a slip loop (see p. 117). Thread your yarn in your left hand and hold the crochet hook with the slip loop in the right hand. Twist the hook first under and then over the yarn to make a loop.

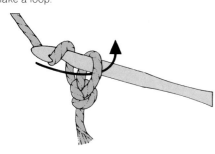

**2** Draw the hook with the yarn on it through the slip loop to form a chain.

## Making a crochet buttonhole

**1** Work from the side edge to the button-hole position (about 3 or 4 stitches in). Make two or more chains, depending on the size of your button. Miss the same number of stitches in the row below.

**2** Re-insert your hook and work in pattern to the end of the row. On the following row, work in pattern over the chains.

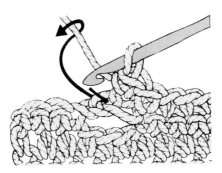

## Single crochet (Sc)

**1** Make a chain row. Insert your hook into the second chain from the hook. Bring your yarn around and draw one loop through (two loops on hook).

**2** Bring your yarn round again and draw yarn through both loops on your hook.

**3** Continue to end, working single crochets into the next and following chains to end.

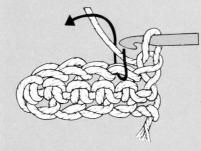

**4** Make a chain and turn. Insert your hook through the first stitch in the row below.

## Double crochet (Dc)

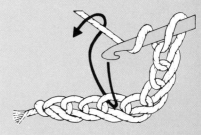

**1** Make a chain row. Bring your yarn round and insert your hook into the fifth chain from the hook. Bring your yarn round again and draw one loop through (three loops on hook).

**2** Bring your yarn round and draw through the first two loops on the hook (two loops on hook).

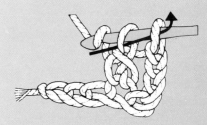

**3** Bring your yarn round and draw through two loops making one double crochet.

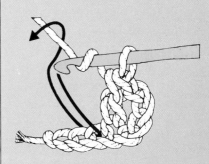

**4** Continue to the end then make three chains; turn. Make first double crochet into second stitch of the row below.

## Finishing off crochet

Complete your final stitch and cut your yarn about 6in from the end of the work. Pull the yarn through the last loop and tighten. Thread the yarn onto a needle and darn the end into the back of the work.

# SMOCKING

Traditional smocking is the most practical way of gathering fullness of a garment across the chest and sleeves for extra warmth and, particularly if worked in a contrast yarn, it can look very attractive. You can work a wide variety of patterns using the basic stitches described below.

Smocking is always worked before you assemble the work, either across fabric gathered into small even-size folds as shown below, or across smocking lines worked into the knitting. To calculate the spacing for the folds either use a printed transfer or cut out a card template with rows of evenly spaced holes marked on it. Lay the template on the fabric and mark through the holes with a dressmaker's pencil.

## Gathering the fabric

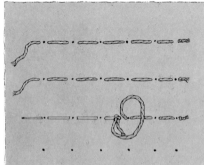

**1** With enough thread on your needle to complete one full row of stitches, knot the long end of the thread. Gather the back of the fabric in rows by picking up a small piece of fabric around each dot.

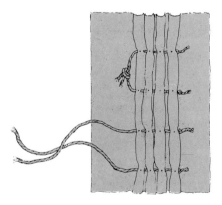

**2** When you have worked all the rows pull up the folds, tie the thread ends together in pairs. (Remove these threads after smocking is completed.)

## Rope stitch

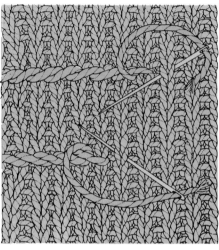

With right side of work facing bring the needle to the surface through the first fold on the left. Work across the row picking up a small piece of fabric on each fold, using stem stitch with the thread above needle. To work stitches with opposite slant, keep the thread below the needle.

## Honeycomb stitch

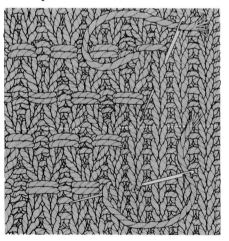

Working from left to right, bring the needle out on the first line and make a back stitch on top line to draw first and second folds together. Then insert the needle and bring it out at the second fold on line below. Make another back stitch to draw third and second folds together. Return needle to the first line to draw third and fourth folds together. Continue in this way to the end of the row. Work other rows similarly.

## Vandyke stitch

Work 2 rows of stem stitch in a chevron pattern, when working upwards keep thread below needle and above needle when working downwards.

## Feather stitch

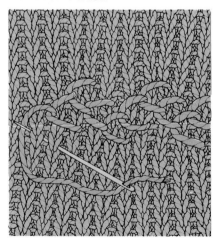

Working from right to left, take needle out at first fold and insert it lower down on same fold. Then take the needle through first and second folds and bring it out over the working thread. Make two more stitches in the same way, making the first over the second and third folds and the next over the third and fourth rows. Working towards the left, make two feather stitches upwards and two downwards drawing in one more fold with each stitch.

# EMBROIDERY

Embroidery is used to enrich a knitting design and add not only color, but texture to a garment. Make sure you always use a blunt-ended wool or tapestry needle to avoid splitting the yarn, and keep your tension the same as the knitting. The most common techniques are duplicate stitch and Cross stitch, but individual stitches can also be worked to create motifs.

Duplicate stitch imitates knitting. It works up quickly and produces a slightly raised design as it covers, or duplicates the knitted stitch. It can be used to add stripes, motifs and letters.

Cross stitch is worked in a similar way as with any woven fabric but care must be taken not to draw the stitches too tightly or the garment will be pulled out of shape.

## Duplicate stitch

### WORKING HORIZONTALLY

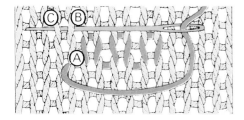

**1** Secure the embroidery yarn at the back of the work and bring your needle out to the front of the work at A. Insert the needle at B, under the base of the stitch above, and bring it out at C.

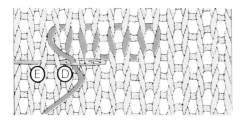

**2** Insert the needle at D and emerge at E ready to embroider the next stitch.

### WORKING VERTICALLY

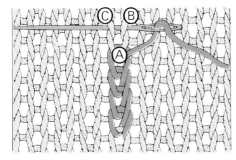

**1** Secure the embroidery yarn at the back of the work and bring your needle out to the front of the work at A. Insert the needle at B, bringing it out at C.

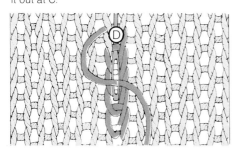

**2** Take the needle under the head of the stitch below and emerge above it at D, ready to form the next stitch.

## Cross stitch

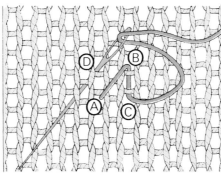

**1** Secure the yarn at the back of the work and bring your needle out at A. Make a diagonal from A to B and bring your needle out at C. Insert at D.

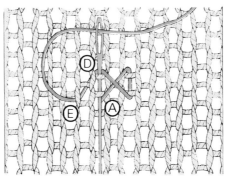

**2** For the second cross, bring your needle out at E, insert again at D and re-insert at A.

### WORKING IN ROWS

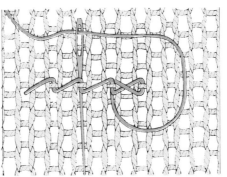

Work one row of diagonals. On the return journey, cross these with a second row.

## Chain stitch

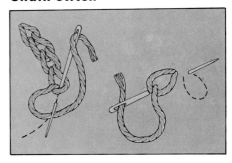

Loop the working thread under the tip of your needle and hold it down with your left thumb while you pick up some of the ground fabric in each stitch. The needle is inserted into the same hole from which it has emerged.

To make a leaf shape, bring out your needle and insert it into the same spot bringing it out with a loop under the needle. Take it over the loop so that you make a small tying stitch to anchor it.

## Back stitch

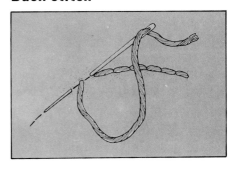

Work in small, even stitches by first making a stitch forwards and then a stitch backwards.

## Stem stitch

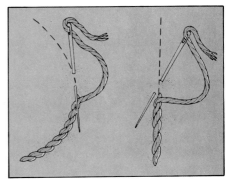

Work the stitch with the thread kept on the same side of the needle. For a wider effect, insert the needle into the ground fabric at a slight angle. The greater the angle, the wider the effect.

The patterns in this book are all easy to follow and where necessary are accompanied by color and pattern charts. However, you can also experiment with different color combinations, sizes and yarns or make up your own designs to embroider onto the garments by following the instructions described on these pages.

## PATTERN CHARTS

While most patterns are written out, those that involve complicated shaping, and almost all color patterns are reproduced in chart form. Charts are extremely effective in conveying the shape and coloration of a garment.

Many designers now chart out both stitch and color patterns on the same grids because it makes them extremely easy to follow. In such a case each square is colored and contains a stitch instruction.

## Reading charts

All charts, whether of color or stitch pattern or both, are read from the bottom of the chart upwards and from right to left on the first and all odd-numbered rows and from left to right on the second and all even-numbered rows. Therefore, the bottom right-hand corner indicates the first stitch.

When knitting in the round, however, the front of the fabric always faces you so the work is always read from right to left.

## Colorwork charts

In these charts each square represents an individual stitch and each line a row or round of knitting. Each color has its own symbol or shading which is contained within the individual squares. The chart may be accompanied by a key that explains the symbols or colors used.

It is essential that you adhere to the current multiple of stitches in a color pattern. This will usually be delineated by darker lines on the grid. If you need to change the size it is often possible to adjust the edges without affecting the pattern repeat.

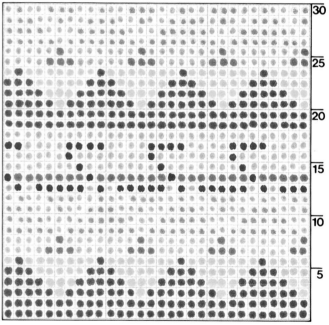

## Stitch charts

In these charts, once again each square represents an individual stitch and each line a row or round of knitting. Each pattern instruction has a different symbol which is contained within the individual squares. The pattern will be accompanied by a key that explains the symbols used.

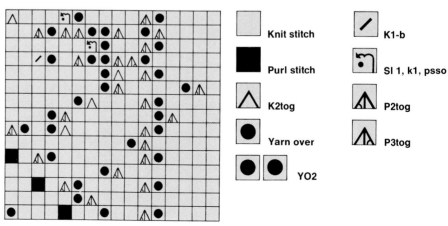

| | |
|---|---|
| Knit stitch | K1-b |
| Purl stitch | Sl 1, k1, psso |
| K2tog | P2tog |
| Yarn over | P3tog |
| YO2 | |

# CHANGING A PATTERN

You can alter any part of a pattern, for example stitch, yarn or size, or even make up your own using the following techniques.

## Altering the pattern stitch

When you change from one stitch to another, for example to a lacy stitch from seed stitch, you must make sure that it will match the multiple of stitches called for in the pattern. For instance, if your pattern calls for a multiple of 8 stitches you can use alternative patterns that consist of multiples of 8, 4 and 2. Therefore, you may be able to work with repeats over 8, 16, 24 or 32 stitches depending on the width of your garment and the number of stitches required.

It is imperative that you make a new tension sample if you change a stitch, so that you end up with an identical size.

## Altering the yarn

| NEEDLE AND YARN TABLE | |
|---|---|
| **Size** | **Yarn type** |
| 2mm<br>no 0<br>no 1 | Fine-weight yarn<br>2-ply, 3-ply baby yarn |
| no 1<br>no 2<br>no 3 | Medium-weight yarn<br>4-ply, baby quick-knits<br>2-ply Shetland |
| no 3<br>no 4<br>no 5<br>no 6 | Knitting worsted |
| no 7<br>no 8<br>no 9 | Thick knitting worsted |
| no 8<br>no 9<br>no 10 | Bulky yarn, mohair |
| no 10½<br>no 11<br>no 13 | Heavyweight yarns |

You can change the type of yarn in the pattern but before you do so you should check that it falls into the same category. *Always* knit up a tension sample before beginning work. The accompanying table will give you some idea of what needles work best with different weights of yarn.

## Changing the size

While most printed patterns come in more than one size, occasionally you will find that you have to adapt a pattern to specific requirements. Here again, a tension sample is vital. Before you begin knitting note the measurements that need changing and adjust the length, width and shaping to match.

If you have to add to the width and length of a sweater, calculate the number of extra stitches needed from your tension sample, add half to the front and half to the back and increase the number of rows until you get to the armhole shaping. Adjust the length and shaping of the sleeves to match. For instance, if you have to add 4in to the width and 6in to the length of a garment and the stitch gauge is 10 stitches and 8 rows to 1in, cast on 20 additional stitches to both front and back and work 48 rows more on both. Add additional stitches to the sleeves adjusting the shaping to match the added length and width.

## Designing with a grid

Begin designing with a simple pattern and fairly straight shapes. Draw the shape, life-size if possible, out on a piece of paper, making sure you have added an excess to the body measurements to ensure a comfortable fit. Then transform your pattern for knitting purposes using a grid which relates to your

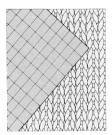

tension sample.

Knit up the sample first using the chosen stitch pattern and calculate the number of stitches and rows to a desired measurement. Draw a grid to match the size of your tension stitch (this is usually rectangular) on a large sheet of tracing paper. Therefore, if you have 10 stitches and 8 rows to 1in, your grid will contain rectangular "boxes" 10 across and 8 deep.

Place your drawn pattern under the tracing grid and trace off the outline, stepping curves to match the grid lines. You will now be able to tell from the grid exactly how many stitches you will need to cast on and where you have to increase and decrease.

## Enlarging designs

Any motif can be enlarged by using the following method. First outline the motif in a square or rectangle and place this at the bottom left-hand corner of a larger piece of paper. Draw a diagonal line from the bottom left-hand corner of the design through the top right-hand corner and onwards to the margin of the paper piece. Determine the desired height of the design from bottom left and mark this point. Then draw a line between it and the opposite point making sure you cross the diagonal line. Where the lines cross at the top right-hand corner draw a vertical line to the base and a corresponding one at the left side. You have now the enlarged outline.

To transfer the motif to the larger piece of paper, divide both the motif and the enlarged outline into an identical number of squares. Draw the motif freehand on the outline, square by square.

# Measuring and Sizing

All the patterns in *Kids Knits* follow the sizing given below. On the whole these sizes are "on the large side", but as children grow at different rates it is advisable to measure the child before you begin and make any necessary adjustments.

## TAKING MEASUREMENTS

The patterns in this book are worked out in six sizes to fit children from birth to 5 years. These sizes are specified with each pattern – i.e., *To fit sizes 1, 2, 3, 4, 5, 6* – together with the measurements of the garment itself. The finished measurements of garments vary according to style because many of them are designed to fit over other clothes. A few of the garments, some hats for example, are worked in one size only. Sizes 1 to 3 allow for diapers where applicable.

### Measuring the body

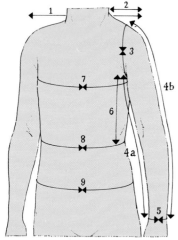

**1** Shoulders – Measure across back from one shoulder tip to the other.

**2** Top of shoulder – Measure from shoulder point to neck edge. From this you can calculate neck shaping.

**3** Armhole – Measure loosely from the highest point of the shoulders.

**4 a and b** Sleeve – Measure with elbow bent from armpit to wrist, and outside arm from shoulder to wrist.

**5** Wrist – Measure around the wristbone.

**6** Waist to underarm – Measure with the arm raised.

**7** Chest – Measure around the fullest part.

**8** Waist – For easy movement, measure with a finger between waist and tape measure.

**9** Hip – Measure around the broadest part (including diaper if necessary).

**10** Inside leg – Measure from diaper or top of leg to foot.

### Calculating hat sizes

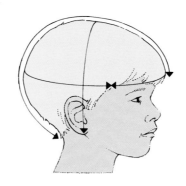

Measure around the head at the widest part to obtain the circumference. Measure across the top of the head from ear tip to ear tip and from mid-forehead to the base of the skull to obtain the diameter.

### Measuring for socks

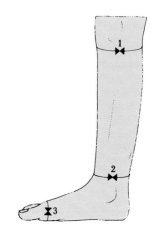

Socks can be knitted to any length by extending the leg and ribbed areas. As a general rule, a knee sock should be double the length of the foot. Always take detailed measurements as follows:

**1** Calf – Measure around the fullest part.

**2** Ankle – Measure around the widest part. This is often the same width as the foot.

**3** Width of foot – Measure around the widest part.

**4** Length of foot – Measure from center back of the heel to the longest point at the toes. When in doubt this measurement should be long rather than short.

**5** Length – Take this measurement up the outside of the child's leg, from the bottom of the heel to the top of the sock.

## SIZING CHART

| Size | 1 | 2 | 3 | 4 | 5 | 6 |
|---|---|---|---|---|---|---|
| Age | 0–6 m | 6–12 | 1–2 yr | 2–3 yr | 3–4 yr | 4–5 yr |
| Weight | To 18 lbs | To 24 lbs | | | | |
| Height | 30" (76cm) | 33" (84cm) | 36" (91cm) | 38" (97cm) | 40" (102cm) | 43" (109cm) |
| Chest | 18" (46cm) | 20" (51cm) | 21" (53cm) | 22" (56cm) | 24" (61cm) | 25" (64cm) |
| Waist | 18" (46cm) | 20" (51cm) | 20" (51cm) | 21" (53cm) | 21" (53cm) | 22" (56cm) |
| Outside leg | 16" (41cm) | 18" (46cm) | 21" (54cm) | 22" (56cm) | 23" (58cm) | 25" (63cm) |
| Inside leg | 9" (23cm) | 11" (28cm) | 14" (35cm) | 16" (41cm) | 17" (43cm) | 19" (48cm) |
| Underarm | 6½" (17cm) | 7½" (19cm) | 8½" (22cm) | 9½" (24cm) | 10½" (26cm) | 11" (28cm) |
| Foot | 3¾" (10cm) | 4¼" (11cm) | 4¾" (12cm) | 5½" (14cm) | 6" (15cm) | 6½" (17cm) |

Before you knit up any garment make sure the measurements given in the pattern are suitable. You will also need to know where to take measurements if you decide to alter an existing pattern or design a new one altogether.

## Yarn fibers

A variety of materials is available to the hand knitter. The natural yarns, especially wool and cotton tend to be more expensive than synthetic yarns but many designers prefer their wearability. The tendency today is for yarns to contain more than one fiber: synthetics are added for strength, elasticity and shape-retention; silk and rayon add sheen.

### Natural fibers

Wool is a pure animal fiber, most commonly available from sheep. It is the classic knitting yarn and most manufacturers produce a wide selection of different yarns, both in blends of individual breeds and from animals of one breed such as Shetland. Other animals also supply us with wool; *mohair*, an extremely warm, fluffy yarn is made from the long silky wool of the Anatolian goat (pure mohair); *cashmere* comes from the Kashmir goat; *angora* comes from angora rabbits; luxury yarns such as *camel hair*, *vicuna* and *alpaca* are also available in limited quantities.

Wool is a very good insulator, because of its curling, twisted fibers, it keeps you warm even when it is wet. It is extremely elastic and supple and crease resistant. "Superwash" wool can be washed in a machine; otherwise dry cleaning or hand-washing is required to keep it from felting and shrinking.

Silk, produced from certain worms, has a shiny, lustrous finish and is often combined with wool to produce a luxury look.

Cotton, harvested from a plant, is a fresh, cool, comfortable and hardwearing fiber which is highly absorbent. It is sometimes mixed with linen, a product of the flax family.

### Synthetic fibers

Manufacturers offer many chemically-produced yarns which are easy care and non-allergic. They are made in the same weights as wool and are easily substituted. Usually a yarn is made up of more than one synthetic fiber.

Acrylic is the most widely-used synthetic due to its lightness and excellent washing properties. It gives strength to wool and by itself is a good insulator and is easy to dye. It never shrinks or felts.

Nylon/polyamide is an extremely hard-wearing and crease-resisting fiber which is very easy to care for and dries quickly. Viscose is a slightly shiny yarn which is rather heavy and helps garments hold their shape. It is non-felting.

## Yarn construction

Fibers are spun in different ways to produce varying textures. They are first made into single threads, called plys, and then the plys are evenly combined to form classic textured yarns. A 4-ply yarn contains four separate strands, a 3-ply yarn contains three. Ply does not indicate thickness since individual plied yarns can vary quite a bit, depending on the thickness of the separate strands.

Special ways of combining strands result in novelty finishes such as: crepe, where the yarns are "locked" together, resulting in a firm elastic twist; bouclé, where one or more of the strands is wound loosely about the others to produce a loopy, raised texture; and chenille, where tightly wrapped strands are cut to produce a velvet-like finish. Some yarns, meche or roving, are spun and pulled together.

## Calculating yarn quantities

Yarns are sold according to weight, not length. How much you get out of a ball depends on a great many factors. The fiber content synthetics normally go further than wool. The fiber texture: fluffy, finer yarns go further than heavy-weight ones. The fiber construction: looser twist yarns go further than tightly twisted ones. Your tension: a loose tension can mean a saving of up to two balls. Finally, the stitch pattern you are using: any variation from stockinette stitch will mean a change in the manufacturer's given length. As a rough guide, the chart below

sets out approximate amounts of yarn for an adult's long-sleeved pullover using different weight yarns, and the same weight yarn of differing fiber content.

| Yarn weight | number of 2oz balls |
|---|---|
| Medium-weight | 6–7 |
| Knitting worsted | 8–10 |
| Thick knitting worsted | 10–12 |
| Aran | 12 |
| Bulky | 14 |

| Yarn fiber | number of 2oz balls |
|---|---|
| Acrylic 80%; nylon 20% | 7 |
| Acrylic 75%; wool 25% | 8 |
| Wool 70%; mohair 30% | 8 |
| Wool 50%; Aran 50% | 9 |
| Shetland 100% | 9 |
| (Tight twist) | 11 |
| Cotton | 12 |

The best way to determine how much you need of a certain type of yarn is to knit up a ball in the chosen stitch pattern. Compare the size of the sample to your pattern: if a 1oz ball knits up to a swatch 8 × 8in (the area is 64in). You then have to calculate the approximate area of each garment section, add these figures together and divide by the area of the swatch. The resulting figure is the number of balls of the chosen weight that you require.

## Substituting yarns

The sweater patterns in this book mostly use 2-ply Shetland, knitting worsted or cotton yarns but they can be knitted up in other yarns. In all cases you should compare your chosen yarns with the table on page 142 which sets out the tension for different weight yarns with specific needle sizes. Compare the information on your yarn band with the chart and the pattern. Remember, the proper tension can often be achieved if you alter the needle size (see p. 114). In any event it is a good idea to knit up a sample beforehand to see if tension and texture are satisfactory.

When substituting wool with cotton, linen or metallics, you will have to add additional stitches for proper fit as these yarns have less elasticity. Yarns that are "interchangeable" may be of the same or different textures, but it's always safest to knit up a sample first.

## Knitting tips

● Always buy sufficient quantity of the same dye lot. If you run out don't continue a piece (i.e. a sleeve) with the new dye lot but knit it from the beginning with a new yarn. A change in the dye lot on Fair-Isles and 2-color patterns is less noticeable.

● Knit to the recommended tension. If you knit too loosely the stitches will rub against each other causing pilling; if you knit too tightly the garment will be stiff and unpleasant to wear.

● To keep your knitting even when using several yarns make certain the yarns are of the same weight (i.e. two or more bulkys, Shetlands, or mohairs etc). If necessary, use double or triple amounts of thin yarns.

● Occasionally, if you're winding lurex around another yarn you may have to change the needle size to preserve tension (the extra strand affects the number of plys).

● When buying a lurex or glitter-type yarn make sure it has a polyester base as other materials will tarnish or the shine will wear off.

● Cotton has a tendency to "shift" while it is being knitted. To correct this when working stockinette stitch change the needle size on the purl row.

# Classic Yarns

Classic yarns are the most enduring and popular yarns as their simple construction and wide color range makes them the most versatile. Previously most often found as wool, price and convenience considerations account for the growing numbers of synthetic yarns on the market today. Generally of a single shade and 4-ply construction, classic yarns are also found as tweeds and variegated mixes, sometimes of more than one type of fiber.

Most of the patterns in this book employ medium-weight Shetland yarns, see top right, but for the purposes of general knitting, the yarns have been classified as fine-weight, medium-weight, knitting worsted, thick knitting worsted and bulky. Not all the yarns listed as bulky are "classic" ones, but they serve to highlight the differences in weight found in this range. A list of manufacturers who produce yarns similar to the ones shown in on page 141.

**100 % synthetic fine-weight**
(Persian-type © Bernat)

**100 % synthetic medium-weight**
(Salukie © Bernat)

**100 % synthetic medium-weight**
(Berella Sportspun © Bernat)

**100 % synthetic knitting worsted**
(Berella 4 © Bernat)

**75 % synthetic/25 % wool knitting worsted**
(Pingofrance © Pingouin)

**100 % wool medium-weight**
(French tweed © Unger)

**25 % wool/75 % synthetic medium-weight**
(Zamira © 3 Suisses)

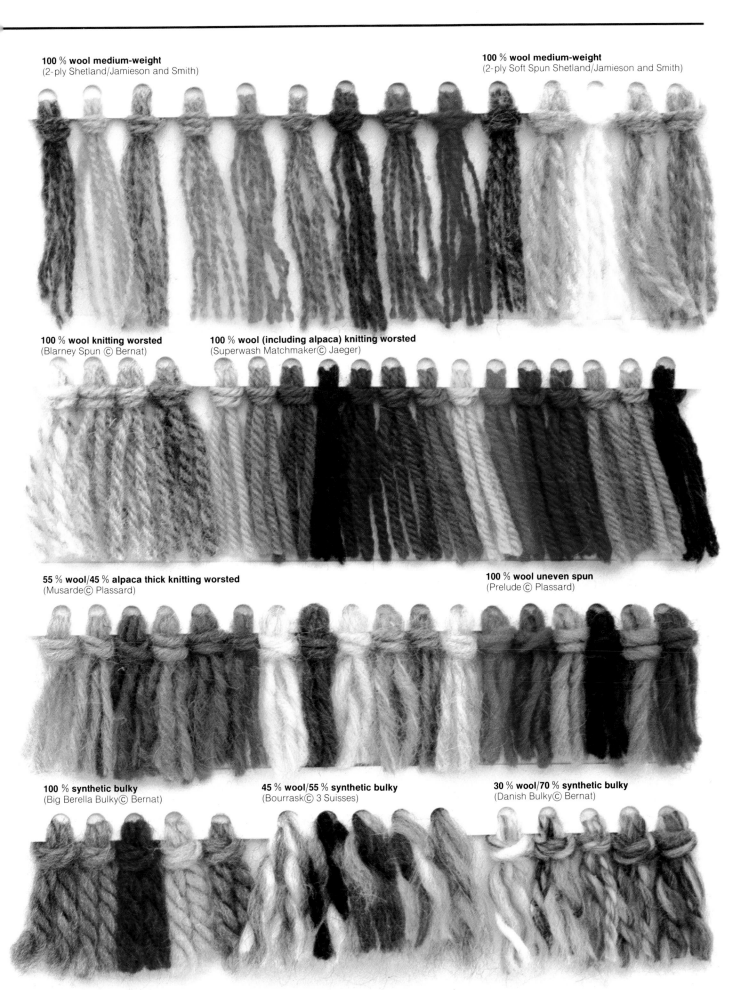

**100 % wool medium-weight**
(2-ply Shetland/Jamieson and Smith)

**100 % wool medium-weight**
(2-ply Soft Spun Shetland/Jamieson and Smith)

**100 % wool knitting worsted**
(Blarney Spun © Bernat)

**100 % wool (including alpaca) knitting worsted**
(Superwash Matchmaker© Jaeger)

**55 % wool/45 % alpaca thick knitting worsted**
(Musarde© Plassard)

**100 % wool uneven spun**
(Prelude © Plassard)

**100 % synthetic bulky**
(Big Berella Bulky© Bernat)

**45 % wool/55 % synthetic bulky**
(Bourrask© 3 Suisses)

**30 % wool/70 % synthetic bulky**
(Danish Bulky© Bernat)

Increased demand by handknitters for cooler cotton yarns has encouraged manufacturers to produce a wide range. Today, cottons and cotton mixes are found in weights ranging from fine to "dish cloth".

Cotton is a practical fabric in that it is washable, making it particularly suitable for children's clothes. Synthetics are sometimes added to improve the decorative effect or to make it more "easy-care".

In addition to the "classic" types, cotton comes in various finishes including bouclés, raggy textures, uneven plys and chenille. More and more deep-dyed colors are being added to the soft pastel shades commonly found.

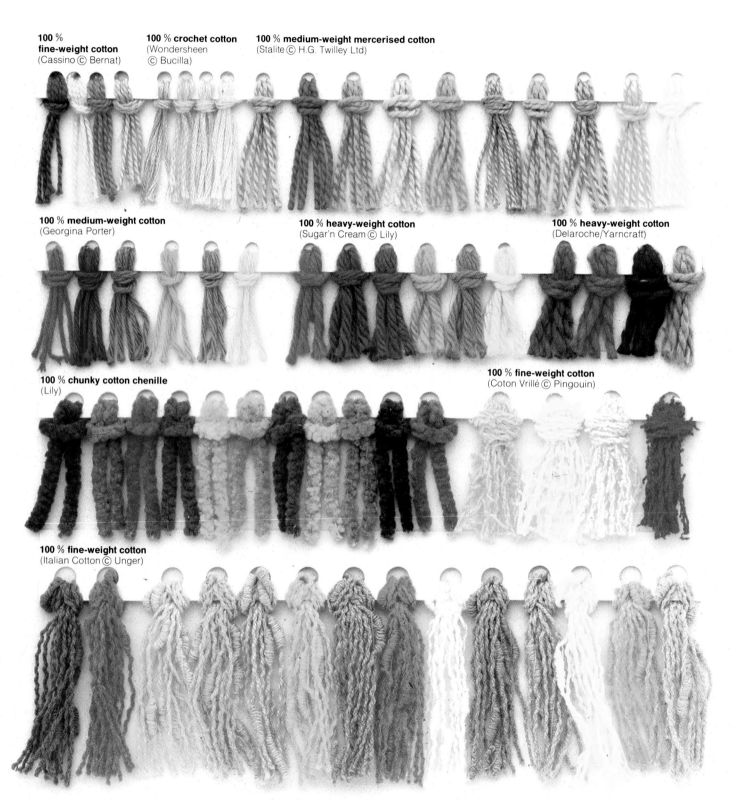

**100 % fine-weight cotton** (Cassino © Bernat)

**100 % crochet cotton** (Wondersheen © Bucilla)

**100 % medium-weight mercerised cotton** (Stalite © H.G. Twilley Ltd)

**100 % medium-weight cotton** (Georgina Porter)

**100 % heavy-weight cotton** (Sugar'n Cream © Lily)

**100 % heavy-weight cotton** (Delaroche/Yarncraft)

**100 % chunky cotton chenille** (Lily)

**100 % fine-weight cotton** (Coton Vrillé © Pingouin)

**100 % fine-weight cotton** (Italian Cotton © Unger)

Silk yarn is expensive to use but comfortable and very hardwearing. Like most yarns, it is generally of 4-ply construction and single shades. Moreover, silk is sometimes added to wool or cotton yarns to give extra strength and a luxurious finish.

Few 100% mohair yarns are produced because they are very expensive, but mohair types are so popular that manufacturers produce yarns with the required fluffy effect but which often contain very little mohair. Mohair normally improves with wear and can be brushed up to make it even more fluffy. Its qualities are best served if it is knitted in reverse stockinette stitch or garter stitch.

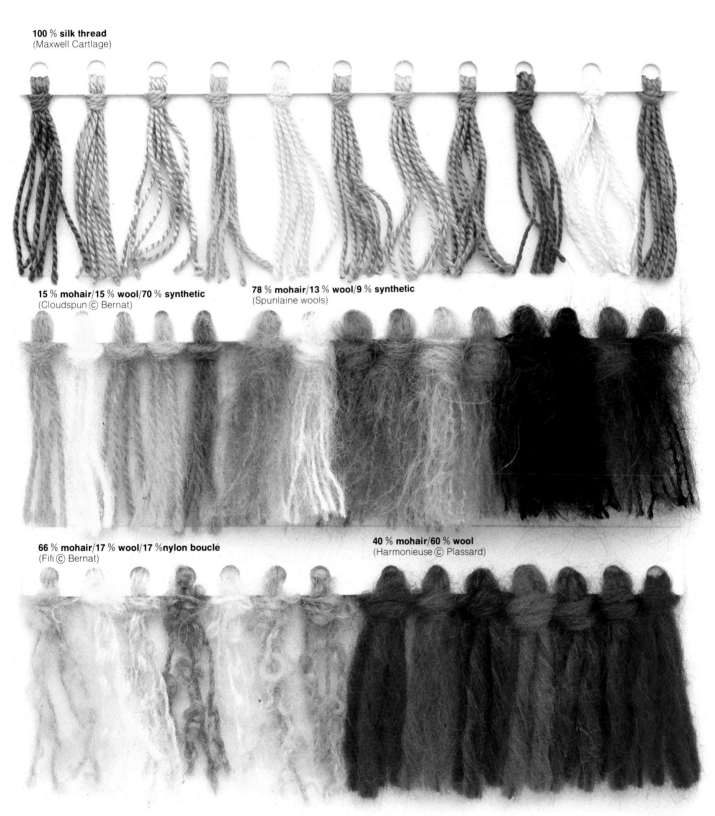

**100% silk thread**
(Maxwell Cartlage)

**15% mohair/15% wool/70% synthetic**
(Cloudspun © Bernat)

**78% mohair/13% wool/9% synthetic**
(Spunlaine wools)

**66% mohair/17% wool/17% nylon bouclé**
(Fifi © Bernat)

**40% mohair/60% wool**
(Harmonieuse © Plassard)

## TENSIONS FOR CLASSIC YARNS

| Needle size | Very fine-weight (2-ply) sts | rows | Fine-weight (3-ply) sts | rows | Medium-weight (4-ply) sts | rows | Knitting worsted sts | rows | Thick knitting worsted sts | rows |
|---|---|---|---|---|---|---|---|---|---|---|
| no 1 | 36 | 44 | 34 | 42 | | | | | | |
| no 2 | 34 | 42 | 32 | 40 | 30 | 38 | | | | |
| no 3 | 32 | 40 | 30 | 38 | 28 | 36 | | | | |
| no 4 | 30 | 38 | 28 | 36 | 26 | 34 | 23 | 31 | | |
| no 5 | 28 | 36 | 26 | 34 | 24 | 32 | 22 | 30 | | |
| no 6 | | | 24 | 32 | 22 | 30 | 21 | 28 | 19 | 25 |
| no 7 | | | | | 20 | 28 | 20 | 26 | 18 | 23 |
| no 8 | | | | | | | 19 | 24 | 17 | 21 |
| no 9 | | | | | | | 18 | 22 | 16 | 19 |

Above, you will find the recommended tensions for the principal classic handknitting yarns for a 4 inch square of stockinette stitch.

## TENSIONS FOR NOVELTY YARNS

| Needle size | Mohair types sts | rows | Bulky sts | rows |
|---|---|---|---|---|
| no 7 | 17 | 22 | 16 | 20 |
| no 8 | 15 | 20 | 14 | 18 |
| no 9 | 13 | 18 | 12 | 16 |

Non-classic yarns, such as mohair, bulky and other novelty yarns have variable tensions which can't be standardized and must be ascertained from information on the ball band, or by knitting up a tension sample. As a guide for using mohair and bulky yarns for the patterns in this book, the above tensions are acceptable.

## KNITTING NEEDLES CONVERSION CHART

| U.S. | 0 | 1 | 2 | 3 | 4 | 5 | 6 | 7 | 8 | 9 | 10 | 10½ | 11 | 13 | 15 |
|---|---|---|---|---|---|---|---|---|---|---|---|---|---|---|---|
| Continental – mm | 2¼ | 2¾ | 3 | 3¼ | 3¾ | 4 | 4½ | 5 | 5½ | 6 | 6½ | 7 | 7½ | 8½ | 9 |
| English | 13 | 12 | 11 | 10 | 9 | 8 | 7 | 6 | 5 | 4 | 3 | 2 | 1 | 00 | 000 |

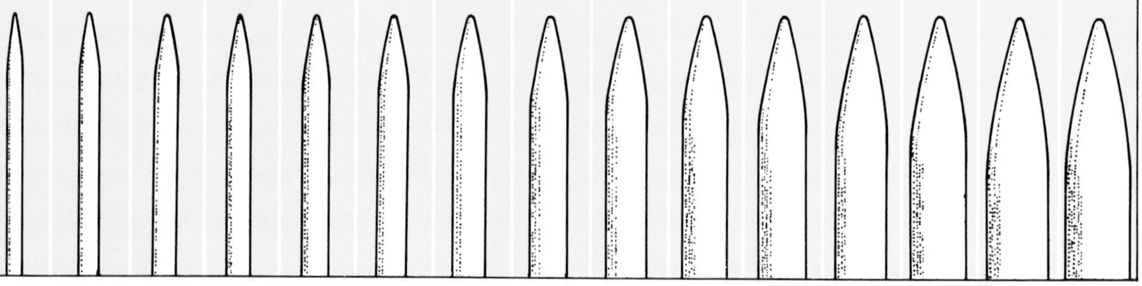

## METRIC/IMPERIAL CONVERSION CHART

Please note that these conversions are approximate to the nearest ¼ inch.

| cm | in | cm | in | cm | in | cm | in |
|---|---|---|---|---|---|---|---|
| 1 | ½ | 11 | 4¼ | 21 | 8¼ | 31 | 12¼ |
| 2 | ¾ | 12 | 4¾ | 22 | 8¾ | 32 | 12½ |
| 3 | 1¼ | 13 | 5 | 23 | 9 | 33 | 13 |
| 4 | 1½ | 14 | 5½ | 24 | 9½ | 34 | 13½ |
| 5 | 2 | 15 | 6 | 25 | 9¾ | 35 | 13¾ |
| 6 | 2¼ | 16 | 6¼ | 26 | 10¼ | 36 | 14¼ |
| 7 | 2¾ | 17 | 6¾ | 27 | 10¾ | 37 | 14½ |
| 8 | 3¼ | 18 | 7 | 28 | 11 | 38 | 15 |
| 9 | 3½ | 19 | 7½ | 29 | 11½ | 39 | 15¼ |
| 10 | 4 | 20 | 7¾ | 30 | 11¾ | 40 | 15¾ |

## GRAM/OUNCE CONVERSION CHART

Please note that these conversions are approximate. One ounce = approximately 28.35 grams.

| grams | ounces | grams | ounces |
|---|---|---|---|
| 25 | 1 | 250 | 8¾ |
| 50 | 1¾ | 275 | 9¾ |
| 75 | 2¾ | 300 | 10½ |
| 100 | 3½ | 325 | 11½ |
| 125 | 4½ | 350 | 12¼ |
| 150 | 5¼ | 375 | 13¼ |
| 175 | 6¼ | 400 | 14 |
| 200 | 7 | 425 | 15 |
| 225 | 8 | 450 | 15¾ |

## Abbreviations used in patterns

| | | | | | |
|---|---|---|---|---|---|
| **alt** | alternate | **Moss st** | k1, p1 to end; next row p1, k1 to end | **ssk** | slip, slip, knit. Slip the first and second stitches knitwise one at a time, then insert the tip of the left-hand needle into the fronts of these two sts from the left and knit them together from this position |
| **beg** | beginning | | | | |
| **cm** | centimeter | **()** | repeat all the material between parentheses as many times as indicated | | |
| **dec** | decrease | | | | |
| **dc** | double crochet | **oz** | ounce | **st** | stitch |
| **foll** | following | **p** | purl | **st st** | stockinette stitch |
| **Garter st** | knit or purl every row | **patt** | pattern | **tbl** | through back of loop |
| **g** | gram | **ppso** | pass previous stitch over | | |
| **inc** | increase | **psso** | pass slip stitch over | **tog** | together |
| **inc 1** | work into the front and back of stitch | **pwise** | purlwise | **turn** | turn the work around at the point indicated, before the end of a row |
| | | **rem** | remaining | | |
| **k** | knit | **rep** | repeat | | |
| **k2tog** | knit two stitches together | **rep from \*** | repeat all the instructions that follow \* | **up 1** | pick up top of stitch below the next one to be worked and work into it to increase |
| **kwise** | knitwise | | | | |
| **m1** | make one (by picking up the loop between the needles and working into the back of it) | **sc** | single crochet | **yfwd** | yarn forward |
| | | **sl** | slip | **yo** | yarn over needle |
| | | | | **yrn** | yarn round needle |

# YARN SUPPLIERS

The following manufacturers all bring out a wide range of natural and synthetic yarns.

**Anny Blatt**
24770 Crestview Ct.
Farmington Hills, Michigan
48010

**Aunt Lydia's**
American
PO Box 3823
Stamford, Connecticut
06905

**Susan Bates Inc.**
212 Middlesex Avenue
Chester, Connecticut
06412

**Belding Lily Company**
Shelby, North Carolina
28150

**Emile Bernat Yarn and Craft Corp.**
Depot & Mendon Sts.
Uxbridge, Massachusetts
01569

**Brunswick Yarns**
PO Box 276
off Sangamo Road
Pickens, South Carolina
29671

**Bucilla**
Sales Service Dept.
150 Meadowlands Pkwy.
Secaucus, New Jersey
07094

**Coats & Clark Inc.**
Attn: CEAD
72 Cummings Point Road
Stamford, Connecticut
06904

**Columbia Minerva Yarns**
Handknitting yarns and crafts
Box 300
Rochelle, Illinois
61068

**Dorothee Bis Yarns**
Knitting Fever Inc.
180 Babylon Turnpike
Roosevelt, New York
11575

**Emu**
Merino Wool Company
230 Fifth Avenue
New York ,New York
10001

**Georges Picaud**
Merino Wool Company
230 Fifth Avenue
New York, New York
10001

**Lion Brand Yarn Company**
1270 Broadway
New York, New York
10001

**Melrose Yarn Company, Inc.**
1305 Utica Avenue
Brooklyn, New York
11203

**Patons**
Susan Bates Inc.
212 Middlesex Avenue
Chester, Connecticut
06412

**Phildar Knitting Yarns**
6438 Dawson Blvd.
Norcross, Georgia
30093

**Pingouin Corporation**
PO Box 100
Jamestown, South Carolina
29453

**Reynolds Yarns, Inc.**
Box 1776
Hauppauge, New York
11788

**Scheepjes**
Ulltex Yarns Inc.
21 Adley Road
Cambridge, Massachusetts
02138

**Studio Yarn Farms, Inc.**
Dept. L
PO Box 46017
Seattle, Washington
98146

**3 Suisses**
Bucilla
Sales Service Dept.
150 Meadowlands Pkwy.
Secaucus, New Jersey
07094

**Unger Yarns**
230 Fifth Avenue
New York, New York
10001

# Acknowledgments

My special thanks go to Amy Carroll for inviting me to spend a very enjoyable year working on the designs for this book. Thank you also to: Ian O'Leary whose beautiful photographs show the clothes off at their best; Michelle, Sheila, Joyce, Sally, Betty, Margaret and Jennifer for their skill and care in knitting up the garments; Jemima Dunne, Anne-Marie Bulat and the rest of the team at Dorling Kindersley for designing the book and for their patience while we worked on the instructions; and my husband and children whose tolerance and forbearance have been deeply appreciated. I offer a very special thank you to Sara Underwood who helped and advised on many of the designs and kept my business running smoothly, and most of all to my dear mother Joy Walker whose skill as a needle woman, encouragement and enthusiasm have helped us bring this book to its successful conclusion.

*Lesley Anne Price*

**Photography**
Ian O'Leary

**Illustrators**
Lindsay Blow
Kuo Kang Chen
Edwina Keene

**Typesetting** Chambers Wallace
**Reproduction** F. E. Burman

*Dorling Kindersley would like to thank:*
Jean Litchfield and others for checking the patterns so carefully; Chantal Esteve, Sue and Ben Hadley, Louise and Charlotte Nery, Alexis, Casper and Amber Price, Ester and Ross O'Leary, and Joanna and Henry Purkis for modeling the clothes; The Button Box, Covent Garden, for lending us a selection of buttons; Galt Toys for lending us props; and Irene Buckingham for knitting the piece for the jacket.